BREAKING THROUGH THE LANGUAGE ARTS BLOCK

Best Practices in Action
Linda B. Gambrell and Lesley Mandel Morrow,
Series Editors

Connecting research findings to daily classroom practice is a key component of successful teaching—and any teacher can accomplish it, with the right tools. The Best Practices in Action series focuses on what elementary and middle grade teachers need to do "on Monday morning" to plan and implement high-quality literacy instruction and assess student learning. Books in the series are practical, accessible, and firmly grounded in research. Each title provides ready-to-use lesson ideas, engaging classroom vignettes, links to the Common Core State Standards, discussion questions and engagement activities ideal for professional learning communities, and reproducible materials that purchasers can download and print.

Breaking Through the Language Arts Block

Organizing and Managing the Exemplary Literacy Day

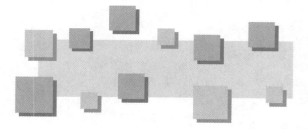

Lesley Mandel Morrow, Kenneth Kunz, and Maureen Hall

THE GUILFORD PRESS
New York   London

Library of Congress Cataloging-in-Publication Data is available from the publisher.

ISBN 978-1-4625-3446-3 (paperback) — ISBN 978-1-4625-3451-7 (hardcover)

About the Authors

Lesley Mandel Morrow, PhD, is Distinguished Professor of Literacy and Director of the Center for Literacy Development at the Graduate School of Education at Rutgers, The State University of New Jersey. Her research, which she conducts with children and families from diverse backgrounds, deals with early literacy development and the organization and management of language arts programs and literacy-rich environments. Dr. Morrow has published more than 300 journal articles, chapters, and books. Her work has been recognized with awards including the Outstanding Teacher Educator in Reading Award and the William S. Gray Citation of Merit, both from the International Literacy Association (ILA), and the Oscar S. Causey Award for outstanding contributions to reading research from the Literacy Research Association. Dr. Morrow is past president of the ILA and is a member and past president of the Reading Hall of Fame.

Kenneth Kunz, EdD, is a Supervisor of Curriculum and Instruction in the New Jersey Public Schools and also serves as president of the New Jersey Literacy Association. He began his career as a third-grade teacher in the New Jersey Public Schools. Dr. Kunz has received recognition as an outstanding teacher through the New Jersey Governor's Teacher Recognition Program and was awarded the Edward Fry Fellowship in Literacy at Rutgers, The State University of New Jersey.

Maureen Hall, EdS, is a part-time lecturer at Rutgers, The State University of New Jersey, and is a literacy coach in several districts across New Jersey through the Rutgers Center for Literacy Development. As a teacher, she was recognized through the New Jersey Governor's Teacher Recognition Program. She serves on the advisory board of the Rutgers Center for Literacy Development and is vice president of the New Jersey Literacy Association.

Series Editors' Note

This book could not have been conceived at a better moment. Its content takes on special meaning at a time when the role of relevance in literacy development is receiving national attention. *Breaking Through the Language Arts Block: Organizing and Managing the Exemplary Literacy Day* will support teachers in reimagining, restructuring, and redefining what it means to engage students in meaningful reading and writing experiences throughout the school day. While this book is grounded in theory and research, it maintains a clear focus on the practical implementation of exemplary language arts instruction for all students. Teaching strategies and techniques are clearly depicted and illustrated with wonderful examples of student work, lesson plans, and other resources.

The authors of this book break with the tradition of treating the language arts separately. They are unwavering in their portrayals of integrated language arts instruction that is research-based and exemplifies best practices in literacy instruction. The authors write in a manner that clearly indicates their awareness of the importance of integrating the language arts to maximize literacy development. Throughout the book, the language arts are braided together in highly motivating classroom reading and writing activities and instruction.

Importantly, this book is also grounded in motivational theory and research that provides a body of knowledge for building the know-how that is needed for exemplary literacy instruction. The authors offer a refreshing look at how to create classroom communities that introduce students to the joy and value of literacy learning.

Teachers' voices abound in *Breaking Through the Language Arts Block*. Indeed, their voices weave throughout the chapters in this book in unique and practical ways to capture methods of organizing and managing exemplary teaching of the language arts. The vignettes of the teachers at the beginning of each chapter add interest, depth, and credibility to this excellent text. This book is an outstanding contribution to the *Best Practices in Action* series because it connects current research findings to exemplary literacy instruction across the language arts.

Public awareness of the need for our students to be highly literate has never been greater. Fortunately, the knowledge base for providing exemplary literacy instruction has never been richer. This book will serve as a valuable, practice-oriented text for teachers and will enhance the knowledge and skills of those who are committed to helping students become passionate and empowered literacy learners.

LINDA B. GAMBRELL, PhD
LESLEY MANDEL MORROW, PhD

Preface

Breaking Through the Language Arts Block: Organizing and Managing the Exemplary Literacy Day is written for any teacher seeking to reimagine, restructure, and redefine what it means to engage today's learners in reading and writing throughout the day. Whether you are a seasoned teacher or new to the field, this book will guide you to rethink what it means to teach literacy. It is appropriate for teachers, reading specialists, administrators, future teachers, and literacy advocates.

WHAT MAKES THIS BOOK DIFFERENT?

This book is unique in that it focuses on the latest formats for organizing and managing a literacy day, providing teachers with practical tips and strategies for making the implementation of these components seamless.

- We bring all the literacy best practices together. The exemplary literacy day puts everything you need for high-quality literacy instruction in one convenient place, with topics ranging from classroom culture to understanding each of the nitty-gritty literacy practices.
- We emphasize the importance of *classroom culture*. None of the components of literacy instruction matter if a learning environment is not a welcoming and nourishing place, filled with language that emphasizes the importance of having a growth mindset.
- We introduce a *vocabulary meeting*. Although vocabulary is an often-overlooked piece of instruction, we provide a special period in the day for

celebrating word learning with students through the use of a vocabulary meeting time.

- We designate a *reading comprehension workshop*. Comprehension and making meaning are the ultimate goals for reading instruction. Therefore the traditional reading workshop should emphasize the explicit teaching of comprehension strategies and skills.

We have spent hours in diverse schools bridging the gap between theory and research and actual practice. We wrote this book as a result of our extensive time and experience with teachers in multiple settings. Teachers within these schools shared a common characteristic: a true passion for providing the best literacy instruction for readers and writers. They also shared a common concern for "putting it all together" and fitting all the components of quality literacy instruction into the school day. Regardless of the standards or programs used, the key features of high-quality literacy instruction are non-negotiable.

In each chapter you will find . . .

- A definition of each literacy practice
- The research behind why each highlighted practice is important
- An explanation of how a teacher might go about setting up his or her classroom for success with each practice
- *Management Tips* and other tools for organizing instruction
- *Breaking Through the Block* tips to help teachers extend literacy instruction throughout the school day
- Snapshots of best practices in action
- A classroom vignette following an exemplary teacher as she grows to develop a cohesive and comprehensive literacy program
- Resources for furthering one's learning about each of the core areas
- Sample lesson plans and activities that can be used in the classroom

Chapter 1 shows teachers the importance of examining their own day to get started with the exemplary literacy day. It provides an overview of the exemplary day and focuses on classroom culture, emphasizing the language that teachers use to promote empathy, responsibility, and a sense of community within the literacy classroom. This chapter sets the tone for establishing respect and rapport with students and gives examples of teacher and student language that promotes a growth mindset.

Chapter 2 introduces discussion of the physical environment. Organizing and managing materials, space, and time are the key elements of the chapter. Suggestions facilitate future student and teacher interactions that enhance instruction. Teachers are taught to think beyond a commercial-print environment to a more student-centered community for learning. The concept of implementing a daily "Do-Now" is also discussed as a way of getting started.

Chapter 3 features the use of formative and summative assessment strategies to guide meaningful literacy instruction. It stresses the importance of starting early in the school year to get to know individual students through the use of several different assessment techniques. Opportunities are provided for teachers to reflect on and track how students are making progress throughout the year.

Chapter 4 shines a spotlight on vocabulary learning through the concept of a *vocabulary meeting.* In the past, vocabulary has been overlooked as a separate entity. For the first time, vocabulary is given space and time like the workshop model. Here, you will learn how to make the vocabulary meeting a daily part of your instruction.

Chapter 5 provides you with a panoramic view of how and when to focus on phonemic awareness and phonics. The word-work session described is short and systematic, yet it is a foundational need for learners.

Chapter 6 focuses on literacy work stations, where students socially collaborate to practice skills and strategies previously taught. Moving beyond "busy work," the chapter provides a plethora of differentiated activities sure to engage all types of learners while the teacher conducts guided reading.

Chapter 7 discusses the latest in guided reading instruction and clarifies the before, during, and after structure of lessons. Lessons are objective-driven and centered on the differentiated needs of students in particular groups.

Chapter 8 features a new look at the reading workshop as the premier place to teach comprehension skills through strategy instruction. Naming the chapter "Reading Comprehension Workshop" is our way of signifying that comprehension is the key focus for instruction. This chapter introduces an explicit way for teachers to help students delve deeper into reading for meaning and includes the topic of close reading.

Chapter 9 summarizes the key elements needed for orchestrating a writing workshop in the K–6 classroom. This chapter mirrors the structure of the reading comprehension workshop, but focuses on working within a community of writers.

Chapter 10 takes content-area literacy to a new level through a discussion centered on the latest knowledge of interdisciplinary project-based instruction. From using informational texts to interdisciplinary teaching, this chapter guides teachers in meaningful ways to ensure that literacy lives beyond the confines of a language arts program.

In *Concluding Thoughts* we summarize key points of the previous chapters and share information on how teachers can continue to learn and enrich their instruction through different kinds of professional development. *Appendix A* provides a comprehensive sample unit plan for an exemplary literacy day, and *Appendix B* contains lists of high-frequency sight words for building vocabulary.

Acknowledgments

We would like to extend our heartfelt appreciation to those who helped with refining our vision of what it means to teach an exemplary literacy day. A special "thank you" is in order for the Califon Public School, in New Jersey, a small school with a big heart and a commitment to ongoing literacy professional development. Mr. Daniel Patton and Mr. Jason Kornegay are administrators who shine as literacy leaders. And the following individuals always said yes to our requests and opened their classroom doors to share literacy best practices: Mandy Araneo, Deborah Beer, Leora Brenowitz, Kristen Charleston, Alison DeMarco, Alyson Ehrlich, Susan Fullilove, Kyle Hoitsma, Kelly Hubiak, Tina Leming, Patricia Tapia Longo, Mary Jane Medea, Lisa Mullin, Eileen Nelson, Jenny Parisella, Amber Pine, Dr. Cynthia Pope, Olga Prymmak, Rachel Smith, Rebecca Waddell, Shira Wasserman, and Matthew Zimmerman.

Contents

CHAPTER 1

Getting Started
with the Exemplary Literacy Day

CLASSROOM VIGNETTE: Meet Ms. Patricia Tapia

After 10 years of teaching students to become better readers and writers, Ms. Tapia starts to question her practices and begins to realize that there are always better ways to improve instruction. She starts to move beyond thinking about literacy instruction as a special "block" and focuses more on organizing and managing literacy throughout the day. Her thoughts turn to working smarter and not harder, with a more responsive classroom that builds a community of learners and empowers the students to be active participants in the classroom. She reads about motivation theory and decides that the cornerstone of her instruction will be choice, challenge, social interaction, authenticity, and success.

A NEW WAY OF THINKING: MOVING BEYOND THE "READING BLOCK"

When this book was first discussed among the authors, many conversations took place about shifting our thinking about literacy as a "balanced" program to a more comprehensive approach with best practices evident throughout the day. We imagined a school day where a child could enter the classroom and experience high-quality literacy instruction across content areas, taking place in an energized, highly organized, and well-managed school environment.

One challenge teachers face is that while many try to take advantage of literacy professional development by attending workshops and conferences, reading professional books, taking coursework, and working with colleagues within professional learning communities (PLCs), the learning that results from these efforts is

1

often out of context and disjointed. Putting it all together to organize and manage an effective classroom makes all the difference. Our work within schools revealed that despite teachers' desire to learn and grow, their efforts to promote balanced literacy was frequently fragmented and inconsistent, with teachers attempting to implement best practices in somewhat disconnected ways.

AN EXEMPLARY LITERACY DAY

The "exemplary literacy day" was created as a result of professional development, research, and fieldwork conducted through the Rutgers Center for Literacy Development. The day was designed to provide a plan for using research-based best practices in literacy instruction. Each component was carefully selected and placed into an appropriate part of a daily schedule. Intentional instruction within these components provides students with experiences to build the skills needed to be successful as literate and critical thinkers. A comprehensive K–6 literacy day includes phonemic awareness, phonics, vocabulary, comprehension, fluency, writing, and motivation. The exemplary literacy day provides a consistent plan that is intended for use across diverse schools and districts.

This can be accomplished when teachers consistently understand and utilize the same terminology for reading and writing instruction. Many strategies for literacy development are interpreted in different ways. This book will help teachers to understand the practices in a consistent, standardized manner. Having a consistent format across grades and schools provides continuity between grades, which allows children to know what to expect when it comes to literacy learning. The skills included in the day are based on common standards that have been adopted and refined across the country.

It is important to understand that the exemplary literacy day is not a prepackaged program. Instead, it is a compilation of best practices that will allow teachers to use data and professional judgment to become experts in their craft. Research has proven that there is no program or material that is best for all children. It is the expertise of the teacher in diagnosing and prescribing instruction for every child that makes the difference.

Studies show that the more literacy instruction and practice children participate in, the more likely they are to do well in school and beyond. Research also tells us that less than 10% of students who are not reading on grade level by the end of third grade will ever achieve grade-level expectations. They will continue to struggle. Therefore, literacy instruction must be a priority and happen all day long in school. To address these gaps, we know that teachers must utilize explicit literacy instruction across content areas that include, but are not limited to, social studies, math, science, art, music, physical education, and technology.

We assume that teachers will differentiate instruction and adapt the format of our design to meet the individual needs of children. Finally, the day was created to emphasize an urgency for learning, where precious school time is used efficiently and effectively.

Research has taught us that changing practice requires a well-designed professional development plan and a commitment of at least 3 years. This allows a plan to become sustainable, so that over a period of time school leaders and teachers witness the exemplary day becoming a foundation of the school culture.

In addition to an exemplary literacy organizational plan, the teaching of skills and implementation of practices will always need to be revisited and refined as new research emerges. Beyond the design of the exemplary day, expectations are that schools will determine appropriate intervention programs for strugglers, encourage family and community involvement, and provide after-school programs to close gaps in achievement. All plans must be flexible and open to change as they are used.

The following is an outline of the exemplary literacy day with definitions of each component. Appendix A at the end of the book presents a complete sample unit plan for a 2-day rollout of exemplary literacy instruction that matches this outline. Two additional features that are not included in the schedule below are discussed in the book: *classroom culture* and *physical environment*. These two vital elements cannot be overlooked, as the achievement of an exemplary literacy day is based in part on the culture and environment of a classroom.

The Exemplary K–6 Literacy Day

Note: Recommended times may need to be adjusted based on teachers' schedules.

Do-Now (10–15 minutes)

Upon arriving at school, children are to . . .

- Engage in an immediate independent or partner activity in reading or writing that sets the tone for the rest of the day.
- Practice skills and strategies previously taught and prepare for the day's lessons. For example, a teacher can decide to allow students to partner- or independently read three times a week and make entries in a writing journal twice a week.

Vocabulary Meeting (15–20 minutes)

- Students participate in an activity centered on a vocabulary-enriched message.
- Students collaborate to deepen their understanding of word meanings.

Reading Comprehension Workshop (time varies, 30–60 minutes)

- Students engage in a comprehension-focused mini-lesson where strategies are taught to help students master grade-appropriate comprehension skills.
- Time is set aside for independent/partner practice concentrating on the strategies and skills taught.
- The teacher confers with readers.
- The teacher and students participate in a group share.

Guided Reading and Literacy Work Stations (minimum of two rotations of 15–20 minutes each)

- Teachers meet with small, homogeneous groups of no more than six students to explicitly teach strategies and reinforce skills as needed.
- Children move through work stations to practice strategies and skills previously taught.
- An accountability piece exists at each literacy station.
- Literacy work stations often include listening (comprehension), word work (vocabulary and spelling), writing (independent or with partner), library (independent or with partner), and technology (skill-based programs).

Word-Work Session (15–20 minutes)

- Teachers provide explicit instruction in phonemic awareness (for early and emergent readers) *or* phonics/decoding (for emergent, transitional, and fluent readers).
- Students often engage in word sorts, word building, and word games.
- Programs vary according to school districts.

Writing Workshop (time varies, 30–60 minutes)

- Students engage in a writing-focused mini-lesson where strategies are taught to help students master grade-appropriate writing skills.
- Time is set aside for independent/partner practice concentrating on the strategies and skills taught.
- The teacher confers with writers.
- Teacher and students participate in a group share.

Interdisciplinary Project-Based Instruction (IPBI) (time varies)

- IPBI is a student-interest–based project that crosses disciplines.

- Long-term activities include research and the creation and completion of a project that demonstrates student learning.
- Reading and writing skills are embedded throughout the project.

Wrap-Up (5 minutes)

At the end of each school day, end on a positive note by saying to the students:

- "What did you learn today in reading/writing that is most important to you?"
- "You can choose to read a poem, riddle, joke, or short story, or to sing a song."

 Breaking Through the Block: Create an area in the classroom for posting a daily learning agenda that all students can see. Laminate cards with the components of an exemplary literacy day. If the agenda is posted on a whiteboard, use a marker to update what students will be learning within each of these components. Referring to the agenda will keep you and the students on task, while ensuring that literacy learning is evident throughout the school day.

CHOOSING OUR EXEMPLARY LITERACY TEACHER

Based on the review of studies regarding effective teachers (Morrow, Tracey, Woo, & Pressley, 1999; Pressley, Rankin, & Yokoi, 1996; Taylor, Pearson, Clark, & Walpole, 1999; Wharton-McDonald, Pressley, & Hampston, 1998), researchers from the Literacy Research Association's Teacher Education Research Study Group (Bahlmann Bollinger et al., 2016) developed a position statement that demonstrates that exemplary literacy teachers . . .

1. Understand the importance of home–school communication.
2. Engage students through small-group, whole-class, and cooperative learning activities.
3. Allow time for independent reading and writing.
4. Teach strategies and skills through authentic and scaffolded high-quality reading and writing instruction.
5. Teach strategies and skills explicitly and spontaneously.
6. Encourage self-regulation through a well-organized and managed classroom.
7. Integrate literacy across the content areas.
8. Have high expectations for all learners.
9. Create print-rich classroom environments.
10. Articulate their reasoning behind all instructional decisions made.

Based on these criteria, we selected an exemplary literacy teacher with whom we have worked. Each chapter begins with Ms. Tapia, a dual-language teacher in an urban school district in the New York metropolitan area, recognizing the needs of her students and researching how best to meet those needs. We will follow her on a journey of discovery as she puts the components of an exemplary literacy day to work for the benefit of her students. It is our hope that after reading this book teachers will feel well equipped and empowered to organize and manage the key components of a comprehensive and exemplary literacy day.

CLASSROOM VIGNETTE: Examining Classroom Culture

Now that Ms. Tapia is getting used to thinking "outside of the block," she considers her classroom culture and wonders how she can effect change in this area. She recalls that a member of her grade-level team recently talked about changes he had made to his classroom culture after having read a book about the power of teacher language. She decides to bring the subject up at their next grade-level meeting. The other teacher allows her to borrow the book that changed his thinking and invites her into his room to observe his new way of speaking to children in action. She comes away from the observation of his classroom impressed by the fact that his students seem to be willing to work hard and strive for independence. She decides that it is time to read up on how he accomplished this and to introduce it in her own classroom.

WHAT IS CLASSROOM CULTURE?

A discussion of the culture of the classroom is critical when talking about organizing and managing a comprehensive literacy day. It is all well and good to establish an environment that is conducive to literacy learning. Without the teacher's modeling and direct instruction in how a classroom functions as a community, however, none of this will work. It is incumbent upon us, as teachers, to be reflective and honest with ourselves as we plan to create our classroom community. To what degree do we need control? How much background noise is acceptable? How do we truly hope and expect our students to behave? Prior planning is the key ingredient to creating a thoughtfully planned community. We need to predetermine what is most important to us as teachers. Are we developing children who can spit out facts? Do we value student input if it varies from our own? What values do we wish to emphasize, and why? A wise teacher reflects both before and after he or she has made decisions. In fact, reflection (for both teachers and students) should be built into every day. When we reflect honestly, we can learn from our errors, replicate what goes well, and meet the needs of all learners within the literacy classroom.

USING LANGUAGE TO CREATE A LITERACY COMMUNITY: WHAT AND WHY?

A classroom is a community of learners, but that community does not develop by itself. Teacher language can encourage the sense of community in a classroom by using inclusive language indicating shared goals ("we" rather than "I"), and requiring that everyone in the room demonstrates and receives respect. It behooves us as teachers to reflect upon the tone and words we habitually use in order to eradicate negativity and focus on language that empowers students to become productive and respectful members of the community. The goal is that every reader and writer feels valued and part of that special classroom community.

A true literacy learning community is based upon the fact that learning is a social activity, and that the teacher is there to create a supportive environment within that social network. The goal here is to "provide children with the means and the desire to construct themselves as responsibly literate democratic citizens" (Johnston, 2004, p. 80). Every student in every classroom has something to contribute. When we plan for those contributions and take them seriously, the child becomes more aware of him- or herself as a learner.

Building a community of readers by posting "selfies" with favorite books.

USING LANGUAGE TO CREATE A LITERACY COMMUNITY: HOW?

Working with children to demonstrate and require respect means that teachers must be completely aware of their own phrasing, body language, and tone. Denton (2015, p. 12) proposes that five guidelines provide the foundation for all teacher language:

1. Be direct and genuine—for example: "We want everyone in our room to feel welcome and part of our reading group. As we gather on the carpet for today's lesson, make sure that all readers have a comfortable space."
2. Convey faith in children's abilities and intentions—for example: "I know you can find a kind way to say that about your writing partner."
3. Focus on action—for example: "Show me how it would look if you helped your station partner solve a problem."
4. Keep it brief.
5. Know when to be silent.

Our primary goal is to obtain and keep the trust of the children in our charge. With trust comes risk taking, which is the basis of growth. Children learn that they can trust us "when we say what we mean and mean what we say" (Denton, 2015, p. 13). We give directions as clearly as possible, using statements (e.g., "Let's all find a comfortable place to stop in our books") rather than questions (e.g., "Can you put your books down?"). We demonstrate our sense of humor, but do not allow it to slide toward sarcasm. Our tone of voice will demonstrate whether we are serious or sarcastic about a statement. "You chose a great book there" could be interpreted in many ways, so our tone of voice must be calm and matter-of-fact. We match our body and verbal language, so that we don't tell a child that we are listening as our eyes scan the room for some other unrelated purpose instead. We focus our attention on the student so he or she knows we are listening attentively. Most importantly, we follow through. When we see or hear a rule infraction, we stop, use an agreed-upon signal to get students' attention, and address the problem quickly and quietly.

> *Management Tip:* Create an attention getter for your students. For example, the teacher can say "Hocus pocus!" The class responds, "It's time to focus!" Move beyond clapping patterns to get students' attention and seek input from your students—for example: "When it's time to gather on the carpet, which of my attention getters is your favorite?"

Language is powerful. We can use it to teach our students that they have potential, and to expand what they think they can be. We use it to convey positive

At the beginning of the school year, students set reading goals and post them.

assumptions and expectations (e.g., "I knew you could beat yesterday's time on task for independent reading. You are within reach of your reading goal!"). We look for opportunities to notice and mention the good things that are happening in the classroom. This shows children not only that we have confidence in them, but that they can also have confidence in themselves as learners. We listen to ourselves speak and reflect on what we say and how we say it. We become more conscious of the wait time, eye contact, and the types of feedback we give to boys versus girls.

Focusing on action means we connect abstract terms (respect, cooperation) with concrete behaviors. We describe children's behaviors instead of their characters. When we create an anchor chart headed "Respect," we describe the behaviors we're looking for:

- What does protecting your reading time look like?
- What does protecting your reading time sound like?
- What does protecting your reading time feel like?

Children need us to translate abstract terminology into actions. It can be frustrating to deal with a student who consistently seems intent upon not following a rule or following through on a responsibility, but it is not helpful to tell the student, "You don't care about your work." This can lead the student to believe that we have low expectations of his or her character. If, instead, we describe our observed behaviors and ask what is going on, or if we describe the desired behaviors, we allow the student to understand that he or she can achieve them. Our words can contain assumptions and judgments stated indirectly—for example: "If you really cared, you'd study harder." This assumption forces a student to be defensive. If, instead, we describe the problematic behavior—for example, "I've noticed that you have not handed in your reading log this week. How can I help? Is everything okay?"—we allow the student the opportunity to explain without feeling defensive.

Learning to be brief when discussing infractions is also helpful. Long explanations can drown children in words, and, even when delivered mildly, make a student feel as though he or she is being yelled at or lectured. Pupil attention can drift during such lengthy talks. Better to ask, "Who can tell us the rule about handling books in the library?" If the teacher and the students have taught and practiced the expected routines and procedures, this reminder will be enough. Leaving out warnings (e.g., "If this continues, we might lose free time") is also recommended, They're not effective, and sound like threats to the ears of children. Threats tell students that we don't believe they can do well, emphasize the teacher's power over student behavior, and make the correction of an error feel like a punishment. Our goal is to grow student capability to self-correct, and not to rely on adult threats (Denton, 2015).

A teacher's skillful use of silence allows student voices to be heard, thinking to be done, and conclusions to be reached.

> *Management Tip:* Provide wait time by designating a 3- to 5-second pause before students are allowed to raise their hands to answer a question. Give everyone a moment to think. Put up your hand to silently remind children they have 5 seconds of thinking time as you count down on your fingers slowly.

We can also model this action by pausing ourselves to gather our own thoughts before we respond to student questions. Research has shown that a slower pace of talking combined with steady eye contact improves literacy and reduces behavior problems. The faster we speak, the more we fit into a specific period of time, but we must ask ourselves how much of what we say so quickly is being retained by the students.

Other times to recognize the power of silence include truly listening to students as they speak. Listening means keeping silence and maintaining eye contact until the speaker has completed his or her thought. In this way, we model the respectful interactions we hope to attain in our classrooms. Interruption has become the norm, but we can model and expect something different.

It is important on several levels to resist the impulse to repeat directions. We give the direction once, allow time for questions, and stop. *The more teachers remind students, the less the children rely on themselves to remember.* Of course, this doesn't mean that we allow confusion.

> **Management Tip:** When a teacher sees students failing to recall a responsibility he or she can say, "Stop . . . look . . . and listen," and then ask the class what they should be doing at that moment. We should make efforts to help students remember directions rather than repeating them. Stating directions only once also requires students to recall that they can learn to do anything (Denton, 2015).

USING STUDENT PRAISE: WHAT AND WHY?

A teacher is also consciously aware of his or her own beliefs about child development, learning, and intelligence. When he or she uses the language of "growth mindset" (Dweck, 2006), he or she demonstrates his or her conviction that perseverance and determination matter more than what we currently call "natural ability." Growth mindset is defined by Mary Cay Ricci (2013) as "a belief system that suggests that one's intelligence can be grown or developed with persistence, effort, and a focus on learning" (p. 3). This definition requires that educators change not only the way they look at student abilities, but also the manner in which they praise children. The shift from "You're so smart" to "I can see how hard you worked to prepare that excellent book talk" changes a child's perspective about intelligence and hard work.

USING STUDENT PRAISE: HOW?

Praising growth and persistence allows students to learn from failure, which eventually encourages them to take on more challenging work. When students persist through challenges, they build resilience. Sending messages that value effort stimulates children's sense of agency and reinvigorates their desire to persevere (e.g., "You can be so proud of your improvement in reading this month. I know how hard you've worked on finishing a book that you've started").

How to Give Praise	
• Name the specific behavior. • Use a warm and professional tone of voice. • Emphasize description over personal approval. • Consider asking a question to extend student thinking.	"The library corner looks wonderful. I see that you remembered to put books back neatly where they belonged. Why is this so important?"

Reinforcing language, which refers to naming the strengths we see in students, requires that we observe children to catch them doing something well (Denton, 2015, p. 90).

Find positives to name in all students. Avoid naming some individuals as examples for others. For instance, instead of saying, "I love how Trinity and Kerlin have cleaned up and are ready to move on," say "Many of you are remembering the rules about cleaning up our literacy stations" (Denton, 2015, pp. 93, 94).

USING LANGUAGE
TO HELP STUDENTS DEVELOP SELF-CONTROL: WHAT AND WHY?

To develop self-control, students need to have a growing sense of autonomy and competence. They also need to have a sense that they are controlled by themselves rather than by a force from outside, and a sense that they are capable of achieving desired outcomes (Deci & Flaste, 1995; Denton, 2015). This thought melds perfectly with having a growth mindset in that it reenergizes students to believe that they can create their own futures through dedicated work—for example: "I noticed that your group moved desks together to make conversation around the reading passage easier. What a great way to get everyone involved!"

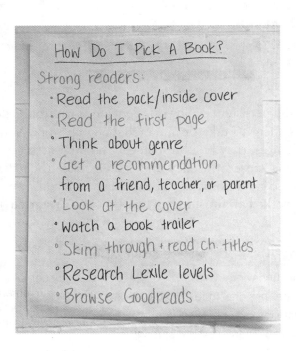

An anchor chart for assisting students with book selection.

USING LANGUAGE
TO HELP STUDENTS DEVELOP SELF-CONTROL: HOW?

A teacher's specificity, using simple and direct language, is the basis of that growing sense of self-regulation. Students learn from adults that they are capable of monitoring and changing their own behavior when we use a calm, but firm voice to remind them—for example: "Show me how you shop for books in our classroom library" or "What should you do when you have finally chosen a book?" (Denton, 2015, p. 69).

TEACHER LANGUAGE: WHAT AND WHY?

In order to be most effective, the language that teachers use is purposeful, empowering, and respectful. Denton (2015) states that teacher language can support children in several ways. Remember that a teacher's word choices should promote good learning habits, encourage children to learn cooperatively, and model the expected language that students should soon use as their own.

TEACHER LANGUAGE: HOW?

When a student hears specific, positive feedback about work or behavior (e.g., "Your use of powerful verbs had a strong impact on your story" or "I have noticed that you're trying hard to make good choices about how you protect your reading time") instead of generic comments (e.g., "Good work today!" or "Good job!"), this empowers the student to replicate and build on what has been done. It also models language that the student can use when working in a small group or with reading and writing partners.

A teacher who asks open-ended questions stimulates both the imagination and the self-efficacy of his or her students. Asking "Did anyone notice what the character said to make us believe that?" provokes children to see "what kinds of things might be noticed, and to name the things being noticed" (Johnston, 2004,

---

The Benefits of Empowering Teacher Language

Your readers and writers will . . .

1. Gain academic skills and knowledge.
2. Develop self-control.
3. Build their sense of community.

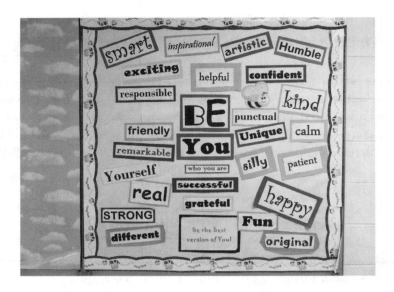

A bulletin board with empowering statements about students as individuals.

p. 13). This eventually leads to more of the talking within the classroom being done by children.

Asking "How else could the author have stated that?" encourages children to understand that the possibility of choice exists, and that learning itself is a matter of choice. A teacher who is able to query, "How did you know that was the statement of the theme in the story?" demonstrates an understanding that student statements are the result of intellectual attempts. The question "How could we check to find another answer?" gives students a sense of responsibility for locating evidence for ideas. A comment like "Do you agree with what Alicia said about the relationship between the two characters, and why?" opens up what is said in the classroom to debate, which shows that, in a democratic society, it is okay to disagree, as long as we have evidence.

Johnston (2004) reminds us that talk is the largest tool in the teacher's arsenal, and that it can be used to help children "make sense of learning, literacy life, and themselves" (p. 4).

BEHAVIOR MANAGEMENT: WHAT AND WHY?

Behavior management is a crucial part of a classroom that works. Without it, little learning can occur. If a teacher is often called upon to "put out fires," precious learning time is lost. In classrooms that work, rules and routines have been established. The teacher demonstrates respect for all pupils by learning about students' lives and being sensitive to their voiced concerns. Expectations for positive behavior must be enforced fairly.

BEHAVIOR MANAGEMENT: HOW?

It is especially important in today's diverse classrooms to recognize and value the story of each student. Culturally responsive teachers (Bensman, 2000, quoted in Gay, 2010, p. 51, summarized here) . . .

- Foster warmth, intimacy, unity, continuity, safety, and security.
- Help students develop a consciousness of their values and beliefs and what they are capable of becoming.
- Build confidence, courage, courtesy, compassion, and competence among all students.
- Are academically demanding, but personally supportive and encouraging.
- Treat everyone with equal human worth.
- Acknowledge differences among students without pejorative judgments.
- Prepare students to understand and deal realistically with social realities, along with possibilities for transformation.
- Teach ethnic, racial, and cultural knowledge, identity, and pride.
- Provide intellectually challenging and relevant learning experiences.

Weinstein and Romano (2015) add that, as teachers, "We are responsible for all the children in the class—not just for those who are easy to teach" (p. 140). As such, we also prepare to work with English language learners, children with disabilities, children who are troubled, those who are living in poverty, and those who are gifted.

A clear set of responsibilities begins behavior management. Once students understand their responsibilities, it is up to the teacher to follow through with consistency and professionalism.

HANDLING DISRUPTIVE BEHAVIOR: WHAT AND WHY?

Of course, there will be times when students misbehave, which can threaten the safety of or impede the learning of other children. At these times teachers will need to use reminding language to help students recall classroom expectations. Denton says that these classroom reminders "prompt children to do the remembering

The teacher provides individual attention and warmth centered on reading tasks.

themselves" (2015, p. 108). She gives several examples of reminders phrased as questions—for example: "What did we learn about choosing an appropriate book for independent reading?" and "What are some things you can do today to protect your independent reading time?" When we do this kind of "reminding," we are calling upon our students to recall what we taught and rehearsed earlier in the school year.

> **Management Tip:** Many teachers draft anchor charts with their expectations at the beginning of the school year. After long holiday breaks or observed points through-out the school year these charts may need to be revisited with the class.

With persistent misbehavior, Denton (2015) recommends that our language become even more "direct, specific, and explicit" (p. 130). Teachers must address the student by name and state not the misbehavior, but the desired behavior. We should keep our statement "brief, calm, and respectful" (p. 130) and should "phrase the redirection as a statement" (p. 132), not as a question. When students are calm, we remind and reinforce them, so that they make the connections between abstract terms (like "respect" and "ready to work") and concrete behavior. When they are actively misbehaving, emotionally distraught, or threatening the safety of others, we need to step in to take immediate action using exact words.

The "must do" for teachers in these situations is to stop and think before speaking. We want to remember to name the desired behavior, not the behavior we see. It's far more effective to say, "Sasha and Marc, it's time to work quietly now," than to say, "There's too much noise in here. Stop talking so much. You know better than this" (Denton, 2015, p. 132).

We also do not want to soften serious redirections, so we use statements, not questions ("Line up now," in lieu of "Could we all line up now?"). For the same reason, we don't use "please" and "thank you" when we are redirecting behaviors. Those pleasantries are used to indicate that someone is doing us a favor. Expected behavior is not a favor.

Redirecting student behavior is simple and serious. Because of that, we need to follow through by observing the behavior of the redirected children, and giving more direct feedback when it is necessary. We must also have logical consequences in mind if students hear our redirection, but do not change their behavior. We avoid, however, naming the consequence while giving the redirection. We have taught logical consequences early in the school year and at other intervals, when students and teacher were both calm, and we have responded consistently throughout the school year. Following a redirection with a warning or threat can lead to power struggles and can communicate to our children that we don't believe they can choose to behave well.

CONCLUSION

In this chapter, we have emphasized the importance of embracing a comprehensive literacy program where students learn to become better readers and writers throughout the entire school day. Implementation of the exemplary day components allows the exceptional teacher to go seamlessly from one activity to the next while keeping students motivated and engaged to learn.

The power of teacher language cannot be overstated. It influences how students see themselves and how they learn. It reinforces their belief in themselves as learners. The language we use can set teachers up as givers of knowledge and students as receivers of knowledge, or it can reinforce the idea that children are constructors of their own learning, and foster a healthy literacy learning climate.

The remainder of this book provides specific guidance for organizing and managing the exemplary literacy day in grades K–6. Each component of the exemplary literacy day is discussed, and we provide a clear pathway for where teachers can go next.

Based on getting started with the exemplary literacy day, you should take time to reflect on the following:

❏ Moving beyond the "reading block," what is your philosophy of comprehensive literacy instruction?

❏ What components of the outlined exemplary day are already in place within your classroom and school community?

❏ In what ways can you enhance your practice to include these components within the day?

❏ Think about the indicators of teaching excellence and identify a colleague in your school community with whom you could work to reflect about and improve on your literacy practices.

❏ Reflect on the language that you use to praise students and their work.

❏ Reflect on the language that you use to redirect students who misbehave in your classroom.

CHAPTER 2

Setting Up
the Literacy Environment

CLASSROOM VIGNETTE: Organizing the Classroom for Learning

When she enters her classroom in mid-August to prepare for a new group of children in September, Ms. Tapia looks around her room and is suddenly dissatisfied with its setup. At home in July she read an entire book dedicated to the literacy environment and she realizes that the room needs a few tweaks to make it a homey, cozy space that is ideally set up for students to dig into reading and writing. Inspired by Debbie Diller, she takes pictures of her classroom "as is." Next, she grabs graph paper, a pencil, and a ruler. She commits the room measurements, doorways, and immovable objects to paper, and imagines herself and her 24 students moving around the room on a daily basis. Once she has her ideal space organized, she asks her custodian for help moving and securing a large piece of storage furniture to the wall. She moves her library section to a corner, leaving the space open for whole-class instruction, moves her guided reading table to a spot from which she will be able to observe everything else going on in her room, and feels satisfied. Later, she will bring in a lamp and a couple of plants to "cozy-up" the reading space.

WHAT IS THE LITERACY ENVIRONMENT?

As stated in Chapter 1, without the support of the classroom's environment, literacy development is not likely to be effective or exemplary. In fact, the creation of a safe and orderly classroom is arguably every teacher's first responsibility. The physical design of any space has a direct impact on the way people within it function. It influences their thoughts and actions. This becomes even more important when we recognize that school rooms are hives of activity, with many children in the process of accomplishing a multitude of tasks at one time within a relatively small area (Weinstein & Romano, 2015). The creation of a physical environment that leads to learning is crucial. When planning the physical environment, teachers keep in mind the functions of each setting.

ORGANIZING THE LITERACY ENVIRONMENT: WHAT AND WHY?

When we speak of the environment of a room set up for literacy learning, we are generally discussing the categories of books and other learning materials, print, space, and furniture placement. In a well-designed elementary classroom, books are clearly in evidence throughout the room, and are sorted in the library area predominantly by genre or author, although a portion of the collection may be leveled. A large portion of the room's books are contained within the cozy, student-friendly library corner, one that invites children to enter and linger by its careful design and display of books, the inclusion of soft elements, like bean bags and stuffed animals, and the hominess of a lamp, a plant, and a rocking chair (Morrow, 2015).

The classroom contains authentic, rather than commercial, print: student work is displayed; environmental print, in the form of labels and directions, is evident throughout the room; and meaningful anchor charts are hung at students' viewing level. These charts remind students of procedures, recap the gist of mini-lessons, name the reading strategies that have been taught, and list students' responsibilities. The Word Wall has a defined spot, and, in primary grades, includes students' names. Words are placed on this wall alphabetically, as they are

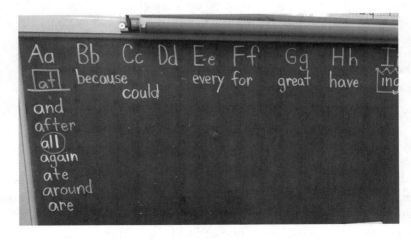

A Word Wall space for high-frequency words and/or commonly misspelled words.

introduced and studied. The words are taken from the Fry (1980) or Dolch (1948) word lists, as appropriate for each grade level. As a word on this wall grows to be used and spelled correctly by students, it is "retired," to make space for new words.

The space within the room has been planned and designed to meet the needs of this year's learners. Materials are clearly organized for student and teacher use and there is a defined large-group area, a small-group table, and a spot for one-on-one teaching. The room's décor does not compete for student attention. The space is not cluttered, and learning spots are comfortable (Diller, 2008). The class establishes routes for moving around the room with the safety and comfort of students in mind. Literacy is evident everywhere. It is embedded in content areas, and instruction in each component of the language arts (reading, writing, speaking, and listening) has a designated time.

There is a sense of urgency on the part of the teachers and the students. This is not to say that work is hurried; time is not wasted. Transitions occur smoothly and without incident. Students and teachers know that time in school is valuable. Distractions are minimal, and everyone present recognizes that this is a room where learning is always taking place. Children know how to work independently and collaboratively, which is evidenced by their focus on the tasks at hand. All of these routines and rituals take practice, which is worked on early and often in the school year.

THE VOCABULARY WORD WALL ✳

In addition to the high-frequency-word Word Wall, the effective literacy teacher builds a word-rich environment in which students are immersed in words (see Chapter 4). To raise awareness for vocabulary, or "word consciousness," a special space in the physical classroom environment should be designated for posting Tier Two words. Using the term "juicy word wall," we stress the importance of including a vocabulary space that is separate from typical sight words and commonly misspelled words. A simple change in the literacy environment is enough to get students wondering about words, their connotations, their uses, and their origins. When designing a space to introduce new vocabulary words for the week, it is important for the teacher to consider his or her own personal interests as a way of getting started.

✳ Ch. 4 (57 - 69)

ORGANIZING THE LITERACY ENVIRONMENT: HOW?

The first weeks set the tone for the entire school year. The adage "Slow down (now) to speed up (later)" certainly applies each September, as teachers meet and acclimate a new class of learners to new procedures and routines. The more conscious a teacher is of how to break down a routine into small, incremental steps, the more successful he or she and the class will become. ~~When those steps are detailed on an anchor chart, developed with the children, they become part of the procedures over which students gain automaticity through carefully orchestrated and explicit direction and practice.~~

Each procedure is introduced on its own, and the review of each procedure is practiced often and to mastery. Putting coats and backpacks away, calling children to the carpet, taking care of the Library Corner, and asking students to line up at the door are each separate procedures with many steps. ~~Once each job has been broken down into its requisite steps and modeled by the teacher, it is easier for children to learn and commit to such procedures as "just the ways we function" within the classroom.~~ Explanation and rehearsal of each routine, often many times over the course of a day in early September, assures that everyone is aware of and knows how to follow the routines.

Student desks are organized. This may take the form of pods of three to six student desks. Some teachers like rows of desks, or a large U-shaped arrangement; however, these arrangements are not conducive to collaborative work. Work stations surround the student desks, and may be closer to the walls. At the small-group table, all of the leveled books for guided reading, small whiteboards, markers, and erasers are located within easy reach.

Management Tip: Keep a guided reading bag with all of the materials you need to keep students motivated and engaged during differentiated, small-group reading instruction.

A "bag of tricks" for engaging students in guided reading.

The teacher's anecdotal notebook is also found at this table. Each station contains the materials needed for work at that spot: the paper, books, writing materials, and directions are centrally located at each station. If materials cannot be permanently settled there because of space, they are in plastic bins that are color-coordinated to match the work stations. Children will place the bins at the correct spots within the room when they are needed.

RESPONSIBILITIES CHART

Good practice dictates that teachers and students create a classroom responsibilities chart together at the start of the school year. This chart is often referenced by both teacher and pupils, and may use icons or photographs of students, which brings it to life. The teacher begins the discussion about rules and responsibilities by asking the children what rules people follow in a community. He or she then narrows it to a discussion of this particular classroom community and asks for student input about their own responsibilities within the classroom. Children may state rules in the negative ("You can't hit anyone"). It helps to restate these ideas in a clear and positive form, and in as few inclusive responsibilities as possible. Our expectations for student behavior must live together with our broader vision for student achievement, for this is our ultimate goal. We do want student input as we create the chart, but we do not wish to generate long lists of rules. Most student responsibilities can be summed up in three beliefs:

- Respect yourself: do your best work and be your best self.
- Respect others: be direct and kind to classmates, teachers, and guests.
- Respect materials and property: take care of materials and keep our classroom neat and clean.

Procedural and specific responsibility charts also exist at literacy work stations. Students know where to go, when to move, and what to do. Diller (2003) suggests small charts she calls "I Can" lists at each station. By detailing what children can do at each work station, we remind them of how to proceed on their own, thus cutting down on interruptions as we conduct running records or guided reading groups with other students.

SETTING UP THE LIBRARY CORNER

One of the most important spaces in the classroom is the Library Corner. This should be an inviting focal area for children. It should allow for privacy as one

Soft Elements to Brighten Up Your Classroom Library	
• rug	• live plants
• big pillows	• rocking chair
• beanbag chairs	• painted bookshelves
• stuffed animals (from characters within books)	• calming, clean, and clear colors with a theme
• soft-light lamp	

reads, which many children might not have access to at home. It should be large enough to allow five or six students to read and move within it. The Library Corner should be the most welcoming and appealing spot in the room. It should be decorated with posters of celebrities reading or posters that go along with books the children love. Many teachers also choose to use the Library Corner for whole-class instruction (see Chapter 8). Pg. 139 – 164

Near the entrance to the corner we might place a book-borrowing spot, so that children may borrow books to take home for the evening and return in the morning. This will require some monitoring and a sign-out system. Many children do not have access to books at home, and this can remedy that situation to a degree.

Bookcases full of wonderful texts of all sorts surround our students in this corner. The books are stored in bins that are labeled "Favorite Authors," "Animals," "Fantasy," "Realistic Fiction," "Stories about Outer Space," "Award-Winning Books," "Fables and Folktales," "Realistic Fiction," and so on. Most of the books are stored by genre, although some (up to about one-third) may be sorted by reading levels. The spines of books are facing outward, if possible, and a few books are displayed so that the entire cover can be seen. These might be books on topics

A well-organized library collection with books arranged by genre.

we are focused on for the week. Other written materials we might want to display in the library include menus, train and bus schedules, travel brochures, advertisements, maps, and anything else that we think might prove relevant to our children. It is our desire here to entice students to fall in love with reading, so we make that easy to do by not restricting their independent reading, if possible.

SETTING UP THE AUTHOR'S SPOT

In another corner of the room we place the Author's Spot, which may consist of a few desks facing each other or a table for writing. It is very important that students feel that their writing is valued. On the walls, or on a trifold on the table top, are samples of what students might want to write and quotes from some of their favorite writers—about the writing process and writing itself. C. S. Lewis said, "You can make anything by writing." "If you want to change the world, pick up your pen and write," was Martin Luther King's motto. E. B. White believed, "Writing is an act of faith, not a trick of grammar."

The "authors' tub," which is also on the tabletop, should contain:

- Colored felt-tip markers
- Crayons
- Pencils

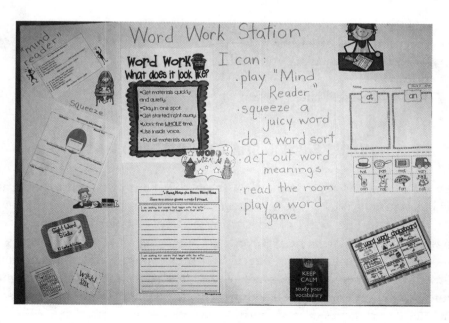

A literacy work station "I Can" list for independent/partner writing.

- A stapler
- Scissors
- Computers
- Paper of many sizes and shapes (lined and unlined)
- Construction paper

Again, our desire here is to instill a love of writing and a desire to write. We might have a few wonderful picture books about writing available as inspiration, including:

- *Ralph Tells a Story* (Hanlon, 2012)
- *Rocket Writes a Story* (Hills, 2012)
- *Click, Clack, Moo: Cows That Type* (Cronin, 2000)
- *Nothing Ever Happens on 90th Street* (Schotter, 1997)

PGS. 119-138

PREPARING FOR LITERACY WORK STATIONS

In Chapter 7, you will be introduced to literacy work stations so that students can independently and collaboratively practice skills and strategies previously learned in class. When designing your classroom environment, be sure to plan ahead to leave space for these commonly used literacy work stations:

- Library (independent or partner)—described above
- Listening (comprehension)
- Word work (vocabulary and spelling)
- Writing (independent or partner)
- Technology (skill-based programs)

USING ANCHOR CHARTS: WHAT AND WHY?

Anchor charts are a staple in most classrooms. What do we need to learn about their creation and use? There is a great deal to learn about creating clear and effective charts. The world of advertising certainly understands how to make things stick in our memories. Advertisers use a set of design principles that include the "picture superiority effect" and the "exposure effect" (Martinelli & Mraz, 2012). Teachers have discovered over time that using bolding, highlighting, pictures, words, and numbers all adds to the effectiveness of the charts we create. Other design principles at work during chart creation are "readability, legibility, constancy, clarity, balance, consistency, icons, patterns, comparison, color, and accessibility" (Martinelli & Mraz, 2012, p. 11). If we hope to have children attend to and utilize the anchor charts we make, we must create them along with our students and frequently make use of the charts ourselves to review a procedure just before we transition to the topic it explains. It also helps to add a rhyme, rhythm, or musical chant to remind children to use the anchor charts to help them as they work.

USING ANCHOR CHARTS: HOW?

Linder (2014, p. 15) reminds us that there are several types of anchor charts: ritual, toolbox, classification, and interactive. Examples of anchor charts include the following:

- *Ritual charts* that detail the steps in procedures that teachers want students to be able to follow routinely.
- *Toolbox charts* that are collections of strategies for student use as they read or write.
- *Classification charts* that highlight unique characteristics (of genre, etc.)
- *Interactive charts* that use student-generated information. Interactive charts require some teacher think-alouds to get them started, and act as a spot to post exemplars of student work.

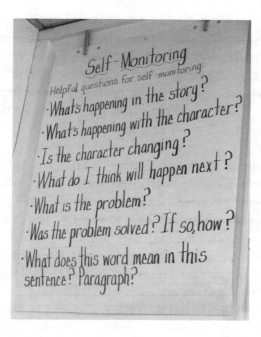

An example of an anchor chart for monitoring comprehension.

According to Martinelli and Mraz (2012), charts act as visuals to help children remember information previously taught. Charts both engage our students and lead them toward independence, since they help them figure out how to solve the problems that continue to arise as students put forth effort in reading and writing tasks.

All anchor charts of value include student input. Teachers listen to the language used by the learners in their classrooms and standardize the meaning of certain phrases and icons, which are used across all charts. To begin to determine what material needs to be displayed on charts, we watch and listen to see what our particular children need and combine that with what is in our curriculum. From there we develop the big ideas and the explicit teaching points we will capture on anchor charts (Martinelli & Mraz, 2012, pp. 2, 3).

The headings of our charts must be succinct. Martinelli and Mraz (2012) suggest that turning a strategy (like "Ways to Predict") into a question ("Wondering What Happens Next?") will capture the attention of our audience (p. 7).

While headings are catchy, the word choices we make within our charts must reflect the language development of our particular students. For primary students, a word and a picture might be appropriate, while in first or second grade, a sentence or bullet points would be useful. Whatever words teachers choose to use on charts, the words themselves must be explained and then used consistently if the charts are to be helpful to those who need them.

Anchor charts take time to build, and time is always at a premium during the teaching day. Therefore, teachers may want to prewrite the headings, and have large sticky notes ready to add as examples on the chart as they discuss each step. Using pictures of our pupils to illustrate the steps within a procedure makes a chart particularly memorable. Learning to draw a few simple icons (an ear to indicate listening, a mouth to show that something requires talking, etc.) is helpful, because we can reuse them across content areas. Remember that the teaching that is captured on the chart has already been done. Quick, easy reminders make charts into tools that children need to see to recall what has been taught.

We have all entered rooms where the charts have "taken over" the space. A cluttered environment cannot be helpful for children, who struggle to locate a chart or a word they may need. This does not foster independence. We rotate charts to reflect what the class needs are currently. Other charts can be stored on skirt hangers, awaiting their time in the spotlight.

Once the physical environment is in place, students will enter the K–6 classroom ready to learn, and the exemplary day is ready to take flight. Working with teachers, we have witnessed that once a positive classroom culture has been established and the room physically supports the philosophy of literacy throughout the day, the Do-Now activity becomes the gateway for executing the exemplary literacy day.

> **CLASSROOM VIGNETTE: From Organizing Space to Implementing the Do-Now**
>
> Ms. Tapia's classroom has undergone an extreme makeover, perfect for her population of students who receive free and reduced lunch. While she understands that breakfast is the most important meal of the day, she notices that many of the students linger while eating breakfast in the classroom or stroll in late at the beginning of the day. She calculates that if 15 minutes of lost instructional time occur every day, over 2,700 minutes (45 hours) will have been lost in just one school year! Her reaction is to include a Do-Now to start school immediately and to demonstrate a sense of urgency for learning within the literacy environment she has created for the students.

IMPLEMENTING THE DO-NOW: WHAT AND WHY?

The purpose of the Do-Now is to provide multiple activities that engage students in independent or partner reading and writing. Teachers must provide appropriate activities that will set the stage for learning to take place. As Plato said, "What is honored in a country will be cultivated there." Teachers who honor the development of literacy demonstrate that attitude by providing within their classrooms a clear agenda for literacy learning that starts the minute students step foot in the door. As mentioned earlier in the chapter, the Do-Now should take approximately 10–15 minutes to get the students started with literacy learning immediately. Based on our work in schools, we recommend that this time be devoted to practicing skills and strategies previously learned in reading and writing.

IMPLEMENTING THE DO-NOW: HOW?

The focus of instructional activities for the day will determine what Do-Now activity works best for the students. Once this is determined, the following steps will assist teachers in making the Do-Now a reality in the classroom:

- Post an agenda on the board that shows what students will be learning throughout the day. This agenda should include the components of the exemplary day that are discussed earlier in this chapter.
- Provide clear directions and project or write them in the same place every day. All students should be able to read the directions from their seats.
- If special materials are needed, they should already be on students' desks.

The Do-Now can take many forms based upon the teacher's objectives. Table 2.1 shows different opportunities for Do-Nows based upon the targeted instructional focus for review.

TABLE 2.1. Opportunities for Do-Nows

Instructional focus	Suggested activities
Reading engagement and comprehension	• Allow students to independent- or partner-read a choice text. • Include a jot lot area (see the photo below) for students to add a sticky note reacting to the text or demonstrating the use of a strategy learned. • Allow partners to take one another on a tour of each other's reading notebooks. • See Chapter 8 for additional ideas for reading engagement.
Word study	• Provide students with a word-sort activity based on patterns recently learned in class. • Practice grade-level sight words on a ring with index cards. In the upper grades, practice decoding multi-syllabic words in context. • See Chapter 5 for additional ideas for reviewing phonics and phonemic awareness.
Fluency	• Partner-read poetry and Readers' Theatre scripts. • Engage in repeated readings of familiar texts both independently and with partners.
Vocabulary	• Choose a vocabulary word from the Word Wall or vocabulary message to define and illustrate in a "word nerd journal." See Chapter 4 for additional review ideas.
Writing	• Free-write for a short period of time, referring to the writer's notebook for topics and ideas. • Allow partners to take one another on a tour of each other's writing notebooks.

A jot lot area for posting students' reactions, questions, insights, and recommendations.

> *Management Tip:* Create a bulletin board space where students can share ideas and inspirations related to their choice reading. Students can read a choice text for homework and jot down reactions, questions, insights, and recommendations on sticky notes for homework. When students enter the classroom, they can finish working on their sticky notes and post them in the "jot lot." The teacher takes a few minutes at some point during the day to share individual contributions from the jot lot. This is a great way for the teacher to engage students in a productive activity while transitioning between lessons, in and out of the classroom, and so on. This ensures that students understand that this is an important activity where all readers' ideas are valued and shared.

CONCLUSION

In this chapter, we extended teachers' knowledge of implementing the exemplary day to include a serious focus on setting up the literacy environment to support learners. If the literacy environment is set up according to our recommendations, the teacher is ready to engage readers and writers according to the suggested exemplary day schedule. This day begins with the Do-Now the minute students enter the classroom.

.... ✋ STOP! THINK! REACT! ✋ ....

Based on your understanding of the literacy environment and Do-Nows, you should take time to reflect on the following:

❑ In what ways does your learning environment support opportunities for whole-class, small-group, and independent/partner work?

❑ How do you set the tone for students to recognize their responsibilities as productive members of a reading and writing community?

❑ In what ways does your library area reflect your literacy beliefs?

❑ What types of recommended Do-Now activities would benefit the students you are teaching?

❑ Is your Library Corner used throughout the day?

CHAPTER 3

Assessment Guiding Instruction

CLASSROOM VIGNETTE

After mastering the use of the literacy Do-Now, Ms. Tapia felt anxious upon reading a new memo from her school administrator about increasing the number of assessments required. She was not alone in feeling overwhelmed. Working with grade-level peers, she decided to take a step back from the exemplary day to focus on assessment. They decided to create a grid for the months of the year to indicate when literacy tests would be administered. After meeting with the school reading coach, they settled on a form for recording scores to keep the information handy. Although the teachers initially felt pressured with all of the informal tests needed to be given, they later felt as though they knew more about their children than in the past once assessments were implemented and analyzed.

ASSESSMENT IN LITERACY DEVELOPMENT:
A GUIDE FOR DESIGNING INSTRUCTION

A critical issue facing educators is assessment. This chapter deals with why we assess, what measures we use to assess, and how to administer the assessments we choose to give. We also discuss when to assess children's literacy development. Finally, we talk about preparing students for the different assessments, especially the standardized tests. How much time should be spent in test preparation will be discussed as well.

WHY WE NEED TO ASSESS CHILDREN'S LITERACY ACHIEVEMENT

Assessment must be sensitive to children's different backgrounds, abilities, interests, and needs in order for teachers to determine what a child has achieved. Assessment is about gathering information to generate data. These data help the teacher to create effective instruction that will meet the needs of a child by selecting appropriate instructional materials and strategies. Therefore, we need to think about instruction as being guided by assessment.

The International Literacy Association and the National Association for the Education of Young Children (1998) issued a joint position statement on learning to read and write that recommends using culturally and developmentally appropriate assessment measures. Additionally, the assessments should align with instructional objectives, while always keeping in mind best practices for the total development of the child.

Administering a single test measure of any type is insufficient for everything teachers need to know about each child. Teachers need to assess performance in many areas and under many conditions. Multiple measures of assessment help teachers, children, and parents to determine a student's strengths and weaknesses and plan appropriate instructional strategies that match educational goals.

In this book we talk about guided reading, reading comprehension workshop, writing workshop, word study session, fluency, and vocabulary meeting. We are also concerned about the child's self-esteem and interest in reading and writing. To determine improvement and to guide instruction we must assess children's development in all of these areas. We discuss many types of assessment in this chapter. Other assessments are included in chapters that address specific areas of literacy development.

Children will handle assessment best when they think of their classroom environment as one that is safe and nonthreatening. This is possible when children know that it will help teachers to plan their instruction. Students need to know that their teacher has high expectations for them and believes that they can be successful when tested (Denton, 2015). Teachers need to give constructive responses to children's work when it is warranted. This provides incentive to get better.

WHAT DOES IT MEAN TO AUTHENTICALLY ASSESS STUDENTS?

Authentic assessment is defined as assessment activities that represent the actual learning and instructional activities of the classroom and out-of-school world. There are several characteristics of authentic assessment perspectives:

- Assessment should be based on a variety of measures.
- Assessment should include observations of children engaged in classroom reading and writing tasks, daily performance samples, standardized tests, and standards-based tests.
- Assessment should focus on children's learning based on the curriculum and standards.
- Assessment should be continuous over a substantial period.
- Assessment should consider student diversity, culture, language, and special needs.
- Assessment should include parent, child, and teacher information.
- Assessment should be a guide to designing instruction.

To accomplish these goals, assessment should be frequent and carried out with varied measures. The main goal is to observe and record actual behavior that provides the broadest possible picture of a particular child (McKenna & Stahl, 2009; Fountas & Pinnell, 2012). Educators should integrate a variety of authentic assessment methods into their instruction. Some of the more common and more useful types include anecdotal observation forms, daily performance samples, audio recordings, videos, pencil-and-paper forms, student evaluations, surveys, interviews, conferences, and checklists (Johnston & Costello, 2005; Purcell-Gates, Duke, & Martineau, 2007; Risko & Walker-Dalhouse, 2010).

AUTHENTIC ASSESSMENT: HOW?

Observation Forms

Use observation forms or teacher-made forms for observing and recording children's behavior. Observation forms usually have broad categories with large spaces for notes about children's activities. Goals for observing should be planned and forms should be designed to meet specific reading and writing goals. Observations should focus on one particular aspect of the child's performance, such as oral reading, silent reading, behavior while listening to stories, or writing. Within the descriptions of behavior, dialogue is often recorded:

> "Although Janet read orally without errors, her reading was without expression. She read, 'The big bad wolf ran away' and every word was said in the same tone. I asked her to listen to me read the sentence and then echo-read it and she did. She said, 'I like doing that. Can we try it again?'"

The template in Figure 3.1 presents a sample form that can be used for several different types of observations, including, but not limited to, oral reading behavior, writing, and more.

Teacher's Name: _____

Student's Name: _____

Date: _____   Time: _____

Location of Observation: _____

Purpose for Observing:

Significant Events during Observation:

Reflective Analysis of Significant Event (this reflection should include what you have learned):

List at least three ways you can use or apply what you observed to your future teaching:

FIGURE 3.1. Sample form for recording student observations.

Rubrics

Rubrics are a great way to communicate expectations to students and to allow them to track growth when achieving specific literacy standards. The teacher can begin with his or her set of literacy standards and essential questions outlined in school and district curriculum guides. It is important to develop rubrics thinking with the end in mind. When unpacking literacy standards, we need to ask what achieving the standard looks like. Therefore, we can develop learning targets and work backward to create concrete and measurable objectives that break the literacy tasks into more student-friendly pieces.

> **Management Tip:** When breaking apart a standard, think about what your students can do to achieve the standard. Draft an "I Can" list, breaking the standard down into steps that a student can take to achieve success. Be sure to use student-friendly language and share the draft as you assign activities throughout lessons.

Your rubric should show what mastery of a skill looks like. Aligned with standardized testing, you may choose to create a rubric with the following indicators:

- Exceeds expectations
- Meets expectations
- Approaches expectations
- Partially meets expectations
- Does not meet expectations

After using the rubric to assess student work, it is important to confer with students to set goals and to provide feedback about their progress.

Daily Performance Samples

In addition to observation forms, teachers can collect daily performance samples. With this type of assessment, teachers organize samples of a child's work in any area of literacy that is taught on a daily basis. Daily performance samples provide data points about how the child is learning and mastering the content (Figure 3.2).

Audio and Video Recordings

Students enjoy the act of performing and having their efforts recorded; thus, these tools simultaneously accomplish the goals of authentic assessment and student participation in intrinsically motivating practices. Audio recordings are an assessment that can determine language development, comprehension through a recorded retelling of a story, and progress in oral reading fluency. By recording

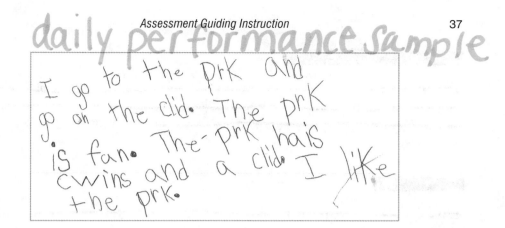

FIGURE 3.2. A performance sample of a child's writing at the end of the kindergarten year.

discussion sessions related to responses to literature, the teacher can better understand how youngsters function in a group. Audio recordings can also be used as a type of self-assessment. Children can listen to their own recordings to evaluate both their story retellings and their fluency.

In addition to audio recordings, videos also allow teachers to view their students in action. Videos are a rich form of assessment because the teacher can hear the child as well as see the child's facial expressions and body movements. Teachers can also use videos to assess their own teaching performance. Because of the wealth of information contained in assessment videos, teachers need to have a specific purpose in mind when choosing video as an assessment tool, and collected recordings should be evaluated with a checklist or observation form.

Teacher-Made Pencil-and-Paper Tests

As the name suggests, teachers design these tests to match instruction. Because it is customized, this assessment can follow the progress of the students and what they are learning.

Student Evaluation Forms

Children should regularly evaluate themselves by collecting samples of their own work and discussing them with their teacher, parents, and other children. In addition, children should use student evaluation (self-evaluation) forms to evaluate their own performance. Completing self-evaluation forms allows children to reflect on their learning experience and helps them become intentional learners and start to develop metacognitive skills. Self-evaluations should be an integral part of authentic assessment and encourage students to reflect on their growth and progress.

Surveys and Interviews

Teachers can prepare surveys to assess children's attitudes about how they think they are learning or what they like or dislike in school. Surveys can be in the form of questionnaires or interviews with written or oral answers (see Figure 3.3 for examples).

Checklists

Checklists and inventories include lists of developmental behaviors or skills for children to accomplish. The checklist should be based on objectives a teacher may have for instruction and designed to determine whether goals set forth have been accomplished. A checklist for evaluating developmental characteristics of children can be used to determine if a child is developing socially, emotionally, physically, and cognitively based on his or her age.

Conferences

Conferences allow the teacher to meet with a child one-to-one to assess skills such as reading aloud, discussing a child's progress, talking about steps to improve, providing individual instruction, and prescribing activities. Children should take an active role in evaluating their progress. The manner in which they can do this is to set goals for themselves.

Reading Motivation Inventory

An important area to find out about is a child's interest, motivation, and self-esteem about reading. A child who struggles often has a low self-esteem when it comes to reading, so knowing if this is an issue is very important. Children with low self-esteem about reading will often "tune out" when instruction occurs or become a behavior problem. It is extremely important for these children to have more instruction in an environment that will allow them to succeed.

> **Management Tip:** Have the children maintain an ongoing record that chronicles knowledge they have constructed over time. Create a chart that hangs on the wall with one pocket for each student. There is a stack of index cards in a pocket for this purpose. At the end of each day, set aside 10 minutes for the children to complete the evaluation task. They are to take an index card, and, for 2–3 minutes, review what they thought was the most important thing they learned that day and tell it to a partner. Then they are to write for 5 minutes about what they discussed. After they write these concepts, they "pair and share" with their partner. When the children leave the class, they put the index cards into their pockets on the chart. The teacher reviews the cards. This gives him or her insight into what concepts the children have understood and recalled correctly. Cards are

Teacher's Name: _____ Date: _____

Student's Name: _____

Ask questions that are age-appropriate for the students you are interviewing.

1. What is a book?

2. What do people do with books?

3. What can books be about?

4. What is your favorite book? Why?

5. What is fun about reading?

6. What is hard about reading?

7. Do you like to read outside of class?

8. What kinds of things do you read outside of class?

9. What are your strengths as a reader?

10. What are your goals as a reader? What plan do you have to achieve those goals?

Teacher's Name: _____ Date: _____

Student's Name: _____

Ask questions that are age-appropriate for the students you are interviewing.

1. What is writing?

2. What do people write about?

3. What are your favorite topics to write about?

4. What is your favorite thing about writing?

5. What challenges do you have with writing?

6. If you wrote a book, what would you write about?

7. Do you like to write outside of class?

8. What kinds of things do you write about outside of class?

FIGURE 3.3. Sample interview surveys.

sent home at the end of a week so parents are kept up to date about what their children are learning. Encourage children and parents to discuss the contents of the cards and to extend the learning at home.

IN-DEPTH INFORMAL MEASURES OF ASSESSMENT

The assessment tools discussed to this point have offered ways to take a snapshot of a student's performance at a particular moment. As informative as they are, teachers also need to incorporate more in-depth tools into their assessment programs. For example, word study knowledge, running records, and informal reading inventories can be used to collect assessments completed. A very incomplete list of literacy assessment tools is shown in Table 3.1.

Assessing Knowledge of Word-Study Skills

Assessment in word study should happen often and take many forms. Phonemic awareness, considered the precursor to phonics, is important in the literacy development of children. When we test a child for knowledge in this area, we try to determine if he or she can segment phonemes in words and we ask him or her to blend words back together again. In tests of phonological awareness and phonemic awareness, we are interested in the child's ability to hear and say the sounds, not the letters. In addition to segmenting and blending, children need to be able to substitute different onsets with rimes to build words and substitute one sound for another. We include an Informal Phonics Inventory, with directions for administering and scoring, in Appendix 3.1 at the end of this chapter.

Running Records

Clay (1993a) created running records for observing and recording children's oral reading and for planning instruction. In this analysis, what a child can do and the types of errors the child makes when reading are recorded. Running records can be useful in determining the appropriate material to use for instructional purposes and for independent reading, and they can also help the teacher identify a student's frustration level. The data collected from a running record, specifically the numbers and types of errors students make, should inform the level of material the teacher uses for instruction and the types of instructional strategies used to deliver it. Having the instruction reflect the information gathered from running records is crucial. One drawback of running records, however, is that they devote more time indicating types of errors students make in oral reading than evaluating their ability to comprehend text.

TABLE 3.1. Sample Literacy Assessment Tools: A Very Incomplete List

Word recognition and vocabulary

Qualitative Reading Inventory, Fifth Edition (QRI-5), word lists (Leslie & Caldwell, 2010)

Informal Phonics Inventory (McKenna & Stahl, 2015)

Dolch Word Lists (*www.kidzone.ws/dolch*)

Diagnostic Assessments of Reading with Trial Teach Strategies (DAR-TTS)[a] (Roswell, Chall, Curtis, & Kearns, 2017)

Dynamic Indicators of Basic Early Literacy Skills (DIBELS) (Deno, 1985; Deno & Fuchs, 1987; Deno & Mirkin, 1977; Shinn, 1989)

Receptive One-Word Picture Vocabulary Test (ROWPVT)[a] (Brownwell, 2011)

Peabody Picture Vocabulary Test, Fourth Edition (PPVT-4)[a] (Dunn & Dunn, 2007)

Expressive One-Word Picture Vocabulary Test, Fourth Edition (EOWPVT-4) (Brownwell, 2011)

Comprehensive Test of Phonological Processing, Second Edition (CTOPP-2) (Wagner, Torgesen, Rashotte, & Pearson, 2013)

Oral reading

QRI-5 narrative passages (Leslie & Caldwell, 2010)

QRI-5 expository passages (Leslie & Caldwell, 2010)

QRI-5 miscue analysis (Leslie & Caldwell, 2010)

Running records (Clay, 2000)

Developmental Reading Assessment, Second Edition (DRA2) (Beaver & Carter, 2013), oral reading section

DIBELS (Deno, 1985; Deno & Fuchs, 1987; Deno & Mirkin, 1977; Shinn, 1989)

Fluency

QRI-5 fluency calculation (Leslie & Caldwell, 2010)

Multidimensional Fluency Scale (McKenna & Stahl, 2015)

DRA2 oral reading section and words correct per minute (Beaver & Carter, 2013)

DIBELS (Deno, 1985; Deno & Fuchs, 1987; Deno & Mirkin, 1977; Shinn, 1989)

Phonemic awareness, phonics, and decoding

Phonological Awareness Test (PAT) (Robertson & Salter, 2018)

Words Their Way primary and upper-level spelling inventories (Bear, Invernizzi, Templeton, & Johnston, 2008)

Qualitative Spelling Checklist (McKenna & Stahl, 2015)

Comprehension

DIBELS retelling section (Deno, 1985; Deno & Fuchs, 1987; Deno & Mirkin, 1977; Shinn, 1989)

DRA2 comprehension analysis (Beaver & Carter, 2013)

(continued)

TABLE 3.1. *(continued)*

Comprehension *(continued)*

Running records literal and analytical questions (Clay, 2000)

QRI-5 literal and analytical questions (Leslie & Caldwell, 2010)

Woodcock Reading Mastery Tests—Revised (WRMT-R)[a] (Woodcock, 2011)

Motivation, affect, and interest

DRA2 reading engagement form (Beaver & Carter, 2013)

Tell Me What You Like! survey (McKenna & Stahl, 2015)

Here's How I Feel about Reading survey (McKenna & Stahl, 2015)

Reader Self-Perception Scale (McKenna & Stahl, 2009)

Motivations for Reading Questionnaire (McKenna & Stahl, 2009)

Strategic understandings

Awareness of Purposes of Reading Interview (McKenna & Stahl, 2009)

[a]This diagnostic tool is also recognized as a screening tool for dyslexia.

Using running records is straightforward. In taking a running record, the teacher asks the child to read a short passage of 100–200 words from a book the child has not read before. Younger children read shorter and easier passages, and older children read longer and more difficult passages. Teachers select a book they believe is at the independent level for the child, that is, a book that he or she can read easily. If the child gets each word correct, he or she then selects a book that is a bit more difficult. The teacher and the student each have a copy of the passage. As the child reads, the teacher marks the passage using the prescribed coding system to indicate whether words are read correctly and what types of errors are made. The types of errors recorded are insertion of a word, omission of a word, repeating a word, substituting one word for another, reversal, refusal to pronounce a word, and an appeal for help. Self-corrections are recorded but are not considered errors. For the running record to be a valid representation of the student's ability, the teacher must know the difficulty level of the materials being used and match students to the appropriate level. Leveled books for difficulty discussed in the chapter on guided reading are commonly used materials.

When collecting the raw data the teacher marks up the passage indicating the types of errors the children make. The teacher analyzes the data by organizing it on a running record form (Figure 3.4). The form allows the teacher to systematically review the errors the students made and classify them as meaning (M), structure (S), or visual (V) errors.

| Name: _____ | Date: _____ |
| Book: _____ | Book level: _____ |

Words: _____   Error rate: _____   Accuracy rate: _____

Errors: _____   Self-correction rate: _____

E	SC	Text	Cues used					
			E			SC		
			M	S	V	M	S	V

M, meaning; S, structure; V, visual; E, error; SC, self-correction.

Reading level

Independent: 95% to 100% accuracy

Instructional: 90% to 95% accuracy

Difficult (or frustrational):   Less than 90% accuracy

Reading proficiency: Fluent _____   Word by word _____   Choppy _____

Retelling

Setting: Characters _____   Time _____   Place _____

Theme: Problem or goal _____

Events: Number included _____

Resolution: Solved problem _____   Achieved goal _____   Ending _____

FIGURE 3.4. Running record form.

Three Types of Miscues

Meaning Miscues (Does It Make Sense?)

When you look at an error, figure out if the child is using meaning cues in identifying the word. If the child is using information from the text, picture clues, or context clues and reads, "The boy *took* the leaf from the tree" instead of "The boy *pulled* the leaf from the tree," he has made an error, but the meaning is intact. This error is marked with an M. The child knows how to use the context to get the word but needs to look more closely at the print.

Visual Miscues (Use of Phonics)

When a child makes a visual error, he or she knows how to use phonics to decode but doesn't pay attention to the meaning of the text. This child reads, "I *stepped* the milk," instead of "I *spilled* the milk." This error is marked with a V. In this situation, ask the child if what he or she reads makes sense and emphasize that it is important to think about the meaning of the sentence when reading, as well as to look carefully at the words.

Structural Miscues (Is the Syntax Correct?)

The child makes a structure or syntax error when he or she intuitively understands the syntax in sentences. For example, if a child reads, "I *went* to the zoo" instead of "I *ran* to the zoo," the English grammar or syntax is correct because a verb goes in that spot, but the word chosen is not correct. Therefore, you mark this error with an S and know the child understands the sentence structure but needs to look more closely at the print.

Calculating an Accuracy Rate

$$\frac{\text{Total words} - \text{errors}}{\text{Total words}} \times 100 = \% \text{ accuracy}$$

In other words:

1. Record the number of words in the testing passage (e.g., 70 words).
2. Count the number of errors made by the child and subtract them from the total number of passage words (e.g., 5 errors subtracted from 70 equals 65).
3. Divide that number (65) by the total words in the passage (70).
4. Multiply that by 100; the result equals the percent of accuracy for the passage read (about 93% in this example).

If a child reads 95–100% of the words correctly (generally 0 to 3 errors in the passage), the material is at his or her independent level when he or she doesn't need any help reading. If 90–95% of the words are correct (roughly 4 to 10 errors in the passage), the material is at the instructional level when the child can read the material but needs some scaffolding from the teacher. Less than 90% of the words read correctly (more than 11 errors) is the child's frustration level when the material is too difficult for him or her. If a child is at the frustration level with the first book he or she tries, for kindergarten, stop testing. If an older child is at frustration level for the first passage, go down as many levels as necessary until you arrive at the instructional material.

Running records should be done about every other month for all early childhood students and twice a year with older students. Teachers should talk to children about the types of errors they make in a running record; teachers should also provide children with strategies such as listening to the meaning of a sentence and looking at the letters in the word to figure out a word.

Informal Reading Inventories

Informal reading inventories (IRIs) are similar to running records, but they place a larger emphasis on comprehension. The purpose of this type of inventory is to determine a student's reading level, like the running record. After reading, children answer several types of comprehension questions. Students should read both narrative and informational text. The comprehension questions focus on main ideas, inferences, and vocabulary.

As with the running record, when teachers listen to the oral reading, they use a coding system to identify and record the types of errors the children make. For example, these codes will indicate if the students omit words, repeat words, reverse words, self-correct, add words, substitute words, and so on. This information helps to guide instruction. One of the most important elements of the IRI, however, is the assessment of comprehension when a child reads or listens to a story (Flippo, Holland, McCarthy, & Swinning, 2009). Children can be tested reading orally and silently for comprehension. If a child gets 0 to 4 of the comprehension questions incorrect, the material is at the appropriate level for his independent reading. Five incorrect questions corresponds to his instructional level and 10 incorrect questions reflects his or her frustration level. Errors are counted and an accuracy percentage is calculated, which indicates if the book the child is reading is at his or her independent, instructional, or frustration level.

When we read aloud to children, material should be above their reading level, but at their level of comprehension. With the use of the IRI, comprehension questions can determine if what is being read is too easy or too difficult for the child's listening comprehension (Gunning, 2003; Hasbrouck & Tindal, 2006; Tompkins,

2003). Teachers can make their own IRIs, but there are also published tests. Some of these tests are:

- *Basic Reading Inventory; Pre-primer through grade twelve and early literacy assessments* (Johns, 2012)
- *Qualitative Reading Inventory–5* (Leslie & Caldwell, 2011)
- *Linking reading assessment to instruction: An application worktext for elementary classroom teachers* (5th ed.) (Mariotti & Homan, 2009)
- *Classroom Reading Inventory* (12th ed.) (Wheelock, Silvaroli, & Campbell, 2012)
- *Analytical Reading Inventory: Comprehensive standards-based assessment for all students* (9th ed.) (Woods & Moe, 2011)

RETELLING TO EVALUATE COMPREHENSION

Having students summarize a text provides the teacher with a unique window into their comprehension of the story. Letting a listener or reader retell or rewrite a story offers active participation in a literacy experience that helps develop language structures, comprehension, and sense of story structure (Paris & Paris, 2007). Retelling, whether it is oral or written, engages children in holistic comprehension and organization of thought. With practice in retelling, children come to assimilate the concept of narrative or expository text structure. They learn to introduce a narrative story with its beginning and its setting. They recount its theme, plot episodes, and resolution. In retelling stories, children demonstrate their comprehension of story details and sequence, organizing them coherently. They also infer and interpret the sounds and expressions of characters' voices. In retelling expository text, children review what they have learned, sequence events, describe new concepts, and recall cause and effect.

Teachers often assess retelling but don't teach retelling as frequently. This can keep children from progressing. Retelling is not an easy task for children, but with practice they improve quickly. To help children develop the practice of retelling, let them know before they read or listen to a text or story that they will be asked to retell or rewrite it (Morrow, 1996). Further guidance depends on the teacher's specific purpose in the retelling. If the immediate intent is to teach or test sequence, for instance, instruct children to concentrate on what happened first, second, and so on. If the goal is to teach or assess the ability to integrate information and make inferences from text, instruct children to think of things from another book they read that are similar. Props such as popsicle stick characters or the pictures in the text can be used to help students retell. Pre- and postdiscussion of text helps to improve retelling, as does the teacher's modeling a retelling for children.

★ GUIDELINES FOR STORY-RETELLING INSTRUCTION

1. Ask the child to retell the story. "A little while ago, I read the story [name the story]. Would you retell the story as if you were telling it to a friend who has never heard it before?"

2. Use the following prompts only if needed:

   a. If the child has difficulty beginning the retelling, suggest beginning with "Once upon a time" or "Once there was. . . ."

   b. If the child stops retelling before the end of the story, encourage continuation by asking, "What comes next?" or "Then what happened?"

   c. If the child stops retelling and cannot continue with general prompts, ask a question that is relevant at the point in the story at which the child has paused—for example: "What was Jenny's problem in the story?"

3. When a child is unable to retell the story or if the retelling lacks sequence and detail, prompt the retelling step by step. For example:

   a. "Once upon a time" or "Once there was. . . ."

   b. "Who was the story about?"

   c. "When did the story happen?" (day, night, summer, winter?)

   d. "Where did the story happen?"

   e. "What was [the main character's] problem in the story?"

   f. "How did [he or she] try to solve the problem? What did [he or she] do first [second, next]?"

   g. "How was the problem solved?"

   h. "How did the story end?" (Morrow, 1996)

RETELLING ASSESSMENT

Retellings can develop many types of comprehension and allows adults to evaluate children's progress. During the evaluative retellings, *do not offer prompts beyond general ones* such as "Then what happened?" or "Can you think of anything else about the selection?" Retellings of narrative text can reveal a child's sense of story structure, focusing mostly on literal recall, but they also reflect a child's inferential and critical thinking ability. To assess the child's retelling for sense of story structure in a narrative story, first parse (divide) the events of the story into four categories: setting, theme, plot episodes, and resolution. Use a guide sheet and the outline of the parsed text to record the number of ideas and details the child includes within each category in the retelling, regardless of their order. Credit the child for partial recall or for recounting the gist of an event (Wasik & Bond, 2001; Whitehurst & Lonigan, 2001). Evaluate the child's sequencing ability by comparing the order of events in the child's retelling with the proper order of setting, theme, plot episodes, and resolution. The analysis indicates which elements the child includes or omits, how well the child sequences, and thus where instruction might be focused. Comparing retellings over a year will indicate the child's progress.

Retellings can be evaluated for many different comprehension tasks. The directions to students prior to retelling and the method of analysis should match the goal. Retelling provides a qualitative analysis form for evaluating oral and written narrative retellings in which checks are used instead of numbers for a general sense of the elements a child includes and to determine progress over time. Also provided in the form is a qualitative evaluation of interpretive and critical responses. A child could engage in self-evaluation (with help from the teacher) by changing the words to "I began the story with an introduction," "I named the main character," "I was able to list other characters," and so on.

PORTFOLIO ASSESSMENT

The portfolio assessment provides a way for teachers, children, and parents to collect representative samples of children's work. It can include work in progress and completed samples. A portfolio provides a story of where children have been and what they are capable of doing now, to determine where they should go from this point forth. The teacher's portfolio should include work selected by the child, teacher, and parent. Each sample of a child's work in the portfolio should include some reflection by the student and teacher. It should represent the best work that children can produce and illustrate difficulties they may be experiencing. The physical portfolio is often a folder that is personalized with a drawing by the child, a picture of the child, and his or her name.

Currently, many teachers are opting to create digital portfolios where all of the students' work is electronic. Computerized assignments can simply be transferred into an electronic folder, and projects that are done by hand can be scanned into a computer file and added to that same folder. A separate digital folder can be used for each child. One benefit of a digital portfolio is that it is easy for the student, teacher, and parents to obtain copies, as the folders can be attached and sent in an e-mail or transferred to removable storage drives. Digital portfolios reduce the amount of paper to store in the classroom.

Whether a teacher opts for a physical or digital portfolio, it should include grade-appropriate work such as:

- Daily work performance samples
- Anecdotes about behavior

- Audios and videos of oral reading
- Analyzed story retellings
- Checklists recording skill development
- Interviews
- Standardized and standards-based test results
- Child's self-assessment forms
- Evaluated expository and narrative writing samples

Some schools have formal schedules for collecting portfolios and administering tests. A portfolio should be prepared by the teacher with the child. Children usually take them home at the end of the school year. Teachers pass portfolios to the child's next teacher (McKenna & Stahl, 2009). The sample progress monitoring form in Figure 3.5 shows one way a teacher can collect comprehensive literacy data over the course of a school year.

STANDARDIZED TESTS: THE PROS AND CONS

In addition to the informal assessments discussed to this point, teachers are also responsible for administering formal assessments. Standardized tests are prepared by publishers and are norm-referenced; that is, they are administered to large numbers of students when they are created to develop norms. *Norms* are the average performance of students who are tested at a particular grade and age level. When selecting a standardized test, it is important to check its validity for your students. That is, does the test evaluate what it says it tests for, and does it match the goals you have for your students? The reliability of the test is important as well. In other words, are scores accurate and dependable? Other features of standardized tests are as follows:

1. Grade-equivalent scores are raw scores converted into grade-level scores. For example, if a child is in first grade and receives a grade-equivalent score of 2.3, his or her performance would be considered above grade level.
2. Percentile ranks are raw scores converted into a rank according to where the child ranked as compared to all children who took the test at the same grade and age level. Therefore, if a youngster received a percentile rank of 80, it would mean that he or she scored better than or equal to 80% of students taking the test at the same grade and age level and that 20% of the children taking the test scored better.

Although many criticisms are associated with standardized measures, they do present another source of information about a child's performance. In addition,

Student's Name: _____	Teacher's Name: _____

Grade Level: _____ Age: _____ School Year: _____ Date: _____

Affective Assessments:

Reading Attitude Survey Score:	Interest Inventory (top-rated topics of study):
(Circle One) Low Motivation / Indifferent / High Motivation	_____ _____ _____

Examiner Word Lists:

Instructional Vocabulary Level: (Grade)   Notes:

Spelling Inventory:

Instructional Spelling/Phonics Group: (Circle)   Letter Name Alphabetic / Within-Word / Syllables & Affixes / Derivational

Running Records:

Benchmark Analysis	% Accuracy	Comprehension Notes
Benchmark Level Tested: (Grade)		
Benchmark Level Tested: (Grade)		
Benchmark Level Tested: (Grade)		

Fluency:

# of Words Correct per Minute (WCPM):	Notes:

Writing Progress: (Holistic Scoring Guide)

Instructional Level: (Grade)	(Circle One) Advanced / Proficient / Below Proficient
Focus/Organization: (Circle One) 1 2 3 4	Elaboration/Details: (Circle One) 1 2 3 4
Grammar, Usage, & Mechanics: (Circle One) 1 2 3 4	Additional Notes:

Additional Assessments:

Name of Assessment:	Notes:

Collecting data over a year

FIGURE 3.5. Literacy progress monitoring form.

taking a standardized test does expose children to another type of literacy situation that they are likely to encounter both in and out of school. Parents like receiving the information from the test because it is concrete information regarding where their child ranks among others in the same grade. It must be emphasized, however, that standardized scores are just one type of information and no more important than all the other measures discussed earlier.

Concerns Associated with Standardized Testing

Because standardized tests represent only one form of assessment, their results must be coordinated with other assessment measures. The standardized test along with informal measures of assessment should all be scrutinized when making important decisions about children's instruction.

Because school districts are often evaluated on how well children perform on the standardized tests, teachers feel pressured to "teach to the test." This situation is often referred to as high-stakes assessment because major decisions are being made from the results of one test score. For example, a teacher's competency might be judged based on test scores; these scores may also factor into the decision to retain or promote a child to the next grade. Some schools prepare children for standardized tests by drilling them on sample tests similar to the real ones. The sample tests are graded, and instruction is geared to remedy student weaknesses. If teachers do not prepare children for the test with practice sessions and do not teach to the test, their children may not score well. Children must have the advantage of knowing what the test is like. They need to learn how to follow the directions and how to fill in the answers. For us to carry out responsible test preparation it must be held in balance with other teaching methods, so that students are not just learning in order to demonstrate proficiency on a high-stakes test.

Breaking Through the Block: There will be assessments that measure students' understanding of reading and writing skills, as well as assessments that measure understanding of content-area information. Refer to your literacy assessments to reflect on each student's strengths and weaknesses. For example, a child who has difficulty with comprehension might struggle solving a lengthy math problem. Perhaps a struggling writer will have difficulty answering open-ended questions in science. Use your literacy assessments to differentiate content-area assessments. Be sure to provide support for students as necessary.

Responsible test prep also means digging deeper into our work, allowing the children to think and respond in several ways, and always requiring their best work. If we do that throughout the year, along with the inclusion of academic vocabulary our children will see on the tests, we are teaching responsible test prep.

Testing has always been an issue in schools. With informal tests we explain to the children that we do them so we can decide what instruction they need to make them better readers and writers. Standardized tests are harder to deal with. If we foster warmth, unity, safety, and security in classrooms, children are more likely to take the tests in stride. Try to instill confidence that says, "Yes, you can do well," to children instead of "If you don't do well, this or that will happen." Let children know that the test is one of many evaluations and they should feel confident that things will be okay. Include parents in conversations about assessment so they understand too.

CONCLUSION

An effective literacy teacher finds ways to balance using formative and summative assessments to guide instruction. The goal of literacy assessment is not just to simply document students' achievement, but to assist students in setting rigorous and realistic goals to become better readers and writers. This information can only be gleaned when the teacher takes time to analyze and reflect thoroughly on assessments that have been administered. Taking the time to get to know each individual learner will allow the teacher to provide the best individualized instruction likely to result in significant student growth.

·· 🖐 STOP! THINK! REACT! 🖐 ··

❑ Refer back to the sample list of literacy assessments at the beginning of the chapter. Determine which areas of literacy development are being assessed and which areas still need attention.

❑ Conduct a literacy assessment on an individual reader. Take the time to reflect on the reader's strengths and areas of needed improvement.

❑ Create a binder with dividers, separating each child's literacy assessments.

❑ Keep a log for parent communication regarding students' literacy development and growth throughout the year.

❑ When designing assessments, ask yourself: What does achieving this standard look like at your grade level?

DIRECTIONS FOR ADMINISTRATION

Consonant Sounds

Point to **S.** Say, "What sound does this letter say?" Go from left to right, repeating this question. It is fine if the child reads across a line without prompting. For **C** and **G**, have the child give both sounds. [*Note:* If the child cannot pass this subtest, consider giving an alphabet inventory.]

Consonant Digraphs

Point to **th.** Say, "What sound do these letters say?" Go from left to right, repeating this instruction. It is fine if the child reads all five without prompting.

Beginning Consonant Blends

Point to **bl.** Say, "What sound do these letters say?" Allow child to proceed with or without prompting.

Final Consonant Blends

Point to **bank.** Say, "What is this word?" Allow child to proceed with or without prompting. Listen for the ending sound. Create a word for each beginning consonant using one of the three endings provided.

Short Vowels in CVC Words

Point to **fit.** Say, "What is this word?" Allow child to proceed with or without prompting.

The Rule of Silent e

Point to **cap.** Say, "If this is **cap**, what is this?" Point to **cape** as you say the second part of this sentence. Go from left to right, repeating the question for each pair.

Vowel Digraphs, Diphthongs, and r-Controlled Vowels

Have the child read each word across each line, from left to right.

Context Clues

Ask child to fill in the words.

(continued)

SCORING

For all subtests and for the total test, use the following criteria:

Mastery	80%+
Needs Review	60–79%
Needs Systematic Instruction	Below 60%

The table below gives the number of correct answers that roughly correspond to these percentages.

Subtest	Total possible	Mastery	Review	Systematic instruction
Consonant Sounds	20	16–20	12–15	0–11
Consonant Digraphs	5	4–5	3	0–2
Beginning Consonant Blends	20	16–20	12–15	0–11
Final Consonant Blends	12	10–12	8–9	0–7
Blending and Creating Words	5	5	5	0–5
Short Vowels in CVC Words	10	8–10	6–7	0–5
The Rule of Silent *e*	4	4	2–3	0–1
Long Vowel Digraphs	10	8–10	6–7	0–5
Diphthongs	6	5–6	4	0–3
r-Controlled Vowels	6	5–6	4	0–3
Context Clues	7	7	7	0–7
Total	**105**	**85–95**	**70–88**	**0–69**

(continued)

INFORMAL PHONICS INVENTORY

Name: _____   Date: _____

Directions: To teach with the initial consonant picture cards, make them the size that works for you by leaving them as is or enlarging or reducing them on a photocopy machine. Copy on firm, colored paper and laminate. Use the cards to alphabetize them, match to words beginning with the same letters, identify initial consonant sounds, or figure out the number of sounds in each word.

   To assess with the consonant picture cards, say the word *boat*. Ask the child the sound at the beginning of *boat*. Read the pictures in columns (e.g., *boat, girl, lamp, queen, van, zebra,* then *circle, house,* and so on). Do not allow the children to see the pictures or words during this assessment. Record incorrect answers.

_____/20 Consonant Sounds

S	D	F	G	H	J
K	L	Z	P	C	V
B	N	M	Qu	W	R
T	Y				

_____/5 Consonant Digraphs

th	sh	ch	wh	ph

_____/20 Beginning Consonant Blends

bl	fl	fr	gl
br	gr	pl	pr
cl	sk	sl	sm
cr	sn	sp	tr
dr	st	str	sw

_____/12 Final Consonant Blends

bank	apt	limp
band	pact	lilt
bang	lift	lisp
bask	lint	list

_____/5 Blending and Creating Words

   Use B, D, F, M, and P with chunks and rimes (*an, it, en,* etc.) to create words.

(continued)

55

_____/10 Short Vowels in CVC Words

fit	led	sup	lap	hug
rot	tin	rag	wet	job

_____/4 The Rule of Silent *e*

cap	tot	cub	kit
cape	tote	cube	kite

_____/10 Long Vowel Digraphs

loaf	heat	aim	weed	ray
gain	fee	coal	leaf	due

_____/6 Diphthongs

town	loud	joy	threw	oil	law

_____/6 *r*-Controlled Vowels

tar	hall	sir	port	hurt	fern

_____/7 Context Clues

The boy r_____ down the h_____.

The cat drank m_____ from a bowl.

The dog p_____ a bone in the y_____.

The girl p_____ with her t_____ in the playroom.

Total: _____/105

CHAPTER 4

Introducing the Vocabulary Meeting

CLASSROOM VIGNETTE: From Assessment to Vocabulary

Ms. Tapia decided that vocabulary will play an important role during instruction each day, so she has set aside 15–20 minutes in her daily agenda to make word learning fun and interactive for the students. Revamping her "traditional" morning meeting, she has decided to focus instead on deepening students' understanding of more challenging academic vocabulary. Read on to learn about how vocabulary comes to life in Ms. Tapia's classroom.

WHY DO WE NEED TO TEACH VOCABULARY?

Beginning at a very young age, children start to acquire and develop language. While having a strong vocabulary background has been linked to greater achievement in school, studies have also shown the effect of vocabulary deficits. We know that children from low socioeconomic families have a vocabulary of about 500 words at 3 years of age, children from working-class families have a vocabulary of about 700 words, and children from professional families have a vocabulary of about 1,100 words (Dickinson & Tabors, 2002; Hart & Risley, 1995; Morrow, 2015; White, Graves, & Slater, 1990). This "word gap" is of great concern to many teachers, particularly because vocabulary knowledge is often recognized as the currency of education and a significant contributor to reading comprehension (Blachowicz & Fisher, 2015). After all, the more children acquire new vocabulary in your classroom, the more successful they are likely to be as they advance through school (Stanovich, 1986). In order for students to meet the demands of reading more complex narrative and expository texts, teachers must focus on broadening and deepening students' vocabulary knowledge.

Fostering a love for learning and acquiring new words in your classroom means that instruction must be authentic, engaging, and relevant to students' lives (Beck, McKeown, & Kukan, 2013). This chapter explores how to transform your vocabulary instruction into a robust part of the day that teaches all students to learn and love vocabulary.

WHAT IS A VOCABULARY MEETING?

As part of an exemplary literacy day, students will benefit from time set aside specifically for vocabulary instruction. Although there is a great "buzz" of excitement when it comes to talking about the reading and writing workshop models in literacy education, few teachers have given vocabulary the spotlight that it deserves in the classroom. It is our belief that vocabulary warrants a similar amount of attention when it comes to planning a literacy-rich day for students.

In this section, we discuss a unique format for gathering students in a group to read and discuss a vocabulary-enriched message (see Figure 4.1). For this 15- to 20-minute meeting time, students are expected to sit in a circle on the floor or in a whole-class central meeting area where text is easily visible and displayed. Prior to conducting the meeting, the teacher deliberately chooses which vocabulary words to teach. The teacher may choose to include new words to teach to the students or embed words to review from previously taught lessons. The key to crafting the vocabulary-enriched message is to write one that is authentic to the students, featuring social events or academic lessons that have taken place in the classroom. The teacher can choose to prepare a text that teaches vocabulary words from graded vocabulary lists, a basal reading story, daily read-aloud, reading workshop text, writing workshop mentor text, content-area text, or other various academic vocabulary lists.

In addition to embedding vocabulary words, opportunities are provided to reinforce previously taught sight words. The teacher also has flexibility with choosing the form of writing that will support the vocabulary meeting. The teacher may choose to write a letter to the class, introduce a riddle, share an informational piece, or write a journal entry. Various forms of writing can support the format of the vocabulary-embedded text. Once students are gathered, the teacher uses a think-aloud strategy to introduce students to the text, connecting back to classroom learning experiences. The think-aloud informs the students about the content (what the vocabulary message will be about) and the purpose (why we are noticing and appreciating these words) of the vocabulary meeting.

Day 1

Reinforced Word Wall Words:	In this part of the template, the teacher considers embedding words that were previously taught.
Tier Two Vocabulary Focus:	What words were intentionally chosen for the vocabulary message?
Setting a Purpose for Learning: ("Today, we will be learning new vocabulary words based on a text that I have written/chosen based on . . .")	Draft your think-aloud. How will you introduce the vocabulary message to your students? Consider various ways to "hook" students into the lesson.
Text Choice: narrative riddle poem informational letter recipe journal list song other	Choose a format for your vocabulary message. Be sure to vary your format throughout the school year.
Opportunities for Differentiation:	Based on your student data, consider various opportunities for differentiating instruction with your students. What are the individual needs of your students?

FIGURE 4.1. Sample lesson plan format for the vocabulary meeting.

 Breaking Through the Block: Although the vocabulary meeting is designed to take 15–20 minutes, time is often of the essence in the classroom. To flexibly include vocabulary instruction in your daily schedule, consider creating vocabulary messages that capture key ideas in a math, science, or social studies lesson. Mix up the variety of your vocabulary messages so that the structure can be included with content-area instruction. For example, you can create a vocabulary-enriched message that lets students know about a science investigation. New vocabulary words will excite your students about participating in the day's lesson.

Many teachers choose to conduct their vocabulary meetings throughout different parts of the school day. There is a great benefit to teachers in that the format of the meeting lends itself to the components of a responsive classroom. If used as a "traditional" morning message, the vocabulary meeting provides a means for bringing students together for academics combined with social–emotional learning. The four components of the vocabulary meeting include a greeting, sharing, group activity, and reading of the vocabulary-enriched message (Center for Responsive Schools, 2015).

VOCABULARY MEETING: HOW?

There are simple steps that a teacher can take to implement vocabulary meeting time in the classroom:

1. *Greet*—Read the text and encourage students to spot the featured vocabulary words.
2. *Share*—Engage students in an open dialogue about the featured vocabulary words, tapping into students' background/prior knowledge.
3. *Group*—Extend the lesson through the use of graphic organizers, games, and vocabulary journal activities.
4. *Read*—Engage the students in a whole-class choral reading of the message to reinforce new words learned and to build fluency.

> *Management Tip:* When choosing a space for your vocabulary meeting, be sure to post your featured words in this area on a weekly basis as new words are introduced. New vocabulary (written on index cards) can be posted in this whole-class meeting area. At the end of the week, be sure to transfer your words to a vocabulary Word Wall in the classroom.

Below is a suggested format for using the vocabulary meeting to support a responsive learning community in the classroom. Each bullet provides additional information about the vocabulary meeting.

• *Greet*—Gather your students in a whole-class area and encourage the students to greet each other by name. Have an open discussion about featured words of the week or words posted on the vocabulary Word Wall. It is helpful to prepare index cards in advance with the featured words of the week written clearly for students to see.

• *Share*—Open a class discussion that allows students to share their ideas about the featured vocabulary words with the whole group. Students can discuss the context of the words they have identified and how the context relates to their thoughts, feelings, or ideas that day.

• *Group*—You may choose to write the message (text) in front of the students and encourage students to carefully decode the text as you write it. For upper-elementary-grade students, teachers will often display a lengthier, more complex text and encourage the students to choral-read the text together at a whispering volume or silently read the text. Once the text is shared, it is important for the teacher to provide an opportunity for students to deepen their understanding of the words. Students may complete a graphic organizer (see the example

Squeezing Juicy Words

Definition:		Picture This!
	Vocabulary Word:	
Synonyms:		Antonyms:
7-Up Sentence:		

FIGURE 4.2. Example of a graphic organizer.

in Figure 4.2) with the whole group, discover the meaning of the featured words through a focused read-aloud, or work in their vocabulary journals to complete an activity related to a word.

• *Read*—At the completion of the lesson, the teacher should encourage the class to echo-read or choral-read the vocabulary-enriched message. At this point, students might be asked to identify challenging vocabulary words that are embedded in the text. Students can also practice academic skills by using context clues to discuss word meanings as the teacher guides a mini-lesson about the embedded words.

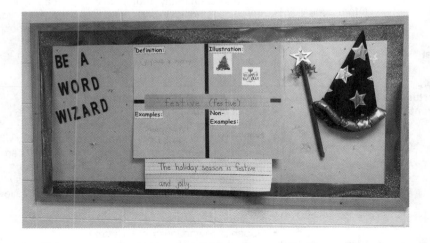

Drilling down into vocabulary with a Frayer model–inspired learning space.

In addition to providing an opportunity for rich discussion around vocabulary, the vocabulary meeting serves as a teachable moment for modeling good writing. It is also an opportunity to foster a growth mindset with your students by reflecting on learning. At the conclusion of the lesson, the teacher might ask:

- "What new words did you learn today?"
- "How do these new words help you as a reader/writer?"
- "In what ways would you like to grow as a vocabulary learner?"

In Figure 4.3, we provide a sample vocabulary meeting for Read Across America Week.

Grade Level(s): Kindergarten/First Grade

Reinforced Word Wall Words:	*and, open, of, that, too*
Tier Two Vocabulary Focus:	*magnificent, fond*
Setting a Purpose for Learning: ("Today, we will be learning new vocabulary words based on a text that I have written/chosen based on . . .")	When we celebrate Read Across America Week, many students are introduced to Dr. Seuss, who was fond of reading for fun. Today I am going to challenge you to decode a text that I have written about the places you will go when you practice reading. See if you can find any unfamiliar vocabulary as you read this text.
Text Choice: narrative riddle poem informational letter recipe journal list song other	Dear *Magnificent* Readers, Dr. Seuss reminds us that reading can take us to great places and open many doors. Most of all, reading is fun too! You have brains in your head. You have feet in your shoes. Reading will take you any direction you choose! What types of stories are you *fond* of? Sincerely, Mr. Ken
Opportunities for Differentiation:	• Vocabulary instruction: *magnificent; fond* • Use of punctuation marks • Rereading for fluency and expression • Follow-up activity: Conduct an interest inventory with the class to learn more about what the students are interested in reading • Read-aloud opportunities: *Miss Malarkey Leaves No Reader Behind* by Judy Finchler and Kevin O'Malley; *How Rocket Learned to Read* by Tad Hills • Sight-word practice • Upper-case and lower-case letters

FIGURE 4.3. Sample vocabulary meeting for Read Across America Week.

TIER ONE, TIER TWO, AND TIER THREE WORDS

When designing instruction for vocabulary meetings, an important consideration involves choosing what types of words to embed in the text or choosing what words to focus on from an existing text. It is important to recognize that words are categorized according to tiers (Beck, McKeown, & Kucan, 2002). Tier One words are words that do not require explicit instruction, primarily because children already come to school knowing the meanings of these words. For example, children who enter school are likely to understand the meaning of *house* and *happy*. As discussed earlier, the teacher must take the prior knowledge and schema of the students into consideration. Teachers who work with English language learners, for example, may discover that Tier One words require additional instruction in class to scaffold students toward mastering a particular lesson. Tier Two words are recognized as high-frequency words that, although they might appear often in texts, students most likely will not understand without explicit instruction. Words such as *impatient, persnickety,* or *incognito* can be the focus of explicit instruction. Tier Three words are often content-, discipline-, or domain-specific, requiring instruction primarily within the content-area classroom. For example, words such as *composer, decomposer,* and *ecosystem* will require special attention in order for students to master a lesson on insects as part of a science curriculum.

INTRODUCING NEW VOCABULARY WORDS: HOW?

One way to introduce new vocabulary words is to utilize the *six-step process* (Marzano, 2004). It involves the following steps:

1. Provide a description, explanation, or example of the new term.
2. Ask students to restate the description, explanation, or example in their own words.
3. Ask students to construct a picture, pictograph, or symbolic representation of the term.
4. Engage students periodically in activities that help them add to their knowledge of the terms in their vocabulary notebooks.
5. Periodically ask students to discuss the terms with one another.
6. Involve students periodically in games that enable them to play with terms.

Teachers use the first three steps when introducing a term to students. For example, assume a teacher is introducing the word *mutualism.* Instead of offering a textbook definition, the teacher describes the term or tells an anecdote that illustrates its meaning (Step 1). The teacher might explain that the crocodile and

The teacher guides a student to participate in a vocabulary meeting.

a bird called the Egyptian plover have a relationship that exemplifies mutualism. The crocodile opens its mouth and invites the plover to stand inside. The plover picks things out of the crocodile's teeth. Both parties benefit: the plover gets fed; the croc gets its teeth cleaned. While explaining this relationship, the teacher might show students images found on the Internet.

In Steps 2 and 3, students try their hand at explaining the meaning of *mutualism*. They devise an explanation or an example from their own lives (Step 2). Next, they draw an image depicting what they think *mutualism* means (Step 3).

A few days later, the teacher reviews the new term using Steps 4, 5, and 6, which needn't be executed in sequence. The teacher might have students compare the meaning of *mutualism* with another previously studied term, such as *symbiosis* (Step 4). Students might pair up and compare their entries on the term in their vocabulary notebooks (Step 5), or the teacher might craft a game that students play using these terms (Step 6).

Recommended Materials
- Large dry-erase board or interactive whiteboard
- Index cards for Tier Two words (optional: color-coded Tier Three words by subject/content area)
- Chart paper
- Markers
- Copies of the vocabulary meeting text (to be used in literacy work stations and for independent reading)

VOCABULARY JOURNALS

Once a space is created for posting vocabulary words in the classroom (see Chapter 2), students can independently reflect on the words and their meanings through the use of vocabulary notebooks, or journals. Gone are the days of having students locate and copy dictionary definitions from long lists of assigned vocabulary words, as this type of instruction does not deepen understanding of words. Instead, vocabulary journals provide a space for expanding upon understanding of new assigned vocabulary words and for jotting down words that students notice and appreciate when independently reading. To maximize time spent on learning, the teacher can create a weekly "vocab-list," or short note containing all of the assigned words of the week for students to paste or copy into their notebooks:

Week 1 Vocab-List
- afraid
- afternoon
- building
- chatter
- discover
- hidden
- nervous
- plenty

Students should be encouraged to have an open conversation with their peers about their familiarity with the words and possible meanings. Introducing the vocabulary journal at the beginning of the year requires a review of procedures. Figure 4.4 shows a sample schedule to guide use of vocabulary journals in the classroom.

Activity Idea

Tape "mystery words" to students' backs and remind students not to peek! Once they are ready to go, students mingle around the classroom and find a partner. Partners then take turns taking the vocabulary words from one another without showing the word. Students then return to their seats to create "7-up sentences" for their partners, as in the sample anchor charts inspired by *Word Nerds* on page 74.

Once students are finished, provide an opportunity for them to reveal and teach the mystery words to their partners. Partners can sign their names in each other's notebooks, symbolizing that they have learned new vocabulary. Allow your students time throughout the week to visit and teach other classmates while

Monday

Carefully paste the weekly vocab-list on a new page in your journal. Underline any unfamiliar words. Discuss words that you might know with a partner in your group.

Tuesday

Choose a word from your vocab-list. Write a student-friendly definition for a friend. Draw a picture to illustrate the meaning of your word.

Wednesday

Write a 7-up sentence for one of your vocabulary words. Be sure to include context clues related to the word's meaning.

Thursday

Choose another word from your vocab-list and write a 7-up sentence for one of your vocabulary words. Be sure to include context clues related to the word's meaning.

Friday

Trade journals with a partner and read their 7-up sentences or review their definitions/illustrations. Write a short note to your partner about his or her work.

FIGURE 4.4. Sample schedule for the use of vocabulary journals.

What Is a 7-Up Sentence?

- Seven or more words to make a complete thought.
- A clue tells about my vocabulary word.
- I can write a telling, asking, demanding, or exciting sentence.
- **Important:** Don't forget to end with a punctuation mark! (. ! ?)

How to Build a Stronger 7-Up Sentence

- Use seven or more words to build a simple, compound, or complex sentence.
- Include context words about the vocabulary word. Choose your words carefully for effect.
- Leave a blank space where the vocabulary word goes so your partner can solve it.

Third Grade: Use punctuation to vary your sentence. Try these: (. , ! ?)

Fourth Grade: Avoid run-on sentences.

collecting more signatures! Students will benefit from repeated exposure to vocabulary words while socially interacting with peers to develop language (Overturf, Montgomery, & Smith, 2013).

EXPLICIT/SPONTANEOUS/CONTENT-AREA INSTRUCTION

An important consideration surrounding vocabulary instruction is striking a balance between teaching words that are assigned from basal reading programs/teacher-generated lists and taking advantage of teachable moments when students are inquisitive about new words they come across while reading. Some words are more important to teach than others (Overturf et al., 2013). While there is much debate about the number of words that should be taught each week, we know that words are learned through repeated exposure and at more than one level (Beck et al., 2002; Jenkins, Stein, & Wysocki, 1984; McKeown, Beck, Omanson, & Pople, 1985; Stahl, 2003). Research shows that children can learn a minimum of 5–10 words per week. The role of the teacher is to explicitly, or purposefully, choose which vocabulary words to introduce, teach, and review.

In addition to explicitly choosing words to teach, the classroom teacher should encourage students to notice and appreciate the power of unfamiliar vocabulary words that they come across spontaneously. For example, students will have a piqued interest when hearing unfamiliar words in conversation. The teacher can provide a student-friendly definition of these words and add them to a list to include in later vocabulary lessons. Similarly, children will come across unfamiliar vocabulary words both when independently reading and when listening to the teacher read aloud. Encourage the students to jot these words down in their vocabulary journals. Students can keep a "Heard a Word" list and later go back to look up their meanings, determine parts of speech, write thoughtful sentences, and feature words through discussion with classmates. Words that students come across spontaneously can contribute to whole-class lessons, individual conference discussions with the teacher, and independent practice in a literacy work station focused on word work.

While building on explicit and spontaneous vocabulary instruction, the teacher should consider the large collection of specialized words that are included in daily content-area lessons (Alverman, Phelps, & Gillis, 2010). With this in mind, teacher-generated word lists, combined with opportunities for unintentional word learning, can guide students' use of content-area notebooks. For example, second-grade students involved in a unit of study on butterflies might paste the word bank on the following page into their science journals.

While the teacher recognizes that special terms will aid in students' comprehension of concepts related to this particular science unit of study, space is

Science Lesson 1: Butterflies	
Words to Know	**Words I'm Wondering About**
butterfly	_____
chrysalis	_____
pupa	_____
metamorphosis	_____
spinneret	_____
larva	_____
entomologist	_____

provided for students to personalize their word learning, collecting additional words and concepts worth recording. Similar opportunities for vocabulary instruction can be applied to mathematics, social studies, art, music, health, the teaching of foreign languages, and the like.

ADMINISTERING AND USING ASSESSMENT TO GUIDE INSTRUCTION

In order to assess students' ability to conceptualize new vocabulary, the teacher should employ both summative and formative assessments that measure the effectiveness of instruction. Within the first few weeks of school, benchmark assessments can provide information about students' prior knowledge of words and schema. Examiner word lists (by grade level) can be used to determine students' familiarity with grade-level-specific terms. For example, in *Assessment for Reading Instruction*, McKenna and Stahl (2009) provide words lists that can be used to calculate whether the grade-level vocabulary words are at a students' independent, instructional, or frustration level. Similarly, tools for vocabulary knowledge can be found within various benchmark tools, including the Qualitative Reading Inventory (Leslie & Caldwell, 2010) and guiding questions used with running records and the Developmental Reading Assessment (DRA; Beaver & Carter, 2013).

CONCLUSION

In a literacy-rich environment, vocabulary is an important part of the effective literacy teacher's repertoire. Begin your school year by designating a space to highlight vocabulary words that are being learned. Feature 5–10 words each week in a whole-class area and transfer these words to your vocabulary Word Wall at the end of each week. Throughout the week, craft vocabulary-enriched messages to deepen students' understanding of the new words being learned. Encourage students to work collaboratively with partners using their vocabulary journals, and, most importantly, celebrate the successes of your students. Before you know it, students will be independently noticing and appreciating the power of vocabulary on their own.

······················· ✋ STOP! THINK! REACT! ✋ ·····················

Based on your understanding of vocabulary development, take time to reflect on the following:

❑ In what ways do you utilize a space in the classroom for celebrating word learning?

❑ How are words introduced, reinforced, and (eventually) retired?

❑ What formats of the vocabulary meeting can be implemented with your student population?

❑ What materials will you use to support vocabulary learning? How will these materials be used?

CHAPTER 5

Word-Study Session

Strategies for Figuring Out Words, Phonological Awareness, Phonics, and More

This chapter follows the basic outline we are using in this book to organize and manage time, space, and materials so that optimum learning will happen. The following list provides the key ideas we discuss:

- Theory and research about word study
- What are the objectives for the children to learn about word study?
- What type of space, time, and materials are important for word study?
- How do we account for individual differences when teaching word study?
- Best practices in teaching word study

THEORY AND RESEARCH CONCERNING FIGURING OUT WORDS

Becoming literate is a process that begins at birth and continues throughout life. Children differ in their rates of literacy achievement; they must not be pressured into accomplishing tasks or be placed on a predetermined time schedule. Researchers have found that children learn that print has *functions* as a first step in reading and writing (McGee & Morrow, 2005).

After functions, the child becomes interested in the *forms of print*. Details about names, sounds, and configurations of letters and words now serve the child's learning more than simple understanding of how print functions.

There are three developmental levels in word recognition: Children first identify words through sight and context, then use letter–sound cues, and finally rely on sounding out words (Cunningham, 2009; McCormick & Mason, 1981). Children's initial questions and comments during story readings are related to the pictures and the meanings of the stories. As they gain experience with story readings, their questions and comments begin to concern the names of letters, the reading of individual words, or attempts to sound out words (Cunningham, 2009; McAfee & Leong, 1997; Neuman & Roskos, 1998).

Some of the strategies for figuring out words are done mostly in grades PreK–2. Standards suggest some skills for grades four and five, and after that phonics only is reviewed. Teachers need to go back to skills that haven't been mastered, but the skills discussed in this chapter are to be mastered in grades PreK–3.

Children are likely to become involved in literacy activities if they view reading and writing as functional, purposeful, and useful. Studies of early reading and writing behaviors clearly illustrate that young children acquire their first information about reading and writing through their functional uses (Cook-Cottone, 2004; McGee & Morrow, 2005). Functional text includes grocery lists; directions on toys, grocery items, and medicine containers; recipes; telephone messages; school-related notices; religious materials; menus; environmental print inside and outside the home; and so on. These represent just a sample of the functional literacy information with which a child comes in contact daily. Young children are also aware of e-mails, text messages, and video game directions, and are interested in digital tools.

OBJECTIVES FOR FOUNDATIONAL SKILLS IN WORD STUDY

We must always have standards to guide us concerning the skills to be taught and at what grade level. Standards suggest that foundational word-study skills are necessary and must be taught as the means to an end. The conventional wisdom is to teach them early and move forward. At the same time foundational skills are being taught, children should be engaged in all other language arts skills such as comprehension, vocabulary development, writing, and fluency. Figure 5.1 provides a brief checklist of objectives for word study.

PHONOLOGICAL AWARENESS AND PHONEMIC AWARENESS

Phonological awareness and phonemic awareness instruction in early literacy leads toward helping students become independent readers. Teaching these skills to children should be done concurrently with other strategies for learning to read,

	Always	Sometimes	Never	Comments
• Knows print is read from left to right				
• Knows that oral language can be written and then read				
• Knows what a letter is and can point one out on a page				
• Knows what a word is and can point one out on a printed page				
• Knows that there are spaces between words				
• Reads environmental print				
• Recognizes some words by sight and high-frequency sight words				
• Can name and identify rhyming words				
• Can identify and name upper- and lower-case letters of the alphabet				
• Can blend phonemes in words				
• Can segment phonemes in words				
• Associates consonant initial and final sounds (including hard and soft *c* and *g*)				
• Associates consonant blends with their sounds (*bl, cr, dr, fl, gl, pr, st*)				
• Associates vowels with their corresponding long and short sounds (*a*–acorn, apple; *e*–eagle, egg; *i*–ice, igloo; *o*–oats, octopus; *u*–unicorn, umbrella)				

(continued)

FIGURE 5.1. Checklist for assessing concepts about print, strategies to figure out words, phonological awareness, and phonics.

	Always	Sometimes	Never	Comments
• Knows the consonant digraph sounds (*ch, ph, sh, th, wh*)				
• Uses context, syntax, and semantics to identify words				
• Can count syllables in words				
• Attempts reading by attending to picture clues and print				
• Guesses and predicts words based on knowledge of sound–symbol correspondence				
• Can identify structural elements of words such as prefixes and suffixes, inflectional endings *-ing, -ed,* and *-s,* and contractions				
• Demonstrates knowledge of the following phonic generalizations:				
a. In a consonant–vowel–consonant pattern, the vowel sound is usually short				
b. In a vowel–consonant–e pattern, the vowel is usually long				
c. When two vowels come together in a word, the first is usually long and the second is silent (*train, receive, bean*)				
• Uses word families often referred to as rimes and phonograms, such as *an, at, it, and ot,* and initial consonants to build words, such as *man, can, fan, ran*				
Fluency • Reads independently with appropriate accuracy, speed, and expression				

FIGURE 5.1. (*continued*)

such as acquiring sight words and learning how to use context and picture clues. Children need to have a holistic view about books and reading, as well as the more abstract skills, as they work on decoding unknown words.

Phonological awareness is the awareness of the sound structure of language. It involves identifying and manipulating larger parts of spoken language such as whole words, syllables, and word chunks such as *at* or *an*. Segmenting, blending, and substituting one sound for another are important skills children need to develop. *Phonemic awareness* is the ability to recognize that words are made up of individual speech sounds (Snow, Burns, & Griffin, 2009; Soderman & Farrell, 2008; Strickland & Schickedanz, 2009; Tompkins, 2013; Shanahan, 2006). The words *hat* and *chat* contain three speech sounds referred to as *phonemes*. The phonemes are not letters; they are sounds. This is different from *phonics*, which includes knowledge of the relationship between letters and sounds. How you teach these is discussed in the next section.

Phonological awareness is an umbrella term and a subset of that is *phonemic awareness*. Phonemic awareness and phonological awareness are considered precursors to phonics and are needed to learn phonics. They are important to achieve successful reading ability. However, they are only one part of a comprehensive program in learning to read (National Reading Panel, 2000). *It is the concurrent use of several word-study skills that creates a proficient reader* (Reutzel & Cooter, 2009). According to the report of the National Reading Panel (2000), a total of 18 hours of teaching phonemic and phonological awareness in the kindergarten year is needed for a child to learn the skills. In a 180-day school year, that would be about 6 minutes a day. Instruction in phonological and phonemic awareness should be playful as teachers read stories, tell stories, play word games, and use rhymes and riddles.

Instruction in the area should be purposeful and planned; we cannot leave it to chance. In the past this instruction was spontaneous and incidental. Of course, it can still be spontaneous when the moment arises and should be; however, it must be systematic and explicit as well. We try as much as possible to make our instruction meaningful and with a purpose (Adams, 2001; Cunningham, 2009; Gambrell, Morrow, & Pressley, 2007).

SCOPE AND SEQUENCE OF PHONEMIC AWARENESS INSTRUCTION

- Phoneme isolation   What's the first sound in *boat?*
- Phoneme identification   What sound is the same in the words *cake, cup,* and *cook?*
- Phoneme categorization   Which word doesn't belong? *run, ring, rope, tub*

- Phoneme blending   What is this word? /p/–/ă/–/t/?
- Phoneme segmentation   How many sounds are in the word *pin*? Let's push and say these sounds: /p/–/ĭ/–/n/. How many sounds are in the word *pin*?
- Phoneme deletion   What is *jeep* without the /j/?
- Phoneme addition   What do you have when you add /s/ to the beginning of the word *nap*? (*snap*)
- Phoneme substitution   The word is *kit*. Change the /k/ to /f/. What's the new word? (*fit*)

When teaching activities that help children learn to rhyme, segment, blend, and substitute sounds, we are strictly working with sounds and not attaching them to letters. Following are activities that will help develop phonological awareness.

- *Matching*: To match sounds, we say, "Which words have the same sound at the beginning, *big* and *boy*? Or *house* and *go*?"

- *Isolating*: When isolating words we say, "What sound do you hear at the beginning of the word *pen*?" (We aren't asking for the letter name; we are asking for the sound.)

- *Substituting*: When we ask children to substitute sounds, we say, "Listen to the word *bat*; it has a /b/ sound at the beginning. Can you say it, /b/, *bat*? Now see if you can make a new word if we say *mmm* at the beginning of *at*. Everyone, *mmm-mat*. What word did we make? *Mat*."

- *Deleting*: When we ask children to delete, we say, "What word do we have when we say the word *snowman* without the *man*? The answer is *snow*." Another deletion is, "When it is rainy outside, we wear a raincoat. If you take the *rain* away from the word, what word do you have left?" The children answer *coat*.

- *Rhyming*: Exposing children to books that contain rhymes, such as *Green Eggs and Ham* (Seuss, 1960) and *Goodnight Moon* (Brown, 1947), helps develop this skill. Teachers can recite rhymes and words that don't rhyme and ask children to differentiate between them. Other rhyming activities are:

  ○ Thinking of words that rhyme with a person's name—for example: "My name is Ann; *fan* rhymes with Ann."
  ○ Singing songs that rhyme, such as "Hickory Dickory Dock,"
  ○ Acting out rhymes, such as "Jack and Jill," and identifying the rhyming words.
  ○ Making up new rhymes in a story song such as "I Know an Old Lady." Let the children decide what else she could swallow and what would happen

to her if she did—for example: "I know an old lady who swallowed a frog; she began to *jog* when she swallowed a frog."

It is a good idea to have some routine rhymes and songs that the class chants repeatedly. The chants should allow children to change the rhymes and to match and substitute rhymes.

• *Segmenting*: Segmenting is an important skill. It is easier for a child to segment the beginning sound (or onset) and then the ending chunk (or rime). Do this with the word *man*. The child should be guided to say *mmm* for the onset /m/ and then *annn* for the rime /an/.

• *Syllabication*: Syllabication is a way of segmenting words or working on phonological awareness. Children can clap the syllables in their names and in the names of their friends. For example, the name *Tim* is one clap or one beat, *Janet* is two, and *Carolyn* is three.

SYLLABLE NAME CHANT

If your name has a beat and the beat is one,
Say and clap your name and then run, run, run.
If your name has a beat and the beat is two,
Say and clap your name and hop like a kangaroo.
If your name has a beat and the beat is three,
Say and clap your name, then buzz like a bee.
If your name has a beat and the beat is four,
Say and clap your name and stamp on the floor.

TEACHING THE ALPHABET

As mentioned earlier, word study includes many skills such as learning the alphabet, gaining knowledge about print, developing a large number of sight words, phonological awareness, phonics, and fluency. We begin with the emergent literacy skills to fluency in the next sections of this chapter.

Learning the Alphabet

Children need to learn the alphabet to become independently fluent readers and writers. It has been demonstrated by research to be a predictor of reading success. When teaching the alphabet the teacher needs to explain what a letter is and can the child point to one on a printed page. The children should also be able to explain what a word is and point to one on a printed page.

Systematic teaching of the alphabet is necessary. A very common practice has been teaching the alphabet from beginning to end with one letter a week. Based on research, two or three letters a week or one letter a day is probably a better way to introduce the alphabet letters. This way the alphabet is introduced quickly and you can go back and review each one again (Levin, Snatil-Carmon, & Asif-Rave, 2006). In a comparison of children who learned a letter a week to children who learned about three letters a week, those in the three-letters-a-day group increased significantly in their letter recognition compared to the letter-of-the-week group. The growth was attributed to the constant review of the letters throughout the year after letters are initially introduced (Reutzel & Cooter, 2009). When introducing letters such as the letter *B*, share both upper- and lower-case. Perhaps the children will do a worksheet that asks them to circle the upper- and lower-case *B*s on the page. At another time the class will bake butter cookies or use clay to make the shape of the letter *B*.

Learning letters in a child's name first is a good way for them to begin learning the alphabet. It has meaning for the child. When teaching thematic units, select a few letters to feature that are used in the context of the theme. For example, in a unit on transportation, feature *b* for *boat*, *t* for *train*, *p* for *plane*, and *c* for *car*. Check children individually using flash cards to determine which letters they know and which they do not know.

Strategies for Identifying Letters of the Alphabet

Explicit teaching is needed for letter identification. The teacher explains to the children that they will be learning to name the letter, say the letter, and write the upper- and lower-case forms of the letter, for example, *Nn*. The teacher writes an upper-case *N* on the board and says, "This is the letter *N*. What is the letter?" The class answers altogether, "*N*." Then the teacher writes the lower-case *n*. She says, "This is the lower-case *n*. What is this letter?" The children respond, "Lower-case *n*." She then points to the upper-case *N* and asks the name of the letter and the children respond. Next, she points to each letter in a different order for a response. This is done at least three times. On a daily basis we allow children to explore letters explicitly, spontaneously, and in meaningful contexts. Here are multiple items and activities for practicing the alphabet that children can do:

- Alphabet puzzles
- Magnetic or wood upper- and lower-case letters using a magnetic board
- Tactile letters made of sandpaper or other textures
- Alphabet board games
- Letter stencils
- Alphabet flash cards
- Alphabet chart posted along the wall of the classroom at the children's eye level

- A large supply of alphabet books
- Taped songs about the alphabet
- Upper- and lower-case letters of the child's first and last name in separate baggie
- Chalk and a chalkboard to write letters
- Markers and a whiteboard to make letters
- Electronic whiteboard for letter games
- Keyboarding letters on the computer
- Finger-painting letters
- Clay for shaping letters
- Food that uses the alphabet, such as alphabet soup, cereal, and pasta.
- Shaping your fingers into letters
- Shaping letters with your body
- Labeling each child's cubbie and desk with his or her first and last name
- Labeling items in your classroom and at appropriate times mentioning letter names in the labels—for example: "Did you notice that the word *desk* begins with a *D*? Whose name begins with a *D*?" Daniel and Deborah raised their hands, and then Leonard said, "My name ends with a *D*."
- Letters in environmental print such as McDonald's, Wendy's, and Burger King.

Digital letter games on the Internet, and websites from professional organizations and other groups, contain a wealth of lessons for learning the alphabet. There are YouTube videos and other such sites for observing teachers teach the alphabet. Useful resources at the website *www.readwritethink.org* include:

A–Z: Learning about the Alphabet Book Genre (*www.readwritethink.org/ classroom-resources/lesson-plans/learning-about-alphabet-book-982.html*)

A Is for Apple: Building Letter Recognition Fluency (*www.readwritethink.org/ classroom-resources/lesson-plans/apple-building- letterrecognition-132.html*)

My Amazing ABC Book (*www.readwritethink.org/parent-after-school-resources/ printouts/amazing-book-30252.html*)

WORD STUDY: TIME, PLACE, MATERIALS

Word study should be taught on a daily basis with a specific time and place for instruction. Word study is taught in a whole-class format when introducing grade-level skills. The teacher will teach the skill and, if it includes a material, show where it is stored so it is accessible to all. For example, in first grade the teacher will be teaching phonics. In fifth grade the emphasis for whole-class instruction would be learning more roots and suffixes to help children read unfamiliar multisyllabic words. When introducing a new concept in word study the teacher will do a mini-lesson that takes about 10 minutes. The children will then have an opportunity to practice the skill taught, either alone or with a partner. This would be for another 10 minutes. If manipulatives are involved, students must complete some written example of the work done. During this guided practice the children can ask questions and the teacher will walk around the room to offer help when needed. After this introduction there will be work in stations to reinforce the concepts. The basic format for lessons is:

- Telling the child what skill is being taught and what it is used for
- Modeling and scaffolding the skill explicitly to show what it is and why it is used
- Allowing time for guided practice with the teacher
- Allowing time for independent practice
- Reviewing the skill often

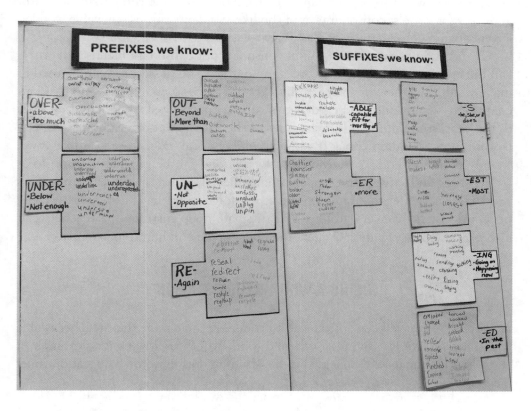

This bulletin board reminds students of their recent word-study units.

We also must take advantage of teachable moments when they occur to reinforce the skills being taught. We purposefully integrate whatever skill we are emphasizing into science, social studies, math, play, music, and art. For example, if children are learning the initial consonant *t* and learning about the temperature in different seasons in a science unit, we point out the consonant *t* in the word *temperature* and remind the children that they were discussing this in their phonics lesson.

A second type of instruction is also needed for word study. When children need more reinforcement for a skill, the teacher will call together a strategy group or focus on that skill in a guided reading group. Strategy groups are about 15 minutes each. In addition to whole-class or small-group planned instruction in word study, when a teachable moment occurs, teachers should take the opportunity to point out a word-study skill any time during the school day.

A third time for word-study materials and practice takes place in a *word-study station*, which contains manipulative materials that the teacher has already introduced to the children where they can practice those skills. The activities are hands-on, and children enjoy working with them. Some materials you will find are scrambled words to be unscrambled, magnetic onsets and rimes to make words, and sorts for vowels, consonants, and the like. Students can use movable wooden letters, foam rubber letters, or flash cards with letters on them. Flash cards can have word endings on them or initial consonants or consonant blends. All onsets can be written in one color and rimes in another. The flash cards can be used to make words on a table or a pocket chart. Board games such as Bingo, Lotto, Concentration, Candyland, and card games can be constructed where children have to use word-study skills within the rules of the game. A popular phonics activity is word sorts. Children can sort words in alphabetical order, based on like vowel sounds, digraphs, and so on. Materials for stations can be purchased from stores for teachers and large school-supply companies. Teachers may create numerous word-study activities that children use to reinforce what they know and use independently when teachers are engaged in small-group instruction. Teachers can also seek the help of parents, aides, and upper-grade children to make materials.

USING A WORD-STUDY STATION

After children have been introduced to the use of materials, their teacher is able to assign word-study activities for them to work on. The following is an example of the activities one teacher assigned to his children during word-study station time:

"Four children made as many words from the word *Thanksgiving* as they could. The letters of *Thanksgiving* had been cut up and placed in plastic baggies for each child. In addition to manipulating the letters to create words, the children wrote the words on an activity sheet. With magnetic letters and their own individual magnetic slates, children created word ladders. They started with one-letter words, then two, then three, and so on. Each child also had a 5″ × 7″ index card to write his or her word from the bottom of the card up the ladder. A partner checked the words. Another group of four children worked with ending phonograms or chunks by creating words with onsets or initial consonants. Finally, children were sorting words with common phonograms, short vowel sounds, long vowel sounds, etc."

All these activities were manipulative. They involved children working with words from individual letters, to letter chunks, beginnings and ends of words, and total sentences. They also required children to work together, check each other's work, and collaborate. All the activities had a pencil-and-paper component for recording what was done—for example, the little words made from the big word *Thanksgiving* were written on a sheet of paper provided by the teacher.

This way the teacher has a record of work done with manipulatives, and the students are responsible for completing tasks. All children have the opportunity to use every material during this period. There are worksheets with the manipulatives that provide more practice. Often, worksheets are regarded as not very useful; however, as long as children are involved in learning through multiple strategies, an occasional worksheet provides practice and reinforcement.

STRATEGIES FOR TEACHING PHONICS

Phonics is the best-known word-study strategy. It is the ability to look at letters and decode them in words. Quite simply, phonics is the connection of sounds and symbols. The use of phonics requires children to learn letter sounds and combinations of sounds (*phonemes*) associated with their corresponding letter symbols (*graphemes*). In the English language there are 26 letters in the alphabet; however, there are at least 44 different sounds. Sound–symbol correspondence is not always consistent in English; there are many irregularities and exceptions to many rules, which are difficult for children to learn. Therefore, we must help children learn words by sight that are difficult to sound out, and we need to give them multiple strategies for figuring out words. Regardless, phonics is the major source to help children to become independent readers.

Teaching Phonics Using Explicit Instruction

Explicit instruction means that a curriculum for teaching phonics is planned, systematic, and follows a scheduled routine to learn specific skills throughout the year. An explicit synthetic phonics lesson will look like this:

Phonics Skill: Connecting the symbol *F* with its sound.

Materials: Picture cards of a *fan, feet, fox, fish, hat,* and *bat.*

The teacher says /f/ and has the children repeat. She explains that *face* begins with /f/. She tells the children to point to their faces and say /f/ each time they hear a word beginning with /f/. She says *"The funny fish has fins."*

The teacher prints **Ff** on the board and identifies the upper-case and lower-case letters. She reminds the children that they both say **Ff**. She says the **Ff** sound and has the children repeat it after her. She asks the children to explain what they do with their mouth and lips when they say the **Ff** sound (*"You open your mouth a little and put your top teeth on your bottom lip and push out the sound of **Ff**"*).

The teacher displays picture cards. She helps the children identify the picture on each card. She asks a child to say the word and the sound of **Ff** separately and place the card on the board.

She gives each child a workbook page with upper- and lower-case **Ff**'s to trace. They are to say the sound of the **Ff** as they trace. On the page are pictures in boxes of a fox, fan, bus, cat, fence, and fish. Each box has a yellow circle under it, except for the first box. There is a fox in that box and the circle has a smiley face with eyes and a mouth. The children are to name each picture and put eyes and a mouth on those that begin with **Ff**. As they make the smiley faces, they should say the sound of **Ff**. The ones that don't begin with **Ff** are left blank.

Many teachers still follow this type of teaching routine to introduce the sound of a letter; however, most go on to do more meaning-based activities as well. This type of lesson alone would not be sufficient for learning the sound–symbol relationship. One reason it is not sufficient is that children need to attach the sounds and symbols of phonics that creates meaning.

> *Management Tip:* Since phonics instruction depends a lot on manipulative materials, be sure they are stored so pieces don't fall out—such as in a plastic baggie. Have phonics materials all in one spot on a shelf so children have easy access to them. Instruct children to put the materials back in the baggies when they are finished and to place them exactly where they were taken from.

Teaching Phonics Connected to Literature

A phonics lesson connected to literature could look like this:

Phonics Skill: Connecting the sound of *Ss* with its symbol.

Materials: Picture cards of a *sun, sand, salad,* and *seal*; children's book *The Snowy Day* (Keats, 1996); alphabet books; magnetic letters with at least one *Ss* for each child.

The teacher projects picture cards on the electronic whiteboard. She asks the children to identify each picture as she shows it. First, she projects the sun and the children respond, "That's a sun." She continues with the other words. She asks, "Is there something the same about each of these words?" "Samantha raises her hand and says, "They all begin with an **Ss**. I know because my name does, too. It is Samantha, like *sun, sand, salad*." The teacher responds, "You are right!" She projects an upper- and lower-case **Ss** on the whiteboard. She asks the children to say the words again and then they talked about what their tongue, teeth, and mouth do when saying **Ss**. More pictures are projected on the whiteboard and two children are called to move all the **Ss** words together and put all those that do not begin with **Ss** in another group.

The teacher asks the children to look around the room to see if they see something that has the **Ss** sound. They get up from their seats and walk around in pairs and when they find a word that has an **Ss** in it, they stop and stand by their **Ss**. James stood at the Word Wall since his name has an **Ss** at the end. Children took turns saying the words they found, such as *sink*, and a poster with the word *summer* on it. A traffic sign on another poster that said Stop, and a book called *Swimmy* (Lionni, 1987) were also found. The teacher had the children come to the literacy center rug and she read the book *The Snowy Day* by Ezra Jack Keats (1996) and asked them to listen for as many **Ss** words as they heard. When the story was over, the children said words they heard as the teacher wrote them on her chart: *snow, snowy, snowsuit, snowman, snowballs, stick,* and more. The children went back to their seats and turned to the **Ss** page in their alphabet books which were originally blank notebooks. They wrote the upper- and lower-case **Ss** on the page. Some copied the **Ss** words; some made pictures of a sun, a seal, and snow. Some wrote sentences with **Ss** words in the sentence. They all added illustrations. At snack time, the children had *sandwich* cookies.

Teaching Consonants

We begin teaching phonics with the most commonly used initial consonant sounds, such as *f, m, s, t,* and *h,* and then use these same sounds in ending word positions. The next set of initial and final consonant sounds usually taught is *l, d, c, n, g, w, p, r, k,* then *j, q, v,* final *x,* initial *y,* and *z.* Most consonants are quite regular and represent one sound. Some consonants have two sounds, such as *g* as in the words *go* and *girl,* often referred to as the *hard g;* and *g* as in *George, giraffe,* and *gentleman,* referred to as the *soft g.* Other consonants with two sounds are *c* as in *cookie, cut,* and *cost,* the *hard c* sound; and *c* as in *circus, celebrate,* and *ceremony,* the *soft c* sound. The letter *x* has a *z* sound at the beginning of a word, as in *xylophone,* but has the *x* sound as in the word *next.* The letters *w* and *y* have one sound at the beginning of a word and act as consonants, as in /w/ in *was* and /y/

in *yellow*. In the middle or at the end of a word, *w* and *y* act as vowels, as in *today* and *blow*. Learning the consonant sounds begins in preschool in a limited way; more instruction occurs in kindergarten; the sounds are mastered in first grade.

Next in the progression we teach blends and digraphs. Consonant blends and consonant digraphs are pairs of consonants that make new sounds. The blends are clusters of two or three consonants in which the sounds of all the consonants are heard, but blended together, as in the words **blue**, **true**, **flew**, and **string**. Consonant digraphs are composed of two consonants that when put together do not have the sound of either one, but rather an altogether new sound, such as *th* in **three**, *sh* in **sh**oes, *ch* in **chair**, *ph* in **photograph**, and *gh* at the end of a word, as in *enou***gh**.

Teaching Vowels

The next phonics element we teach are the vowels. We teach vowels in the middle of kindergarten and reinforce them if needed in first grade. The vowels are *a, e, i, o,* and *u*. We teach the short vowels first: *a* as in *cat, e* as in *bed, i* as in *hit, o* as in *hot,* and *u* as in *cut*. Next we teach the long vowels: *a* as in *hate, e* as in *feet, i* as in *kite, o* as in *boat,* and *u* as in *cute*. Long vowels have the sound of the name of the letter. As mentioned earlier, *w* and *y* act as vowels in the middle and at the end of words. The letter *y* has the sound of a long *e* when it comes at the end of a word, as in *baby*. The *y* has the sound of a long *i* when it is at the end of a one-syllable word such as *cry* and *try*.

Vowels change their sound when they are *r*-controlled. They become neither long nor short, as in *car* and *for*. As with consonants, there are vowel pairs that we teach. The first vowel pairs are called *digraphs*. Vowel digraphs include two vowels that have a single sound such as *ai* in *pail* and *ea* in *sea*. The next vowel pairs are called *diphthongs*. Diphthongs are composed of two vowels that form a gliding sound as one vowel blends into the other, such as *oy* in *toy* and *oi* in *oil*. Vowels can be difficult to learn, since they have many sounds and combinations of sounds that make the sounds change.

At each grade level, teachers should review what has been learned in earlier grades and add on additional work in medial consonants, variant consonant sounds, and blends. The phonic elements to deal with next include some structural aspects such as compound words, syllabication, contractions, prefixes, and suffixes. Eventually children will learn about synonyms, antonyms, and homonyms.

Children find it easier to learn about word patterns or chunks rather than individual sounds. Word patterns help in decoding many different words that contain the same patterns, but may have a different beginning or ending sound. Teachers should help students learn familiar word patterns at the end of words called *rimes*—also referred to as *phonograms, word families,* and *chunks*. There are many common rimes, such as *an, at, et, en, in, it, op, on, ut,* and *un*.

There are many phonics generalizations and rules. Here we list those that will apply to many words:

1. When a one-syllable word has only one vowel in the middle of the word surrounded by two consonants, the vowel is usually short. Words such as *hot, cut,* and *bet* follow this consonant–vowel–consonant (CVC) word pattern.
2. When there are two vowels in a word with one syllable, and one of them is an *e* at the end of the word, the first vowel is long and the *e* is silent. This is called the consonant–vowel–consonant–*e* (CVCe) pattern or the final *e* rule. Some words that demonstrate the rule include *plate, cute,* and *bone.*
3. When a consonant is followed by a vowel, the vowel is usually long, as in *be, go,* and *because.* This is called the consonant–vowel rule (CV).
4. When two vowels are together, the first is long and the second is silent. This is the consonant–vowel–vowel–consonant (CVVC) rule. Some say, "When two vowels go walking, the first one does the talking," such as *meat, boat,* and *rain.*

At the beginning of the chapter, we discussed the necessity for teaching phonics within meaningful contexts, along with a systematic and direct presentation of skills, synthetically, and with meaning. It is also important that children have continual practice to learn sound–symbol relationships. A single lesson is never sufficient. Therefore, teachers should provide several experiences with letter and letter–sound combinations and review them with children as often as possible.

MEANING-BASED PHONICS STRATEGIES

How can we help children recognize the sound–symbol relationships of consonants and vowels in a meaningful context? Science and social studies themes lend themselves to featuring letters that appear in units. For example, when studying farm, pet, and zoo animals, we can feature the letter *p*, because it is used frequently in this context. The following types of activities then can follow and be used with other consonants as well:

1. Read *Pet Show* (Keats, 1974) and *The Tale of Peter Rabbit* (Potter, 1902) during the unit, and point out words that begin with the letter *p* in these books.
2. Make word charts using words from the books that begin with the letter *p.*
3. On a field trip, bring peanuts to the zoo to feed the animals.

4. Make lists of animals that begin with the letter *p*, such as peacock, panda, and pig.

5. Read the book *Animalia* (Base, 1987) and study the *p* page about peacocks.

6. Collect sensory items about animals that begin with the letter *p*, such as Puppy Chow to smell, peanuts to eat, peacock plumes to touch, a purring kitten to listen to, and the book *Petunia* (Duvoisin, 2002) to look at and read.

7. List words from the unit that begin with the letter *p*.

8. Write an experience chart of activities carried out during the unit, and highlight the letter *p* when it appears in the chart.

9. Ask children to add to their Very Own Words collection with favorite words from the unit that begin with the letter *p*.

10. Make a collage of pictures featuring things from the unit, and mark those that begin with the letter *p*.

11. Print the song "Peter Cottontail" on a chart. Sing the song and highlight the letter *p* when it appears.

12. Have children help you make up nonsense rhymes for featured letters and chant them, such as the following:

    My name is Penelope Pig.
    I pick petals off of petunias.
    I play patty-cake
    and eat pretzels with pink punch.

13. Add a page for the letter *p* to a class "Big Book" entitled "Our Own Big Book of Letters, Sounds, and Words." Have children draw pictures or paste in pictures of words that begin with the letter *p*.

14. Complete a worksheet for the letter *p* that requires students to trace the letter, write the letter, and circle pictures that begin with the letter *p*, such as *pig* and *popcorn*.

15. Encourage children to write about their experiences during the unit, such as their visit to the zoo, the books they read, and the songs they sang. In their writing they will be using the letters emphasized and, although their writing may not be conventional, through the use of their invented spellings, they are indirectly enhancing their phonics. The more children write, the better they become at segmenting sounds in words. This point is demonstrated in this example of Justin's story about the panda bear at the zoo. He wrote, "*I saw a prte panda ber pik up her babi panda at the zoo.*"

The teacher can highlight the sounds of words in themes. Be careful not to abuse the stories by overemphasizing the sounds featured; however, do not pass up the opportunity to feature letters in this natural book setting. For example, in a unit on food, Ms. Fino, a first-grade teacher, featured the letter *b* and read *Blueberries for Sal* (McCloskey, 1948), *Bread and Jam for Frances* (Hoban, 1964), and *The Berenstain Bears and Too Much Birthday* (Berenstain & Berenstain, 1987). These and similar activities can be carried out for any initial consonant.

When we read, we use several skills concurrently to decode and derive meaning from the printed page. We therefore need to encourage children to use multiple skills, rather than isolated skills, in their approach to reading. Children should be taught to use context clues and phonic clues simultaneously. One strategy that accomplishes this goal has already been suggested—reading a sentence in which you pause and leave a "blank" to be filled in by the child. For example, say, "The *b* _____ flew up to the tree and landed on a branch." Supplying the initial consonant for the word, either by sound or by sight, draws on a child's skills with phonics, context, syntax, and semantics.

LOOKING FOR PATTERNS

We learn by looking for patterns. The brain takes what it knows and tries to apply it to the unknown. Patterns such as familiar word endings help children deal with unknowns. Therefore phonics activities that engage children with groups of letters or patterns in words makes decoding easier. This type of phonics is often referred to as using onsets and rimes. An *onset* is the beginning sound of the word that could be a consonant, a consonant blend, a consonant digraph, or a vowel. A *rime* is a group of letters that form word endings. Some familiar rimes are *ake, an,* and *it.* Rimes often are used in several words. With the onset *b* at the beginning of the words and the three rimes *ake, an,* and *it* as potential endings to a word, we can make the words *bake, ban,* and *bit.* This type of activity helps children learn letter–sound relationships by analyzing the elements in a word or picture and selecting critical features as they place the words or sound pictures in piles. Through sorting, students clarify words and pictures on the basis of sound and spelling and construct an understanding of our spelling system and consequently are able to decode unknown words (Strickland & Snow, 2002; Bear, Invernizzi, Templeton & Johnston, 2008).

The following are game-like activities that use onsets and rimes to sort words, make words, classify words, find little words in big words, blend, segment, and substitute letters to make words. In these activities children are learning patterns in words, and the manipulative nature of the hands-on activities are appealing. When working with manipulatives, it is important for children to write down the words they create so the teacher can assess progress.

Making Words

Many of these activities can be done for a different purpose. The teacher sets the purpose and models the strategy before the child carries it out. All of these activities involve the manipulation of letters and letter patterns.

Another popular type of word-making activity uses onsets and rimes. With younger children, the teacher provides a few well-known rimes, such as *at*, *an*, or *in*, and asks the children to make as many words with these endings as they can think of by adding different initial consonants or consonant blends to the beginning of the rimes. With the rime *at*, for example, children created the following words: *cat*, *sat*, *mat*, *rat*, *hat*, *fat*, *vat*, *pat*, and *bat*.

Another word-making game provides children with letters. In this lesson they were *a*, *d*, *n*, *s*, and *t*. With these letters children can be asked to make the following words (Cunningham, 2009):

Use two letters to make *at*.
Add a letter to make *sat*.
Take away a letter to make *at*.
Change a letter to make *an*.
Add a letter to make *Dan*.
Change a letter to make *tan*.
Take away a letter to make *an*.
Add a letter to make *and*.
Add a letter to make *sand*.

Word Sorts

Help children learn to decode through patterns. The teacher decides on the purpose of the sort. Sorts can be done over and over for different skills. The activity allows children to practice skills they have been exposed to. Sorts can be done with pictures or letters and words. Let children know the purpose of the sort by placing a target card at the top of a column. For example, if you are sorting long and short vowels, the picture and/or word at the top of one column would be a *sock* for short vowels, and the picture at the top of the second column would be *cake* to sort the long vowels (see Figure 5.2).

You can also sort words for blends, digraphs, and numbers of syllables, which are all ways to help students see patterns. Words can be sorted for meaning by categories, such as colors and types of food. Words can also be sorted using rimes. Other games to practice decoding skills include Bingo, Concentration, and Lotto. Just decide the skill and distribute letter cards, blends, digraphs, long or short vowels, beginning sounds, or ending sounds, and play the game.

FIGURE 5.2. Example of word and picture sorts for long and short vowels.

In addition to the materials discussed, some quality phonics websites with more teaching ideas are:

- *http://teacher.scholastic.com/clifford1*—This website has phonics games using Clifford the dog. The games offer videos, read-alongs, and even options to hear stories in Spanish.
- *www.netrover.com/~kingskid/phonics/phonics_main.htm*—This website has an interactive exercise where kids experiment with words. The exercise asks students to spell a word and then gives the sounds of each letter provided.
- *www.kizclub.com/phonicsactivities.htm*—This website has various printable activities to teach children phonics.

- *www.kizphonics.com*—Here is a program with a systematic phonics approach.
- *www.phonics.com*—This website has printable activities, videos, and games and is arranged by levels from ages 3 to 8.
- *www.turtlediary.com/kids-games/english-topics/phonics-games.html*—This website has both games and printable activities that can help kids learn letter sounds, rhyming words, and lots of new words.

OTHER STRATEGIES FOR FIGURING OUT WORDS

Using Environmental Print

Environmental print is a way for children to learn to read words in familiar print found in the child's surroundings such as logos, food labels, and road signs. They are in the home, outside on the roads, and in restaurants and stores. When very young children associate the McDonald's logo with the word *McDonald's* and try to read it, they are learning that a group of letters makes up a word that can be read and thus provides information. The ability to read environmental print also gives the child a sense of accomplishment and usually elicits positive reinforcement of the child's achievement by caring adults.

Early childhood classrooms need to have environmental print brought in from outside, and teachers need to label items in their child-care centers, nursery schools, kindergartens, and first and second grades. The print should be traced and copied. This print will become part of a child's sight vocabulary.

The environmental print that children know best appears on food containers for cereal, soup, milk, cookies, detergent, and other items in the home. Teachers point out fast-food logos, road signs, traffic signals, and names of store chains, supermarkets, and service stations. Mail, magazines, newspapers, storybook readings, TV channels, and telephone numbers are all excellent sources of environmental print. We collect logos and make them available in our classrooms by posting them on charts, pasting them onto index cards, and creating loose-leaf books of environmental print (see Figure 5.3). Teachers can photograph environmental print in the neighborhood and bring the photos to the classroom. We then suggest that children read the words, copy them, and write them in a sentence or a story.

Including environmental print in the classroom should start at the beginning of a school year with only a few signs, such as children's names on their cubbies, and the words *Block Center* to identify that area of the room. We make labels with 5″ × 7″ index cards and dark felt-tip markers. We begin each word with a capital letter and continue with lower-case script, thus providing youngsters with configuration clues. Teachers hang labels at heights easy for children to see. They point out the labels to the children, and suggest that they read them to friends and copy them. As the school year progresses, teachers label new items, but do this with the children.

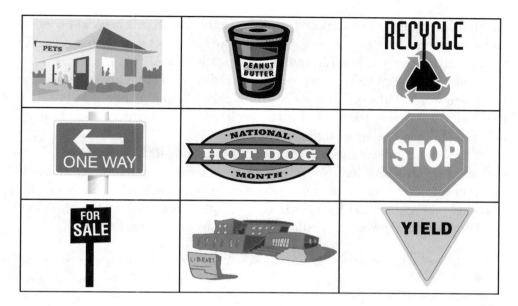

FIGURE 5.3. A chart of environmental print helps children as they write.

We encourage the children to let us know what to label. Then we put up the labels when the children are watching. We refer to the labels as part of our normal routine so that they are used and will then add to the child's sight vocabulary. We use labels for relating messages such as *Wash Your Hands Before Snack*. We refer to the labels often so that the children will identify them as useful and functional. We label items related to content-area topics. If the class is studying dinosaurs, we display model dinosaurs and label each with its name. Long, difficult words such as *Brontosaurus* and *Tyrannosaurus* will become sight words for many early childhood youngsters. It is common to observe preschool, kindergarten, first-grade, and second-grade children reading labels to themselves or to each other. Post messages and assignments for children daily in a permanent spot on the chalkboard or on chart paper (see Chapter 4 for some examples of appropriate messages).

This routine will teach children to look at the chalkboard each day for a special message. From the messages they will learn that print carries meaning that is interesting and useful. Some teachers refer to this practice as the *morning message* and have formalized it into a lesson when the school day begins (Morrow, 2003a).

Using Context and Pictures

Experiences with literature can lead children to use contextual clues and illustrations to figure out words and recognize that they have meaning. Literature experiences can take place in whole-class, small-group, or one-to-one settings, using directed listening (or reading) and thinking activities, shared book experiences, and repeated readings of stories. For example, we can select a story that is predictable, in which the text and illustrations are closely related. We can ask the children to look at the pictures on a page before reading it to them and ask what they think the words will say. Then we read the page to demonstrate that print and illustration are closely related and that the pictures provide information that can help the children as they read the story.

The syntax and semantics of a sentence (its grammatical structure and meaning) also help children identify words. We can encourage children to use these elements of written language by stopping our oral reading at predictable points in a story and asking them to fill in words. For example, when reading *The Three Little Pigs* (Brenner, 1972), you can first read the complete repetitive phrases:

> "'Little pig, little pig, let me in,' said the wolf. 'Not by the hair of my chinny, chin, chin,' said the first little pig. 'Then I'll huff and I'll puff and I'll blow your house in,' said the wolf."

The second time say:

> "'Little pig, little _____ let me in.' 'Not by the hair of my chinny chin _____.' 'Then I'll huff and I'll _____ and I'll blow your _____ _____' and so on."

HIGH-FREQUENCY WORDS AND SIGHT WORDS

Sight words are those found frequently in reading materials for children. Sight words allow for quick recall. These words do not carry meaning, but they hold sentences together. They are often difficult to decode because they have irregular patterns in their spelling. Having these words as sight words makes them easy to read since they are learned by memory. Sight words should be taught in a systematic and direct manner. The teacher selects several (three to five) words for the children to learn each week. To learn these words, the following activities are used:

- Words are said aloud and used in a sentence.
- The sentence is written on a chalkboard or flip chart and the sight word is underlined.
- Features of each word, such as the letters or its similarity to other words, are discussed. The teacher points out any regular or irregular patterns the word may have.
- Children are asked to spell the word aloud, spell the word in the air with their finger, and write the word on paper.

- Children chant the letters as they spell words. They may learn movements that go along with some words, which helps them remember those words easily.
- The teacher has a high-frequency word box. While sitting in a circle, each child has a turn to pick a word, say it, use it in a sentence, and show it to the group.
- The words can be written on index cards similar to Very Own Words and stored with the child's other cards.

There are sight-word lists by Fry or Dolch, which were created by combing through books looking for the words used most often in children's literature. According to Adams (1990), the following 13 words represent 25% of the words children find in early literacy texts. These should be first on the list to learn: *a, and, for, he* (or *she*), *in, is, it, of, that, the, to, was,* and *you.*

To ensure that children are acquiring sight recognition of high-frequency words, sight-word games should be used daily and they should be tested on their ability to read them. The teacher should ask them to identify the words with flash cards and find them in context within passages to read. This testing can be done several times during the school year (Allington & Cunningham, 2007; Cunningham, 2009). There are children who are not able to segment and blend. These children will need hundreds of sight words. However, even when a child can use phonics in beginning reading, sight words are an important way to understand what reading is, to build confidence, and then to build an extensive reading vocabulary. Appendix B at the end of the book has 300 sight words listed by order of difficulty to learn in first, second, and third grade.

Developing Sight Vocabulary

An extremely important skill for beginning readers is to learn sight words. There was a time when the most common way to teach children was through sight and repetition of those words. Sight words enable children to read books immediately and then understand what reading is. *Learning as many sight words as possible is very important.* Many children can learn phonic sounds and rules but are unable to apply them in context. In the book *Teacher*, Sylvia Ashton-Warner (1986) describes a method for developing sight vocabulary called Very Own Words. She encourages children to write their favorite words from a story or content-area lesson on 5" × 7" cards, with each word on a separate card. Very Own Words are often from a child's home life: *Mommy, Daddy, Grandpa, Grandma, cookie.* They also reflect emotional feelings: *naughty, nice, good, punish.* After Very Own Words are recorded on index cards, they are stored in a child's file box, or in a plastic baggie.

A good way to start Very Own Words collections is through a discussion of pets, toys, friends, and parents. Let children know that after this discussion you will ask them to name their favorite word in the conversation. Here is how Ms. Rosen does it.

> MS. ROSEN: (*Holds up an index card box of her favorite Very Own Words.*) This is my Very Own Words [VOW] box. I collect words about my family, friends, things I like to do, and new words I learn. This one says *bicycle*. I like my bicycle so I made a VOW card for it, and I'll put it into my VOW box. On one side you can see the word; on the other side is the word with a picture of the bicycle. What are your favorite people, things, pets, toys?
>
> JAMAL: I love my grandma; I would like to have the word *grandma*.
>
> KIM: I love oatmeal cookies, I want that word.
>
> AMAD: I like it when my mom reads books to me. I want the word *book*.

Ms. Rosen has cards ready and a marker and wrote *Grandma* for Jamal with a picture of a lady's face; on the other side she just wrote *Grandma* without a picture. She wrote *oatmeal cookie* for Kim on one side with a picture, and on the other just the words. For Amad she wrote *book* with a picture and on the flip side only the word.

Children also can choose a favorite word in a storybook or words generated from the study of social studies and science units. Soon children will request their Very Own Words without being asked.

We should encourage children to do things with their words—read them to friends or to themselves, copy them, and use them in sentences or stories. Because words are based on a child's expressed interests in situations at home and in school, the collection of Very Own Words is a powerful technique for developing sight vocabulary.

Teachers can encourage children to study the letter patterns in their Very Own Words. They can discuss consonant and vowel sounds, blends, digraphs, and structural elements such as prefixes and suffixes, as well as phonic generalizations that may be evident. When a child studies letter patterns in words he or she has selected, it will mean more than doing the same task with words selected by the teacher or found in a textbook.

 Breaking Through the Block: In the upper grades, many vocabulary words that students might come across in the content areas may be difficult to decode, especially as these words become more complex. Special words are featured in math, art, and gym classes, and so on. In addition to becoming familiar with the meaning of the words, students should be able to recognize and read them in context. For example, the word *rhythm* will come up in music class. It has a silent *h* and a silent *y* as well as the digraph *th*. The unusual spelling and irregularities in its pronunciation should be pointed out in music class. Content-area teachers should embrace the foundational skills that students need to master their content.

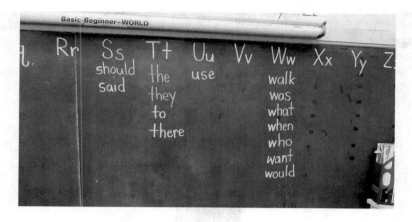

Word Walls help children read and spell commonly used words.

Using a Word Wall to Teach High-Frequency Words

A traditional *Word Wall* typically has the letters of the alphabet posted across a wall at the children's eye level. As high-frequency words are introduced, they are posted under the letter where they belong in alphabetical order. The featured words are ones teachers select as being a priority to learn. Other words may be ones that children are having difficulty with reading and spelling. Before putting words up, note their characteristics, such as their pronunciation, spelling, and letter patterns. Suggest to children that the Word Wall can be used as a dictionary when writing.

The Word Wall can be used to play word-study games. For example, if the teacher wants to work with substitution of sounds, he or she points to a word such as *went* and says, "This word says *went*. If I take away the *w* and put in a *b,* what does it say?" or "This word rhymes with *look* and begins with a *b.* Can you find it on the Word Wall?"

Word Wall words can be sorted by word families, rhyming words, words that have the same vowel sounds, and so on. This can be done on paper or on an electronic whiteboard by moving the words around or writing them down on a sheet of paper. Many different lessons for using the wall independently should be provided (Cunningham, 2017; Moustafa, 1997; Xu & Drame, 2007).

Although the Word Wall was designed to teach high-frequency words, teachers use it for new words learned in themes, from books read, and from daily discussions. With very young children, the first words on the Word Wall will be their *names.* Some additional Word Wall activities that the teacher can lead are as follows:

- Have students sort words by pattern—for example, words with the letters *an* or *at.*
- Classify words into colors, names, animals, or the like.

- The Secret Word game with the Word Wall provides the student with a series of clues such as these:

  "The secret word has an *at* pattern at the end."
  "It has three letters."
  "It is an animal."
  "It has fur and little pointy ears."
  "It lives in people's houses."
  "It likes milk."
  "It is a __ *at*."

FLUENCY

A skill that needs more emphasis in literacy instruction is *fluency*. According to the National Reading Panel (2000), helping children become fluent readers is crucial for literacy development. Some teachers merely assess fluency by timing students, which does not capture the true meaning of the term. *Fluency* is a combination of accuracy, automaticity, and prosody when reading. More simply, a child who reads fluently is able to decode text automatically and accurately. He or she does not have to labor over every sound. In addition, the child reads with the appropriate pace and expression. This aspect of language is referred to as *prosody*. Prosody suggests that the student is comprehending the text, since he or she is reading with appropriate expression and rate (Kuhn & Stahl, 2003; Kuhn, Schwanenflugel, & Meisinger, 2010). Time needs to be set aside for 10 minute of fluency lessons embedded into word-study time or comprehension development. The ultimate goal for reading instruction is that students be fluent readers. Research has shown that the following strategies are useful, fun, and help to develop fluency.

Echo Reading

The teacher or more able reader reads one line of text, and the child then reads the same line. The number of lines read is increased as the child's reading improves. When reading, we must be sure to model with good accuracy, pace, and expression and be sure the children are looking at the words and reading the words, instead of just listening and repeating. Ask them to look at and follow the print on the page with their finger. Try to echo-read a few times a week.

Choral Reading

When choral reading, the entire class or a small group of children reads an entire passage together along with the teacher. The teacher ensures that he or she provides a model for pace and expression. Short passages and poetry are good for choral reading. When choral reading, the child "feels" the correct pace and expression necessary in reading fluently. Try to choral-read a few times a week.

Paired Reading

Paired reading involves a more able reader in the same classroom or from another classroom as a model of fluent reading for less fluent readers. When they read together, the more able reader acts as the tutor. The children should read material that is easy for the child who is less fluent. The readers should take turns; for example, the tutor can read a page and then the less fluent reader repeats the same page. They can alternate reading page by page. The tutor helps the less able reader with accuracy, rate, and expression.

Readers' Theatre

Readers' Theatre is the oral reading of a short play. The children have assigned parts and practice the parts for the presentation. Children work not to memorize their parts, but work toward fluency. They can hold their books as they present. This provides a model of what good fluent reading sounds like. We can invite parents to school to hear the class perform a Readers' Theatre piece and take the opportunity to introduce them to the concept of fluency. They can be taught some of the strategies by having them participate with the teacher and their children. Young and Rasinski (2009, pp. 244–246) provide a Readers' Theatre script along with face puppets with directions for carrying out the activity.

Antiphonal Reading

Antiphonal reading is a form of choral reading in which parts are taken by groups. Poetry with conversation works well with this activity. Teachers divide their class into two, three, or four groups. They assign each group a different part to read. Students practice each part and then read together (Johns & Berglund, 2002). Sometimes antiphonal choral readings can be judged as to which group had best expression and pace.

Tape-Assisted Reading

Listening to fluent reading samples on CDs while following the written text provides an excellent model for children. These CDs can be purchased or made by teachers, parents, and other students who present fluent models for reading.

Repeated Reading

Read the same story three or four times in 1 week. When a story is repeated, it offers the opportunity for fluent reading because of its familiarity. When children can read a text well, they will understand what fluent reading is. Select a short story. On the first day, read the text to the children as they follow along. On the second day, do an echo reading. On the third day, do a choral reading, and on the fourth, do a partner reading. Help support the reading of the text and use challenging books with rich vocabulary.

Children should participate in fluent reading activities daily. They are easy to do, they don't take much time, and they are fun. Fluency can be worked on as early as preschool. Preschoolers can participate in all the fluency activities, but as listening activities rather than reading ones. They are exposed to the rhythm, pace, and expression involved in fluent reading. Preschoolers can echo-speak instead of echo-read. The teacher recites, and they repeat. Choral speaking can be done with memorized pieces of poetry. They can be involved in paired listening with an older child, listening to excellent models of storybook reading on tape, and repeated readings.

MATERIALS FOR FLUENCY TRAINING

Reading materials for reading instruction, such as basal selections or leveled books, are good for fluency training. They can be read using echo and choral reading as part of the instructional routine when new text is introduced. Books with conversation, such as fables, are good for Readers' Theatre since the characters provide parts for children to read. Short pieces of text and poems are best for choral, echo, repeated, and paired reading. A book of poems by Mary Ann Hoberman called *You Read to Me, I'll Read to You* (2001) has delightful poems with at least two characters talking to each other in every poem. The poems use different-colored print for the different characters and are perfect for Readers' Theatre, echo reading, choral reading, antiphonal reading, paired reading, and repeated reading. For example, the poem "I Like" uses purple print for one character and pink for another (shown as *italics* in the excerpt below), and blue to represent both characters reading together (shown here as **bold**)*:

---

*From *You Read to Me, I'll Read to You: Very Short Stories to Read Together* by Mary Ann Hoberman. Copyright © 2001 Mary Ann Hoberman. Reprinted by permission of Little, Brown and Company.

I like soda.	*I like milk.*
I like satin.	*I like silk.*
I like puppies.	*I like kittens.*
I like gloves.	*I like mittens.*
I like to slide.	*I like to swing.*

We don't agree on anything.

CONCLUSION

In this chapter we have discussed research that identifies why we need to teach phonics. We have also discussed at length strategies for teaching different ways to figure out words by sight, through context clues, by pictures, by phonemic awareness, and through phonics. Some concerns teachers have about teaching phonics include when to teach it, how much time to spend on word study, and how to differentiate instruction when teaching word study. We used to view phonics as the most important skill in teaching reading. We now know it is only a skill to help us decode and ultimately comprehend. Teach it quickly and early, and review when necessary.

················· ✋ STOP! THINK! REACT! ✋ ·······························

Based upon the work in this chapter, you should ask yourself and reflect on the following questions:

❏ What research-based best practices in word study do you already use and which do you need to add to your work?

❏ Do you have all of the materials you need for word study? If not, are you able to speak to someone within your district about ordering materials?

❏ Are you currently implementing all of the phonemic awareness work mentioned in the chapter?

❏ If you do not already teach the sounds in the order recommended in this chapter, are you able to make changes to your practice?

CHAPTER 6

Literacy Work Stations

CLASSROOM VIGNETTE

Ms. Tapia was worried about having stations in her classroom. She had tried them once before and just felt as if the classroom was out of control. She didn't like the noise level and the movement in the room, finding the practice to be somewhat "chaotic" at times. Now, however she has learned how to set rules and put routines in place for working in stations, and her children are able to follow them. They know where to go and when, and their independence at the work stations is fantastic. Students complete their work, and the noise in the room is good noise, with children engaged in practicing skills they have been taught while collaborating with their peers.

WHAT ARE LITERACY WORK STATIONS?

In order to understand the current context of literacy work stations, it is important to look to past influences on this common literacy practice. Dewey (1966) significantly influenced programs in U.S. early childhood and elementary education. Classrooms reflecting Dewey's ideas contained "centers" for different activities and content areas. For example, classrooms would have a science center that might include shells, rocks, plants, a class animal, magnets, and the like. The items in the center might reflect what was being studied in science or social studies at that time. There would be an art center, music center, social studies center, and, of course, a literacy center. The literacy center would have bookshelves filled with children's literature and soft pillows to lean on for when children were looking at books. Dewey's centers had minimal rules. His concerns were that children would be able to explore, experiment, collaborate, and interact to learn. The focus was on the social, emotional, physical, and intellectual development of the whole child.

Our centers, now "work stations," may look a bit like Dewey's did; however, the focus now has changed. We will discuss the following about stations:

- *Purpose:* What are work stations and why are they used?
- *Role:* How do we help children to learn to work independent of the teacher in stations?
- *Transitional Methods:* How are children assigned to stations and how do they move from one station to the next?
- *Need:* What kinds of stations do we need in classrooms?

SHIFTING FROM "CENTERS" TO WORK STATIONS

First things first: the literacy stations are called "literacy work stations" because the term better denotes that student work will be occurring in these areas. What we used to call "centers" were more a combination of games around a particular weekly theme, or merely students moving to separate parts of the room to produce more "seatwork." Centers have had more of a *keep-the-child-busy* reputation. Centers have been elaborate, which made them time-consuming for teachers to create, and often required a good deal of space. Many of the center activities did not have an accountability component, enabling the teacher to see what children accomplished, and sometimes routines were not clear.

Students occupied at a meaningful work station.

The material at work stations is based on strategies or skills that have previously been taught, usually in whole-class lessons, to the class. Each station has an accountability piece built into the material and typically at least one station requires produced work to be collected. Students know that they are to accomplish the work product in order to practice skills and strategies they will need as readers and writers. As such, literacy work stations serve many purposes:

- Allow for differentiated practice of work that has been taught (different-colored folders may denote work for each group of learners at a particular station).
- Allow for collaborative work in small groups (we want children to learn to work together, and stations encourage this).
- Allow independent work habits to form (students learn to work on their own, or to "ask three before me," so that the teacher is able to conduct small-group work).
- Allow the teacher to focus on one group for guided reading.
- A work station is a space where children work with each other within the classroom. The work station is a place for working with peers or alone to practice skills taught by the teacher (Diller, 2003).

Work stations that actually function in the manner we wish them to take lots of prior preparation on the part of teachers and many practice sessions with the children in their classrooms.

A most important element in stations is that the activities are differentiated so that students of high and low achievement can work on them. This means children with high achievement are challenged, and those with lower achievement levels can also work on them and be successful. For example, if the station activity involves writing a short informational text describing farm animals (the topic being studied in science), children who are high achievers are expected to research the topic and present a sophisticated product. Low-achieving students might instead choose from a menu of opportunities to demonstrate their learning and mastery of a standard. Students are encouraged to work with partners so they can help each other. When children work in stations they are usually *heterogeneously* grouped, making it possible for all children to interact with each other.

HELPING CHILDREN MANAGE THEIR BEHAVIOR DURING STATION TIME

For stations to be productive a good deal of time and effort goes into helping children learn to be independent of the teacher. The effort early in the year to help children become independent when using stations will prove to be extremely beneficial throughout the year when teachers work with small groups. During instruction all children, except for a few who are working with the teacher, need to be on task and productively involved in independent literacy activities. To achieve this goal, rules need to be created by the teacher and her class, and children need time to practice how to manage their behavior during station time. Children need to know what to do, how to do it, and where to go and when, without the help of the teacher.

LITERACY WORK STATIONS: HOW?

During the first several weeks of school, we need to set up management strategies. Teachers approach this task in different ways at different grade levels. These rules are practiced the first few weeks of school. During station time children move from place to place, handle materials, work in collaborative groups, and clean up. Here are some examples of how Ms. Tapia gets her children ready for stations and other areas of learning throughout the school day.

Ms. Tapia rings a chime to let the students know that it is time to transition from a whole-class lesson to time for literacy work stations and guided reading. She reviews a station chart to show who will be working and where. Time is taken to review the activities suggested at each station and appropriate use of materials is noted.

The sound for transitional times should be unique to the desired action so that the children can decipher that a change is to come and there should be another sound that allows them to know to move about the room. Teachers may consider chimes, bells, the stroke of an instrument, and the like to differentiate the sound to an action. The key to it all is being consistent and modeling each different section of the day.

To allow children to move responsibly about the room, teachers will want to be sure to physically model the desired behavior while orally expressing their thought process—for example: the teacher places her index finger on her head and tells the children, "When my finger is on my head, I am sharing with you my thoughts," and then says, "I am going to stand, push in my chair, and with my arms by my side I will move to the next station." After, she repeats the physical model without speaking to reinforce to the children all of the intended actions. She has them notice what she modeled and other behaviors that she might not have pointed out such as how quietly she moved about the room, how she walked rather than ran, or that she didn't make any stops. Finally, she has some children model the desired behavior. This should be repeated and modeled as needed, but initially teachers should spend 5 minutes or less during several days with gentle reinforcements.

Opportunities for Modeling Desired Behaviors and Expectations

- Circle time
- Vocabulary meeting
- Lining up at the door/entering and exiting the classroom
- Walking throughout the halls
- Using time effectively for literacy stations
- Protecting independent reading and writing time

This method of modeling desired behavior can and should be applied to all aspects of the classroom to set the precedent of structure and discipline in a clear, concise manner. When station time is starting Ms. Tapia will announce that the timer is set for 3 minutes and that she expects that the children will be engaged in their work at stations when the bell on the timer rings.

To start, Ms. Tapia models each expectation to the class over the course of the first weeks of school. She models how to respond to the sounds, how to physically transition, and how to close up the station prior to transitioning. Ms. Tapia has the children practice walking from one station to the other. She puts yellow tape on the floor that provides paths to get to the next station efficiently. In the past, students would bump into each other when moving from place to place. She tells the children to walk as if they had "marshmallow feet." This, of course, makes moving quieter. Children are asked to reflect on their transitions and will model for others more effective methods so that everyone can independently travel about the room.

Moreover, children are given turns to be in charge of observing the behavior of their fellow students. The observer for the day is in charge of looking for on-task behavior. He or she will put a popsicle stick into a pocket on the Good Citizen chart for a child who is transitioning quickly from one activity to another, on task, and completing work. Ms. Tapia provides constructive comments and praises appropriate behavior often during station time and during the entire school day.

Management Tip: Using what is often called the *fishbowl technique,* Ms. Tapia will arrange in advance with a group of children who have demonstrated positive behaviors the opportunity to be models for the remainder of the class. This technique has the other classmates looking into the "fish bowl" of the model classmates actively working in a station. The observing children will point out what is going well, note the positive behaviors, and praise their classmates. Ms. Tapia utilizes this opportunity for constructive comments to the whole class, and reinforces behavior with an explicit example provided by the children. *Note: Ms. Tapia tells her class that if she comes to observe the group, they* are to continue their activities as though she isn't present. It is important that her presence isn't viewed negatively or as a means to find fault in their actions.

Some great resources to check out include:

- *Literacy Work Stations: Making Centers Work* (Diller, 2003)
- *Practice with Purpose: Literacy Work Stations for Grades 3–6.* (Diller, 2000)
- *The Literacy Center* (Morrow, 2003b)
- *Literacy Development in the Early Years: Helping Children Read and Write (8th Edition)* (Morrow, 2015)

ORGANIZING FOR PRODUCTIVE STATION TIME

The success of station time depends to a large extent on how it is organized, designed, and managed. Even creative and knowledgeable teachers struggle unless they carefully plan and prepare the environment and employ managed daily routines. A list of suggestions follows to help organize stations and other parts of the school day:

1. Teach children management routines to help them transition from one activity to another.
2. Be sure that children know where to go and when.
3. Work on self-regulation of behavior appropriate for school.
4. Prepare the physical environment, including selection of materials and their placement in the classroom.
5. Discuss student responsibilities
6. Provide expectations for behavior during whole-class, small-group, and station time.
7. Give students a method or tool to utilize when they are stuck or have completed a task, without asking the teacher for help. If the children "run out" of things to do, it could cause unnecessary disruptions in the classroom.

For a classroom to work well, teachers need many different strategies to help children regulate their behavior. At the beginning of the school year, teachers should spend a good deal of time on management skills through modeling so that learning can take place. When children can follow these organization and management routines, optimum learning can take place (Reutzel & Clark, 2011). Taking the time to slow down at the beginning of the school year will enable you to speed up later.

RULES AND RESPONSIBILITIES FOR USING STATIONS

Rules for using stations can be made by the teacher with the children. If students are involved in the preparation and rules for the station, they will feel more responsible about following them. The management of station time is crucial for its success. Students must know how to:

- Speak in soft voices.
- Share and use materials appropriately.
- Take turns.
- Help others who may need it.
- Keep the station materials in good condition by handling them carefully.
- Put materials back where they found them.
- Record completed tasks on forms provided (see the sample "passport" in Figure 6.1)
- Put their completed work in the station basket.
- Choose from a list of differentiated activities to demonstrate understanding of a skill or strategy previously taught.

When station time takes place during guided reading, these additional rules are important:

- Unless there is an emergency, do not interrupt the teacher.
- Ask designated class helpers to answer questions when you have one. If an answer cannot be obtained, then the child can go to the teacher. Make an anchor chart with rules to follow, such as the one Ms. Tapia made, shown in Figure 6.2.

Helpful Things to Do When Working in Independent Groups	
• Select a leader to help the group get started. • Select a recorder to write down what the group does. • Select a reporter to share the accomplishments of the group.	• Give everyone a job. • Take turns talking. • Share materials. • Listen to your friends when they talk. • Stay with your group.
Helpful Things to Say When Working in Independent Groups	
• "Can I help you?" • "I like your work. I notice how you . . ."	• You did a good job on this part . . ."

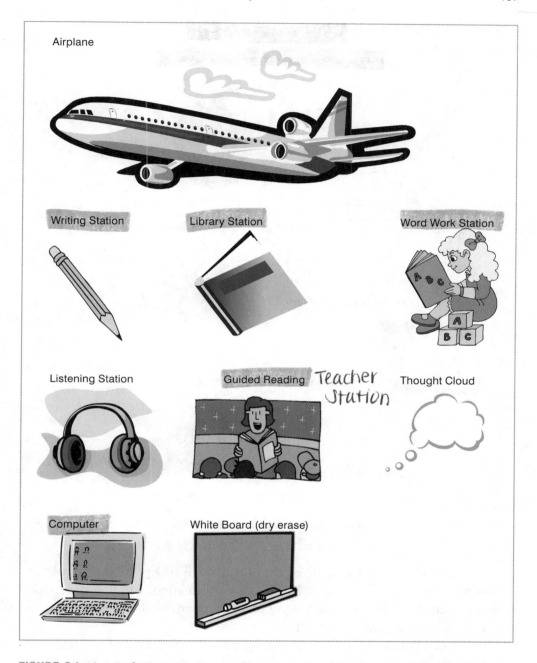

FIGURE 6.1. A sample "passport" to encourage accountability for on-task behavior during work station time.

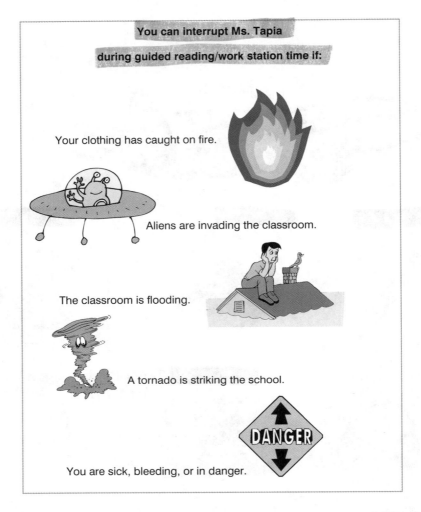

FIGURE 6.2. Anchor chart with rules to follow during work station time.

Children in grades 3–6 will often work in small groups in their station to accomplish one big task together. In this type of situation, children have group tasks to complete. When working in groups that require collaboration to complete a task the following guidelines will help.

At times when a teacher is unavailable, with the exception of an emergency situation, teachers should consider implementing the Parking Lot Questions system, which is simply creating a designated spot for children to grab a sticky note, jot down their question and name, and place it in a parking lot of questions. As the teacher becomes available, she can address the questions. Students should know what to do while waiting and can even remove their question if they find an answer.

ASSIGNING CHILDREN TO STATIONS

There are many ways that teachers assign children to stations or have children themselves select stations. This task often depends on the children in the class and the teacher's preferences for management. Some teachers are more structured than others, while some classes can handle more independence than others. What is good one year may have to change for another. Following are some suggestions for student assignment to stations.

If teachers choose to allow children a choice of activities or stations, no more than two or three choice activities should be available lest one risk confusion within the classroom. We must keep in mind the fact that choice promotes motivation. If only five children can fit in a work station because of the size of the area and materials, there must be directions explaining how to handle this issue.

> **Management Tip:** Create a *star station chart*. The chart should be about 11″ × 17″ with five stars on it. If a child wants to use that literacy station, he can take a post-it at the chart, write his name on it, and put it on a star to request visiting that station. If there are five post-its on the chart, there isn't room for any more children. If there are fewer than five, others can use it. When finished with work in a station, the child removes his or her post-it and discards it so other students can come in. *Remember: Stations are an opportunity for students to practice skills and strategies previously taught. It is not important for students to complete each and every station within a week.*

STATION ASSIGNMENT CHARTS

There are many variations on this type of system. The *station assignment chart* is one that provides several choices for three or four different heterogeneously grouped children (see Figure 6.3). You can use a pocket chart that includes illustrations representing station activities or create your own chart. At the top of each row is a place to put names of children. The figures are movable, as are the name cards (Reutzel & Cooter, 2009; Fountas & Pinnell, 1996).

Some teachers have children change stations when they are ready to see

Evaluate Yourself during Small-Group/Partner Work	
• Did you say helpful things? • Did you help each other? • Did you share materials? • Did you take turns?	• Did you all have jobs? How well did your jobs get done? • What can you or the group do better next time?
(Morrow, 2015)	

Jasmine, James, Darren, Jack, Peter	Helen, David, Kenneth, Max, Lilly	Dylon, Tammy, Isabel, Samantha, Jason	Susan, Kevin, Josh, Len, Jovanna
Partner reading	Listening comprehension	Vocabulary	Writing
Writing	Computer center	Word-study manipulatives	Partner reading
Vocabulary	Word-study manipulatives	Partner Reading	Listening comprehension
Word-study manipulatives	Partner reading	Writing	Computer center
Listening comprehension	Vocabulary	Computer center	Word-study manipulatives
Computer center	Writing	Listening comprehension	Vocabulary

FIGURE 6.3. A sample work station chart.

another small group for guided reading instruction. The teacher can simply ring a bell for children to make the change. Some teachers allow children to move from one station to another on their own when they have completed the required assignment. Children can only go to a station that has room for them. This is the time that the child uses the star chart discussed earlier. If there is no space for a child in one station he or she can choose another.

WHAT IF STUDENTS DON'T FINISH THEIR WORK?

Again, teachers are often concerned if children don't finish all station work during a station time. The teacher sets the expectation and rotation of children so they get through all station materials in a period of a week. Those who do not get to finish all of the assignments can be given additional time, if the teacher so wishes. If there are children who don't finish regularly, the teacher needs to confer with the child so he or she can find out the difficulties to try and find a solution.

There is always more noise in the room during station time, since children are encouraged to collaborate. We know the difference between productive noise and bad noise; therefore we can determine when guidance is needed in stations.

Before beginning any station time, review the rules quickly and review special activities to concentrate on in stations based on recent lessons. Before you have children use stations without your guidance, be sure they have adequate time to use them when you can watch and help. During the first 4 to 6 weeks in school, children need practice working in stations with the teacher as a "guide on the side." The children will soon learn to use them independently without guidance.

ADDITIONAL SUGGESTIONS FOR ACCOUNTABILITY

There must be accountability for work done at stations; therefore, at least one station activity needs to involve passing in some type of work to the teacher. Each child should have a log (see Figure 6.4) or a "passport" to track progress in work stations. The children indicate on the log what they plan to do during station time. When a child completes a task, he or she indicates on the log that the activity has been completed.

Management Tip: Gather students in the whole class to reflect on the following questions:

- "What did you do well during work stations today?"
- "What are you working on in work stations?"
- "How can I help to improve a work station in the classroom?"
- "What were you able to accomplish as a reader/writer with your peers?"

Discussing and reflecting on these types of questions with your students can serve as a form of accountability.

WHAT KINDS OF STATIONS AND STATION ACTIVITIES DO WE NEED IN THE CLASSROOM?

The classroom literacy stations should include:

- Word-study station
- Independent/partner reading (library) station
- Listening comprehension station
- Writing station
- Optional stations

ACTIVITIES I WILL DO
AND ACTIVITIES I COMPLETED AT STATION TIME

Student's Name: _____ Date: _____

"I Can . . ." (Activities chosen to be completed)	Literacy Work Station Visited	Accomplished Work
	Independent or Partner Reading (Library Station)	
	Word Study	
	Listening Comprehension	
	Computer	
	Writing Station	
	Optional: Literacy Games	
	Other Station Activity	

FIGURE 6.4. Sample activity log.

Classrooms can have stations for all content areas and purposes; however, space is always a problem. Teachers have learned to store station materials in baskets and bins, or on the front and backs of closet doors. Teachers have found that some household goods such as shoe bags provide spaces for children's work or storing station activities. School supply companies have devised many types of storage for written activities, manipulative activities, children's writing journals, and other station activities and completed work.

The following section outlines important stations with activities that teachers have found to be productive.

SAMPLE LITERACY STATION ACTIVITIES

Library Station

I can . . .

- Read or look at a book, magazine, or newspaper.
- Tell a friend why he or she should read what I read.
- Partner-read a book.
- Retell a story to a friend.
- Rate a book using a five-star system. (Other children can sign up to read it by jotting their names on post-it notes on the inside cover. The book will circulate down the list.)

Word-Study Station

I can . . .

- Use a word-study game for learning the alphabet.
- Build words with onset and rime tiles.
- Make little words from big words.
- Complete a word sort or speed sort with friends.

Vocabulary Station

I can . . .

- Write a definition, draw a picture, write a sentence, and write a synonym for a vocabulary word using my "Word Nerd" journal.
- Write a story using five new vocabulary words from the week.

- Utilize all content-area vocabulary for discussion.
- Look at the list of "juicy words" in my reader's notebook and complete a graphic organizer for a choice word.

Listening/Reading Comprehension

I can . . .

- Listen to a book on a headset and fill in a graphic organizer with the setting, theme, episodes, and resolution.
- Create a PowerPoint or Powtoon presentation for a book that I have read.
- Retell a story I read with a partner.
- Make up questions about what I have read for others who have read the same book.

Optional: Fluency Station

I can . . .

- Choral-read a poem.
- Echo-read a story.
- Participate in a repeated reading of a favorite book or text.
- Participate in a Readers' Theatre with my classmates.
- Record myself reading and rewind and reflect on my fluency (expression, etc.).

Writing Station

I can . . .

- Write a story.
- Draw a picture about a story I wrote.
- Make a book for a story I wrote.
- Create a PowerPoint for a story I wrote.
- Write a puppet show and perform it for friends.
- Write to a pen pal.
- Write a recipe.
- Write a joke or a riddle.
- Use Animoto to make a video and act out the story I wrote.

- Write an advertisement for a story I wrote.

- Write an expository text about a science topic I am studying using a mentor text.

- Write blogs or, create podcasts, webinars, or videos for what I have written (looking back at my writing journal).

- Use three stickers to incorporate into my drawing or picture, and write a "sticker story"

Management Tip: Stations will work best when all components are well organized. Children must know how to do the activities, how to store materials, where to place completed work, and so on. Bins from thrift stores are a great tool for organizing such materials. Colorful labels for stations can be laminated and applied to the bins.

Teachers should share station activities with other teachers to increase their supply of materials. Children can be involved in making materials for the literacy stations. One activity children can create is a taped story they can read well, to which others can listen. Participation in creating station activities promotes a feeling of ownership and respect for the area. There are, however, wonderful materials that can be purchased from teacher supply companies, and we have the benefit of online teaching channels and websites to provide new activities for stations. Some online sites that can be used for station activities are Volki, Puppet Pals, Wall Wisher, and Blogster.

Teachers can move stations from one place to another because they find a space that is bigger, brighter, or quieter. New items need to be added frequently to

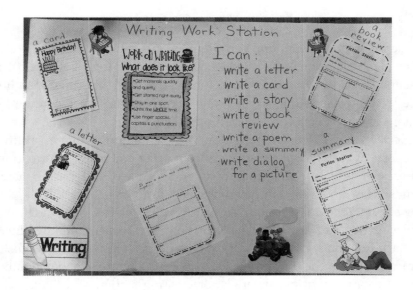

An "I Can" chart reminds students of what they can focus on at a station.

motivate interest; we can put some away for a while and bring them out again at a later date.

To illustrate how one teacher manages station time, we will observe Ms. Tapia's classroom. The activities that Ms. Tapia models for her class for station time are often skill- and theme-related. In the beginning of the school year, she spends time introducing children to the stations in the room and the types of activities they include. She has her class practice working on the different activities. At this time, Ms. Tapia does not work with small groups during station time; rather, she helps the children so that they eventually will be able to work independently. The children are assigned tasks and in some cases have choices when they complete required activities. The tasks engage the children in reading and writing to help with skill development. Her children never run out of work to do at stations. There should always be something else to participate in, such as select another book to read or write in your journal.

INTERDISCIPLINARY/CONTENT-FOCUSED STATIONS

Based on space and what is being studied, teachers can optionally create stations for content areas. These stations motivate interest and they also enable the teacher to embed literacy activities into content areas. The same rules apply to content-area stations as to literacy stations. When a specific theme is being studied (such as weather) the teachers may create a station for that theme or add materials to an existing one. Examples of types of materials to be found in different content areas are:

- *Science station:* aquarium, terrarium, plants, magnifying glass, class pet, magnets, thermometer, compass, prism, shells, rock collections, stethoscope, kaleidoscope, microscope, narrative and informational literature reflecting topics being studied, and blank journals for recording observations of experiments and scientific projects.
- *Social studies station:* maps, globe, flags, community figures, traffic signs, reports of current events, artifacts from other countries, informational and narrative literature reflecting topics being studied, and writing materials to make class books or your own books about topics being studied.
- *Math station:* scales, rulers, measuring cups, clocks, stopwatch, calendar, play money, cash register, calculator, dominoes, abacus, number line, height chart, hourglass, numbers (felt, wood, and magnetic), fraction puzzles, geometric shapes, math workbooks, children's literature about numbers and mathematics, writing materials for creating stories, and books related to mathematics.

- *Art station:* easels, watercolors, brushes, colored pencils, crayons, felt-tip markers, various kinds of paper, scissors, paste, pipe cleaners, scrap materials (bits of various fabrics, wool, string, etc.), clay, play dough, food and detergent boxes for sculptures, books about famous artists, and books with directions for crafts.
- *Music station:* piano, guitar, or other real instruments; CD and/or tape players and tapes and CDs of all types of music; rhythm instruments; songbooks; and photocopies of sheet music for songs to sing.

 Breaking Through the Block: Teachers can include stations beyond times for reading and writing. You can include stations for art, music, math, science, social studies, and so on. Based on current topics of study, teachers should provide narrative and expository texts for students to read. Students can partner-read about these topics and jot down things they are still wondering about. To promote writing in content-area stations, be sure to provide students with paper, writing utensils, and access to technology.

Ms. Tapia believes strongly in the integration of literacy into all content areas. Her class is learning about dinosaurs, which is reflected in her stations. She embeds the topic being studied into literacy activities in all stations. Before beginning station time, she spends a few minutes reviewing the station materials that are new for the exploration of dinosaurs. Stations have materials that are in place over a period of time as those discussed recently. However, the current theme embedded into stations makes the station activities more interesting and relevant for students. Literacy skills that need to be practiced are utilized in theme-based stations. A description of what has been added to each of Ms. Tapia's stations related to the dinosaur theme follows:

- *Writing station:* Dinosaur-bordered writing paper, dinosaur-shaped books, a dinosaur dictionary, a dinosaur-shaped poster with words about dinosaurs, pencils, crayons, colored pencils, markers.
- *Literacy station:* Fiction and informational dinosaur books, dinosaur books with accompanying CDs, a dinosaur vocabulary puzzle, a dinosaur concentration memory game, a teacher-made dinosaur lottery game.
- *Computer station:* A video about fossils(*www.teacherplanet.com/links/redirect.php?url=http://www.kidsturncentral.com/links/dinolinks.htm*).
- *Science station:* Small skulls and old animal bones, along with a magnifying glass and rubber gloves to examine the bones and draw what they think the entire animal may have looked like; dinosaur pictures to sort into meat eaters and plant eaters; other pictures to be sorted into "walked on two feet" and "walked on four feet." There are recording sheets for all activities.

- *Math station:* Measuring tools in a basket and sheets to record the measurement of various plaster bones of dinosaurs; dinosaur counters; little plastic dinosaurs in an estimation jar; a basket containing 50 little dinosaurs numbered from 1 to 50 to be put in sequential order.
- *Art station:* Dinosaur stencils, dinosaur stamps, clay models of dinosaurs, and many pictures of dinosaurs to help students make their own sculptures.
- *Dramatic play station:* The dramatic-play area is transformed into a paleontologist's office with chicken bones embedded in plaster of paris, carving tools and small hammers to remove the bones, safety goggles, paper and pencils for labeling bones, trays to display them, dinosaur books, and posters of fossils and dinosaurs.
- *Social studies:* Using geography and directions, follow the path of fossils in the United States and around the world. Create maps for others to find the fossils based on N, S, W, and E directions.

CONCLUSION

For a classroom to work well, teachers need many different strategies to help children regulate their behavior. At the beginning of the school year, teachers should spend a good deal of time on management skills so that learning can take place utilizing literacy work stations. When children can follow the organization and management routines, optimum learning can take place in a collaborative social setting (Morrow, Kuhn, & Schwanenflugel, 2006).

·· STOP! THINK! REACT! ··

Based on your understanding of literacy work stations, you should take time to reflect on the following:

❑ How can you implement the core literacy stations in your daily agenda?
❑ What strategies and skills have been taught and can be reinforced in your classroom literacy stations?
❑ What materials can be used to support your learners?
❑ What areas of the classroom could be designated for productive station work?
❑ Identify a grade-level colleague with whom to brainstorm ideas related to grade-appropriate standards taught and potential opportunities for differentiated stations.

CHAPTER 7

Guided Reading

Grouping for Differentiation of Instruction

CLASSROOM VIGNETTE

Since Ms. Tapia began using guided reading, she started to know her students better. In a small group, she was able to learn not only their reading skills but more about their lives outside of school. The small-group setting allowed her to build close relationships with the children, making everyone feel comfortable in the classroom and willing to share their concerns. This also fostered a "closeness" that wasn't there before. Not only does guided reading help Ms. Tapia with differentiating instruction within the literacy development of her children, but it also creates a social and emotional bond with the students.

WHAT IS GUIDED READING?

The purpose of this chapter is to discuss ways to meet the individual needs of children in small guided reading group instruction. Guided reading is a form of explicit instruction that takes place in small groups that are led by the teacher. Fountas and Pinnell (1996) discuss it as follows:

> In guided reading a teacher works with a small group. Children in the group are similar in their literacy development with similar skill needs. Groups have children in them whose instructional reading levels are also similar. The emphasis is on improving skills and reading levels. Children are grouped and regrouped in a dynamic process that involves ongoing observation and assessment. (p. 4)

Furthermore, Spiegel (1992) writes:

> The overall purpose of guided reading instruction is a way to meet individual needs. Guided reading instruction is systematic instruction with a scope of skills and objectives to accomplish. Activities are designed to meet the objectives. Skill instruction is not left to chance; it is assured. Although there is a systematic plan, guided reading instruction should allow for "teachable moments." (p. 40)

Literacy instruction is viewed in tiers of achievement levels with regard to the response-to-intervention (RTI) model. Tier 1 instruction is at grade level and is usually done with the whole class (see Chapter 8). Tier 2 attends to individual differences with small-group instruction led by the teacher to meet the student's achievement level. Finally, Tier 3 instruction is for children who are not achieving on grade level, but who do not have learning disabilities and are not receiving special services. Many of these students are potential candidates for special services, and therefore need to receive additional literacy instruction in small groups directed at their needs. Within this model, struggling readers receive instruction in reading three times a day. Guided reading is considered Tier 2 and Tier 3 instruction. To be sure of a clear understanding, Table 7.1 shows the relationship between RTI and literacy instruction.

Researchers found that in small-group instruction, teachers are better able to retain students' attention. The small group offers the opportunity for more student participation (Combs, 2009; Lou, Kinzer, Coiro, & Cammack, 1996; Slavin, 1987; Sorenson & Hallinan, 1986). When teachers use small-group instruction they have the opportunity for differentiating instruction. Teachers can change instructional methods and materials to meet the needs of each student in the group. When groups are homogeneous, it is possible for teachers to provide more individualized instruction at the appropriate level (Jalongo, 2007; Slavin, 1987). In small groups, instruction can be paced for students' rate of learning, and teaching styles can be modified to meet different learning styles (Combs, 2009; Hallinan & Sorenson, 1983).

The use of a variety of organizational strategies is important because some children's reading needs change as the year progresses. To that end, the use of several different grouping schemes within the same classroom tends to eliminate the stigmas attached to a single grouping system. Variable grouping will ensure that children will interact with everyone at some time in one group or another. Teachers need to use a variety of strategies for organizing classroom space and strategies to meet individual needs through *differentiation of instruction*. With our diverse population, the "one-size-fits all" curriculum will not meet the needs of all children (Walpole & McKenna, 2007). For teachers to provide instruction that is

TABLE 7.1. The Relationship between RTI and Literacy Instruction

RTI tiered models	How does this translate into literacy instruction?
Tier 1: Core instruction	
All students in Tier 1 receive high-quality, scientifically based instruction, differentiated to meet their needs, and are screened on a periodic basis to identify struggling learners who need additional support.	The teacher uses assessment data to design whole-class lessons suitable for the entire class. Expert teaching is provided through small group instruction, and the teacher confers with learners as part of the daily schedule.
Tier 2: Group interventions	
In Tier 2, students not making adequate progress in the core curriculum are provided with increasingly intensive instruction matched to their needs on the basis of levels of performance and rates of progress.	The teacher designs high-quality guided reading lessons to target groups based on needs related to skills and strategies being learned. This extra intervention takes place outside of the literacy schedule to provide an extra dose of instruction.
Tier 3: Intensive interventions	
At this level, students receive individualized, intensive interventions that target the students' skill deficits for the remediation of existing problems and the prevention of more severe problems.	A daily "extra dose" of guided reading instruction is provided by a reading specialist and an intervention program is implemented.

Note: Based on *www.rtinetwork.org/essential/tieredinstruction.*

attending to the needs of all children, they must assess their students' achievement and then implement instruction tailored to the different needs.

OUR SHARED BELIEFS ABOUT GUIDED READING

We became strong believers in guided reading because of our teaching and coaching experiences. There are vast differences between the children in classes in terms of background experiences and achievement. For example, a teacher might have a student who speaks very little English or is unable to read in his or her first language. Classrooms will also have students who are below grade level. The opposite is true as well, since many students are on advanced reading levels and need additional attention, time, and support. Some students have difficulty paying attention or staying on task, and others have specific needs diagnosed as learning disabilities. Regardless, these students, and many more, constitute the general makeup of classes all across the United States.

HOW DO WE PREPARE FOR GUIDED READING?

There is a good deal of organization and management necessary to carry out guided reading lessons well. Teachers need to know how to assess student achievement and form groups for instruction. Appropriate assessments must be available in the school and used on a regular basis (see Chapter 3). When children progress or need additional help, their group placement needs to change. Teachers should have forms for taking anecdotal notes about children and also to record what groups have worked on. Teachers need leveled books for guided reading. Stations must be developed that have productive independent work in them and be changed to meet the needs of children (see Chapter 6). Children must be taught to work in stations independent of the teacher.

Children need a place to store their guided reading materials, which would include the leveled books they are using for instruction, writing journals, vocabulary words, and the like. Students are responsible for keeping their materials neat and organized. There needs to be a table in the room (either round or kidney-shaped) for guided reading groups to meet away from the rest of the class so there is quiet in the room. Teachers must plan lessons for the different groups. Guided reading lessons cannot be spur-of-the-moment activities. Materials for lessons need to be at the teacher's fingertips when teaching.

A guided reading corner, set to go.

HOW DO WE GROUP FOR INSTRUCTION?

Whole-class instruction, often referred to as *shared reading experience*, has always been one of the most common forms of teaching in school. It is quite appropriate when information needs to be introduced to all the children. Whole-class instruction is mostly at grade level in the form of mini-lessons to introduce new ideas and concepts. Whole-class instruction provides and builds a sense of community in the classroom. The types of activities that are appropriate for the whole class are mini-lessons for teaching grade-level strategies, reading stories, singing songs, and having short class discussions.

Guiding reading groups, on the other hand, are for explicit instruction of skills. Teachers should plan for many types of groups so that children get to work with others in the class and to avoid the stigma attached to being associated with only one group. Children should work in many different groups; however, groups should change as children improve in skills.

There are some disadvantages of grouping. For example, if groups are inflexible, once a student is tracked in a particular group that placement may never change throughout his or her school career. This practice affects self-esteem and the type of instruction a student receives (Antonacci & O'Callaghan, 2003; Slavin, 1987). Another disadvantage of grouping occurs when only one measure determines a child's group placement.

Using Assessment to Better Determine Groupings

With such a variety of group formations, many teachers ask, "How do I select children for each type of group?" Small groups for explicit instruction for teaching of reading and writing skills are formed by the teacher based on students' needs and achievement. There are many assessments to determine reading level, word-study knowledge, and so on. Assessment helps to discover achievement levels and skill needs to establish group placement.

The following measures, previously discussed in Chapter 3, serve to benefit teachers when determining groups:

- Running records (to determine text reading level, types of strengths and weaknesses in word analysis, comprehension, fluency, and self-monitoring)
- Letter-recognition tests
- High-frequency word tests
- Standardized test scores
- Informal reading inventories
- Comprehension evaluations
- Attitudes toward reading

These students have similar interests.

When selecting children for groups, the assessments and teacher judgment are important. Guided reading groups are homogeneous. Of course, no two children are the same, but like characteristics in skill needs and reading level are key to a successful group. When building a team or group of readers to work together, their sense of community and feeling that they belong is key to their participation. Consider the personalities within the group, and how they mesh with one another.

Group Size

The number of groups in a classroom when differentiating instruction depends on the differences among the children. Typically, three to five groups are found in classrooms, with no more than six students per group. When there are more groups, effective instruction might not be as manageable.

MATERIALS FOR SMALL-GROUP GUIDED READING INSTRUCTION

Teachers select the instructional materials for small-group reading instruction based on meeting the skill needs of the children. Selecting the appropriate book for instruction also can be done with the use of a running record. The test is administered with leveled material. Teachers will make critical decisions about the right levels of materials for the children he or she is teaching.

Leveled reading books are materials used for small-group explicit instruction during guided reading. These books have been leveled for difficulty, which helps teachers to select materials that are just right for instruction. The texts should be at the child's instructional reading level. When a child's word recognition and comprehension is 90–95% with a particular book, the level of that book is at his or her reading instructional level. If the child scores higher than 95%, the book is for independent reading. A score below 90% indicates that the book is too difficult to be used for instructional purposes (Clay, 1993a). If the text is too easy, there is no opportunity to teach new strategies; if the book is too difficult, it will be a frustrating experience for the child. Leveled books were created for instructional purposes and do not take the place of quality children's literature (Taylor, 2008). During independent reading time, children need to be given an opportunity to read materials they choose based on their own interests.

Commercial publishers level their materials. Publishers may designate a difficulty level using letter-, color-, or number-based systems. Using Lexile frameworks also provides a way to evaluate the readers and texts being used. Lexiles for difficulty are based on multiple criteria (Morrison & Wilcox, 2013; Fountas & Pinnell, 1996). There are quantitative and qualitative measures. Quantitative measures include:

- Length of a book, including number of pages and words
- Word length and frequency of use
- Number of different words
- Number of syllables in words
- Size and layout of the print

Qualitative measures include:

- Levels of meaning or purpose
- Structure of text and genres
- Language conventionality and clarity
- Syntactic complexity
- Abstract concepts
- How well illustrations support the text

Teachers should be aware that there are some differences between how books from different companies are leveled. Books from one company may be labeled more difficult than books from another company that is using another measuring system. The chart in Figure 7.1 shows how the same book is rated differently based on the system being used for leveling. Remember that the leveled books are for instructional purposes mostly during guided reading. During other parts of the day, children should have choices about what they will read.

Category	Grade Level	Letter Level	Number Level	Lexile Range
Emergent	K	A B C	A & 1 2 & 3 4	Below 200
Emergent/Early	K/1	D E	6 8	Below 200
Early	1	F G H I J	10 12 14 16 18	190–530
Early/Fluent	1/2 2/3	K L M	20 24 28	420–650
	3 4	N O P Q	30 34 38 40	520–820 740–940
Fluent	4/5	R S T	40 40 44	
	5 5/6	U V W	50 50 60	830–1010 925–1070
		X Y Z	60 70 80	970–1185

FIGURE 7.1. Reading-level conversion chart (original in color). Compiled by Kimberly Taybron and Marie Lee, PCS, ELA, curriculum resource specialists, September 27, 2012.

PLANNING FOR GUIDED READING LESSONS

When planning for guided reading we need to think about many things:

- Where will the lessons be taught in the classroom?
- How much time will be spent teaching guided reading lessons?
- Where does it fit in the school day?

Guided reading lessons should focus on a systematic sequence of skills to be developed based on the needs of the children in the group. The objectives for the lessons, like the selection of the text, depend on the students' reading achievement (Reutzel & Cooter, 2009). Keep in mind that the students are more important than the leveled text. Small-group guided reading instruction is characterized by the following:

1. Children are assessed regularly during guided reading. For example, teachers may do a running record for a child. The teacher evaluates the child's reading needs

and reading level and determines whether the child should remain in his or her present group or move to a group where the work is easier or more difficult.

2. The number of groups formed is not preset; it is determined by the number of different ability levels in a given classroom.

3. Books selected for instruction meet the needs of the students, regardless of their grade level, to differentiate instruction.

4. Small-group instruction is designed to provide children with strategies for becoming independent, fluent readers.

5. A guided reading lesson can teach almost any skill or strategy. The major concern is that it is designed to meet the needs of the children in the group.

6. Guided reading lessons are *15–20 minutes maximum*.

7. Children reading below grade level should meet daily, but also need additional intervention. Children who read on grade level should meet two to four times a week. High-achieving students should meet once or twice a week so they can reach their fullest potential. Teachers should also do a short check-in with these readers daily.

8. Activities provided for children who are not in guided reading groups are often in stations. Children are actively engaged in interesting, productive, and active work practicing skills learned in guided reading lessons. Station activities attend to differences in children since they can be completed in a complex way for the advanced reader or in a less complex manner for the struggling reader (see Chapter 6).

9. The teacher often writes notes to parents about the guided reading lesson for children to take home. The note suggests homework for the child and how parents can help. These notes are also used to guide conversations during parent–teacher conferences.

THE GUIDED READING LESSON

Guided reading lessons must be planned. We provide a sample planning template in Figure 7.2 and a template for recording anecdotal notes in Figure 7.3. The structure and components of a guided reading lesson are as follows:

Before Reading (3–5 Minutes)

The teacher names the objective or skill to be learned during the lesson. The teacher sets a purpose for reading related to the mini-lesson skill. A warm-up activity is used to review skills and strategies previously taught.

Working with students in the "before" section of guided reading.

During Reading (10 Minutes)

The children whisper-read the book in the primary grades. This is not round-robin reading when children take turns reading aloud, nor is it choral reading. When children whisper-read they read at their own pace in soft voices. Older children should be encouraged to read silently. While the children read, the teacher listens to provide guidance or scaffolding when a child cannot figure out a word. The teacher takes notes about the children's reading strengths and weaknesses. The teacher has a focus child in the group sitting next to him or her and takes more careful notes on that one student. The next day a different focus child will sit next to the teacher during guided reading. Teachers who choose to listen to more than one student should limit anecdotal note taking to no more than two students, as quality is more important than quantity.

> *Management Tip:* If students have a difficult time paying attention during whisper reading, have your students turn their seats around at the guided reading table. If space allows, permit students to choose a comfortable spot to read in the classroom and come back later for the after-reading component.

After Reading (5 Minutes)

Revisit the purpose for reading or the objective. Students should have an opportunity to discuss the comprehension focus question. Engage students in a brief activity using the skill or strategy taught during previous whole-class lessons. Help students refine their practice with that skill or strategy. Be sure to ask students how today's instruction helps them as readers.

Group Level: _____   Text Title: _____

Standard(s) Addressed	
Before Reading ( ) **Phonics** ( ) **Vocabulary** ( ) **Genre intro** ( ) **Purposeful book walk** ( ) **Prediction**	
Guided Language to Focus Instruction	*This book/chapter is called . . .* *It is about . . .* *You will read today to find out . . .* (Pose a general comprehension question to set the focus for independent reading.) *Our strategy today will focus on . . .* (Name the strategy using student-friendly language.)
***During Reading**	• Students will whisper-read or read silently. • Teacher will listen in on one or more student(s) and will provide reading strategies (teaching point) based on their individual needs, collect anecdotal notes, or conduct a running record.
After Reading **Discussing the text**	Turn and talk—discuss (comprehension question from earlier).
Teaching point **Including strategy instruction**	*Today I'm going to show you how to . . .* (modeling instruction). Make the standards accessible to the learner with support.
Lesson Closure	Review skills from the Before Reading component of the lesson (optional). *How does today's strategy help you as a reader?*

FIGURE 7.2. Sample planning template.

Student's Name:
Date:
Book level:
Phonological awareness:
Phonics:
Vocabulary:
Comprehension:
Fluency:
Writing:
Comments:

FIGURE 7.3. Anecdotal notes template.

The following is a description of two different guided reading group lessons in Ms. Parisella's first-grade classroom:

Ms. Parisella believes strongly in the need for small-group instruction to find out what individual children know and what they need to learn. She has organized the class into five groups of four to five children (each who have similar reading needs and are reading at about the same level). She moves children from one group to another based on her assessment of their progress. A typical lesson could be about any literacy skill such as (1) repeated reading to develop fluency, (2) working on a word analysis skill, (3) developing comprehension strategies, or (4) reading a new book with teacher support.

Ms. Parisella assesses one child's reading development during each reading group lesson by taking a running record of their oral reading fluency. The running record will help her understand the child's skills/needs.

Ms. Parisella engages the rest of the class with station work. When students are working well on their own, she calls on her first group for guided reading instruction. She follows the outline for a guided reading lesson.

Before reading, Ms. Parisella discusses her objective for the lesson, which is to learn four new vocabulary words for a new book they will begin to read. She writes four sentences on the whiteboard, leaving one word blank in each. She asks the children to predict what word might make sense in the blank. She then asks them to write the words on their own whiteboards. They discuss the new words and how they figured out their meaning from the context of the sentences. Ms. Parisella introduces a new book about animals selected from her leveled books and asks the children to whisper-read and look for the new vocabulary. When they find them they write them on a post-it, and when they finish reading they copy the words into their Very Own Dictionaries. She also poses a focus comprehension question to the group related to one of the words, carefully making sure that she can assess students' understanding of the text.

During reading, Ms. Parisella reads the first page of the book to the children and then asks the group to whisper-read the story at their own rate. She listens carefully to support those in need of help. She selects a focus child for the day for which she takes a running record as she listens to her read. The next time she meets with this group, another child will sit by her side to be assessed.

After reading, the children and teacher discuss the story. Ms. Parisella asks questions that relate to the new vocabulary and to ensure that students were able to comprehend the text. Ms. Parisella prepared another practice sheet with four more sentences that have the new vocabulary words missing. She asks the children to fill in the missing words. A strategy is introduced to help students better use context clues when reading. As the lesson ends, Ms. Parisella writes a short note to one of the parents of the children she sees in a group about his or her progress, what he or she was learning, what he or she needed help with, and what his or her homework is.

GUIDED READING IN THE UPPER GRADES

If we teach in grades 3–6, the guided reading approach will entail some similar and a few different procedures. Similar to the primary grades, leveled books are used for instruction to meet the reading level of children in a group. For example, there are sixth-grade children who are reading on a second- or third-grade level. The challenge is finding the appropriate materials for them. It is important that both the achievement levels of the child as well as social and emotional sides are equally addressed with the elementary grade children. The children don't want to be viewed as receiving *extra help* or reading "baby books." Their perception of themselves can affect their overall esteem and their attitudes toward reading. In the middle grades strategy groups are used in lessons. In these cases, children with similar difficulties, but perhaps on varying reading levels, work on a particular strategy.

 Breaking Through the Block: When it comes time for content-area instruction, remember the skills and strategies that were worked on with students during guided reading. When possible, remind the students of what they have been practicing and assist students as they practice when reading articles and content-area textbooks or writing challenging essays.

Access to quality literature is crucial for strategy groups. You might be able to acquire books through book clubs, by taking out books from public libraries and the school library, or by pooling resources together with a group of colleagues. Some schools dedicate a room or closet to *host* the materials. Whether the storage is in your classroom or in a communal area, adequate time must be dedicated to selecting materials. Quality literature has a myriad of skills within the text that are waiting to be discovered, illuminated, and will allow for a natural, genuine conversation with the book.

Management Tip: Because planning guided reading lessons takes a considerable amount of time, we should consider creating an online database of guided reading lessons to share with our colleagues at school. If these lessons are stored in a shared folder, teachers will have access to specific lessons when determining appropriate books matched to individual readers.

The following lesson highlights what a strategy group might look like in the upper grades. There is a difference in what happens during the before/during/after structure between guided reading and strategy group instruction. Sample menus for strategy instruction using both fiction and informational texts are provided in Figure 7.4.

Before Reading

Set clear objectives and precedence for what the group will work on. Mrs. Medea starts her lesson as follows:

> "We have been working on inference questions and answers. Let's review what an inference is and how we might find them. Inferences are clues that the author gives us, but doesn't just say it outright. For example, let's look at this picture [holds up a picture of a child who has fallen off a bike in a park setting]. What can you tell me about how this child is feeling right now?"

The children raise their hands and suggest he is feeling "sad" or "upset." Mrs. Medea asks, "How do you know that the child is feeling this way?" One student observes that he or she has fallen off his or her bike. Whereas another child notices that the illustrator shows tears on the child's face. However, when a child says, "Mad, because their parents weren't watching them," Mrs. Medea draws the group in to say:

> "It is possible that his parents weren't watching him, but we cannot infer that based on the clues in the pictures or the text; therefore we don't have enough information to draw that conclusion.
>
> "Let's try this again with another picture. What clues in the picture can we find to tell us about something this little boy is hoping for. . . ."

She holds up the image and again has the children make inferences based on the picture.

She then begins to read two to three sentences excerpted from various books. Here is an example of how this could be done:

> "Now let's read some sentences without pictures to see if there are any clues here. This is different than a picture where we can see the clues. This time, we will have to use words to help us. Let's look at this example. Close your eyes and visualize what I am reading. I will read it two times:
>
> "'Where's Papa going with that ax?' said Fern to her mother as they were setting the table for breakfast. 'Out to the hoghouse' replied Mrs. Arable. 'Some pigs were born last night.' [Pauses.]
>
> "How do you think Fern is feeling? What information in the text suggests that Fern is feeling upset, but doesn't tell you in words or show you with pictures?"

The teacher should follow with questions that are inference-based. For example, after reading more to give the students additional context and information about Fern's character, Mrs. Medea asks, "If Fern were given three wishes, what

Strategy Menu for Fiction

Self-Monitoring	Accuracy/Decoding	Fluency
Teacher asks, "Did that make sense? • **Was anything you read tricky for you to understand?"** • Back up and reread. • Think about what you have read so far. • Slow down when reading. • Ask, "What did that just say?"	**"This word was tricky for you to sound out . . ."** • Look for a "little" word within the word, add the rest. • Take off affixes—find the base word. • Break into smaller chunks, sound out, and put back together. • Does it look right, sound right, and make sense?	**Rate—Expression—Phrasing—Dialogue** • Stop at end marks, pause at commas. • Look at end marks—what would that sound like? • Put words together as if you were talking. • Change your voice when you see dialogue. • Listen to me (model), student repeats.

Comprehension	Vocabulary	*Conferring Options
Literal <u>Teacher asks, "What did you just read?"</u> **Strategy:** Students stop and ask . . . • Who? What happened? • Who's telling the story? • Who's talking? • What's the problem? **Inferential** <u>Teacher asks, "Why?"</u> **Strategy:** Students stop and think . . . • It says . . . I know . . . , and so I think . . . • The character (says, thinks, acts, feels), so I think . . .	**"Do you know what this word means?"** • Context: read the sentence before, the sentence it's in, and the sentence after (or more). • Cover and insert a word that would make sense. • Keep reading, it may not matter (skip it until you miss it). • Keep track of unknown words.	**"Are you paying attention to . . . "** • what the character is like? • what the character is doing to solve his or her problem? • how the character is changing? • what the character is learning? **"Have you noticed . . . "** • anything repeating (line, word, ideas, feelings)? • when a character has an important realization, an epiphany? • if the character has acted differently than he or she normally does? • if the character has been given any advice from another character? • if the character is thinking back to another time?

Strategy Menu for Informational Texts

Self-Monitoring	Accuracy/Decoding	Fluency
Teacher asks, "Did that make sense? Was anything you read tricky for you to understand?" • Scan and plan. Back up and reread. Think about what you have read so far. • Slow down when reading. • Ask, "What did that just say?"	**"This word was tricky for you to sound out . . . "** • Use the pronunciation key. • Look for a "little" word within the word, add the rest. • Take off affixes—find the base word. • Break into smaller chunks, sound out, and put back together. • Does it look right, sound right, and make sense?	**Rate—Phrasing—Expression** • Stop at end marks, pause at commas. • Look at end marks—what would that sound like? • Put words together as if you were talking. • Listen to me (model), student repeats.

Comprehension	Vocabulary	*Conferring Options
Teacher asks, "What did you just read?" **Strategy:** Students stop and ask . . . • What's the topic? • What do I already know about this topic? • What's most important about this topic? • How does _____ (text feature) help me understand the text? • It says . . . , I know . . . , and so I think . . . <u>Main Idea</u> • Turn headings into questions. • Use the topic sentence, first paragraph, or chapter. • Use the concluding sentence, paragraph, or chapter.	**"Do you know what this word means?"** • Use the glossary for bold-printed words. • Context: read the sentence before, the sentence it's in, and the sentence after (or more). • Cover and insert a word that would make sense. • Keep reading, it may not matter (skip it until you miss it). • Keep track of unknown words.	**"Are you paying attention to . . . "** • unfamiliar words and trying to determine their meaning? • the headings/subheadings? • the text features (illustrations, diagrams, bold words, etc.)? • what the text is mainly about? • the questions you have about the text/topic? **"Have you noticed . . ."** • new information you are learning? • if what you thought you knew has changed? • if the author's viewpoint is clearly stated or implied? • bias on the part of the author?

FIGURE 7.4. Sample menus for strategy instruction.

would they be? What evidence in the book do we have to make these conclusions?"

This would guide the students to use text evidence to support their claims as well as to explore character development qualities that the author has put into place without simply stating it to the reader. This 5-minute mini-lesson paves the way for learning about inference.

During Reading

Mrs. Medea says:

> "We are going to begin reading this book, and you will notice that there is a sticky note on this page. This is where I'd like you to stop reading. If you finish before the rest of your team, you can reread the section again or look at the pictures. Since we are acting like detectives today, you may find clues in the pictures or when you reread the pages."

Place the sticky notes at a designated stopping place and include an inference question on the sticky note. This will prepare the children for a later discussion.

After Reading

As the facilitator of the discussion, Mrs. Medea keeps the conversation about inference going on as long as needed. She has the children make up inference questions to ask each other and asks the children to describe what an inference means and how making inferences helps the students as readers.

ADDITIONAL CONSIDERATIONS FOR GUIDED READING

We discussed earlier how preparing the environment is an important part of guided reading. It is imperative that the teacher is familiar with the text being used, and has preplanned appropriate stopping points for discussion. Guided reading lessons taught "on the fly" are a recipe for disaster.

Teachers should also have each child's reading portfolio readily available so that he or she can add anecdotal notes to it. All of the materials necessary to make the guided reading session efficient should be within arm's reach to eliminate distractions. Simple systems like a rolling cart, file folder organizers, cabinet, plastic shelving, and bins near the guided reading table make a major difference and set the tone for the students.

Sitting around a table seems to be an effective way to reach each child. If you don't have a table, gather in a cozy setting on the floor by forming a circle, or move desks together to create a pod. Children who are not in the guided reading group need to be productively engaged in independent activities so that the teacher can devote all of his or her attention to the group.

AVOIDING CONFUSION

There are many strategies and organizational structures for reading instruction. Often they are confused. For example, reading comprehension workshop (Chapter 8) does have children conferring with the teacher about what they are reading. The children are discussing a book they chose to read, which may or may not be at their instructional reading level. The discussions that take place during the conference are not substitutes for guided reading. There are other small-group reading instructional strategies that are intended for children to build and practice their skills, but they are not teacher-led; therefore, they are not guided reading. *Literature circles* also enhance comprehension skills and are led by students. The circles are formed sometimes by a child's interest in reading a particular book. The manner in which the children participate does involve them in literacy strategies they have learned and allows them to practice them. Literature circles consist of a group of children who have read the same book. The children have their discussions independent of the teacher. Teachers need to model literature circle activities so that children can carry them out independently. Literature circles are organized as follows:

1. The teacher forms small groups. Each group selects one book from the list provided by the teacher. The groups will read and discuss their chosen book.
2. The teacher helps the students with discussion by using prompts.
3. The students may or may not be given jobs within the group to carry out. In classrooms where independence is fostered, students will often guide their own inquiry within groups. However, when assigned roles are needed, common jobs include:
   a. The *discussion director* is responsible for the opening and closing remarks, reminding members to refer to their books to find support for their comments, and ensuring that everyone participates. The discussion director asks questions that the group will discuss.
   b. *The word finder* selects words that are important to the book. He or she lists the words, and they are discussed.
   c. The *illustrator* draws something related to the reading.

   d. The *creative connector* finds the connection between the book read and the outside world. The connections can be to themselves; to another student in the class, a friend, or a family member; or to other books.

   e. The *summarizer* writes a summary of the reading. It should be short and to the point (Harvey & Daniels, 2009).

After the teacher helps children to understand the procedures, the literature circles are led by the students.

CONCLUSION

Guided reading is one of the most important parts of the literacy day. It allows the teacher to differentiate instruction to meet the individual needs of the children. It is necessary to have some type of guided reading to help children with skills and strategies they have not mastered. The best way to really get to know our children's achievement and needs is to plan instruction through small-group guided reading instruction.

- 🖐 STOP! THINK! REACT! 🖐 -

Based on your understanding of guided reading instruction, take the time to reflect on the following:

❑ Examine your daily schedule to determine how to fit guided reading into your exemplary day. Where can you find 30 minutes to ideally meet with two groups for 15 minutes each?

❑ Collaborate with your peers around a leveled text to design lessons with the guided reading using a before/during/after structure.

❑ Teach a guided reading lesson and time yourself to reflect on whether or not certain parts of the lesson are exaggerated or could use more refined language to guide student learning.

❑ After teaching a few guided reading lessons, take a look at your anecdotal notes. Draft a friendly note home to a parent to celebrate a student's reading successes and provide tips for further practice at home.

❑ Mark a date on the calendar for examining the current structure of groups. Ask yourself: Do any of the students need to move based on performance within the leveled group?

CHAPTER 8

Reading Comprehension Workshop

CLASSROOM VIGNETTE

After analyzing her running records and Developmental Reading Assessment (DRA) data, Ms. Tapia notices that more than 60% of her students continue to struggle with finding evidence from the text to support their thinking. She knows that the time is right for a whole-class lesson and begins to think about where to go to find a strategy matching the needs of her young readers. As she begins planning, she seeks input from a reading specialist at her school who recommends a perfect workshop mini-lesson. Ms. Tapia is one of many teachers embracing the structure of a workshop model geared toward her individual students and their immediate reading needs. When planning, she asks, "What will help these students sitting in front of me today?"

WHAT IS READING WORKSHOP?

Once the teacher has collected and analyzed literacy assessments and students are familiar with the previous components of the exemplary day (a high-quality literacy environment, Do-Now choice activities, vocabulary meeting, etc.), he or she is ready to bring the workshop model to life in the classroom. Many school districts have embraced the "workshop" model because it provides a research-based structure for engaging young readers and writers in instruction that gradually releases responsibility and builds confidence for independent practice. Because the term "workshop" is sometimes misinterpreted, and quality across implementation may vary, we have developed a series of helpful guidelines for organizing and managing

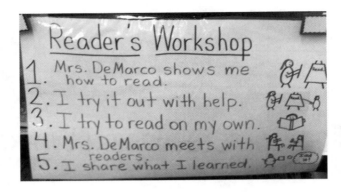

This anchor chart lets students know the structure of the reading workshop.

the workshop model within the classroom. To get started, it is important to recognize that the term "workshop" connects to a sequence of activities that occur within a specific amount of time (depending upon the teacher's schedule). The components and timing of the workshop include:

1. A high-quality mini-lesson *or* read-aloud with think-aloud strategies modeled (30% of the allotted time).
2. Independent/partner practice with a taught comprehension skill (50% of the allotted time).
3. Conferring with the teacher.
4. Sharing learning (20% of the allotted time).

Because the foundations of literacy instruction are embedded across the literacy day, we decided to focus on comprehension for the reading workshop model. Comprehension is the ultimate goal of reading instruction, and therefore the focal point of our workshop model. Uncovering the meaning of a text requires explicit modeling, with the teacher emphasizing a select set of strategies in greater depth and then gradually releasing responsibility to the students. To make this happen, a specific time must be designated for comprehension instruction where students have the "gifts" of choice and response within a community of avid readers (Miller, 2002).

HOW TO PLAN FOR THE WORKSHOP

What Is the Purpose of the Lesson?

As we mentioned at the beginning of this chapter, it is our belief that if 60% or more of students are in need of working on a comprehension strategy or skill, then

Ten Strategies for Comprehending Texts	
1. Setting a purpose for reading the text	6. Identifying text structure
2. Connecting to prior knowledge	7. Evaluating content
3. Predicting	8. Monitoring comprehension
4. Inferring	9. Questioning
5. Relying on visualization	10. Summarizing and synthesizing

the time is right for planning a workshop lesson. Generally speaking, 10 strategies are often relied upon for explicitly teaching students to comprehend text (Duke & Martin, 2015). These strategies are adaptable for reading both narrative and informational texts.

Determining the purpose of the comprehension lesson will depend on a number of factors. First, the teacher should reflect on what students have previously learned. Next, the teacher will utilize learning standards to set a purpose for the lesson, ensuring that students receive a balanced diet of instruction using narrative and informational texts. A teacher who explicitly designs comprehension instruction recognizes that students need many opportunities to apply the strategies being learned and that it is more advantageous to teach fewer strategies in greater depth. Utilizing the guidelines in the box "Ten Strategies for Comprehending Text" is a helpful way to get started when planning a comprehension lesson, primarily because strategies ("the how") teach students to master skills ("the what").

 Breaking Through the Block: Some of the most challenging skills for students to master are those related to reading and comprehending informational text. Find "one-page" texts that engage and motivate students. For example, a class studying life science will be interested in articles found through resources such as *wonderopolis.org*. Set a purpose for reading articles with partners and remind students about the skills and strategies that have been taught for understanding informational text. After they read the article, students should be instructed to reflect on their confirmed ideas or changed thinking related to the topic. By reading and analyzing nonfiction, students can generate more questions they wonder about and read, research, or reach out to experts on the topic.

A challenge that exists across schools often involves setting a purpose for comprehension instruction. For example, many school districts enforce policies that require teachers to follow prescriptive programs with fidelity, creating a system where students are often seen as "products, detached from their own learning processes" (Almasi & Hart, 2015, p. 257). Teachers can also be faced with the opposite problem, where an overwhelming autonomy caused by a "loose"

curriculum, or no curriculum at all, leaves many options open for teaching reading comprehension.

Regardless of varying circumstances, we advocate for best practices that provide explicit strategy instruction for students based on their diverse needs and the unique contexts of the classroom learning environment. The exemplary reading teacher uses data thoughtfully to determine a purpose for the reading comprehension lesson and can articulate his or her reasons for choosing that path.

Once a purpose has been determined, a few preferred resources for comprehension strategy instruction top our list of recommendations:

- The *Comprehension Toolkit* series for grades K–2 and 3–6 (Harvey & Goudvis, 2013)
- *Growing Readers: Units of Study in the Primary Classroom* (Collins, 2004)
- *Units of Study for Teaching Reading* (Calkins, 2016)
- *The Reading Strategies Book: Your Everything Guide to Developing Skilled Readers* (Serravallo, 2015)
- *Notice and Note: Strategies for Close Reading* (Beers & Probst, 2013)
- *DIY Literacy: Teaching Tools for Differentiation, Rigor, and Independence* (Roberts & Roberts, 2016)

Focusing on strategy instruction will help students master skills that are commonly linked to reading comprehension (see Table 8.1).

TABLE 8.1. Skills Related to Reading Comprehension

Skills for reading literature	Skills for reading information
<ul><li>Asking and answering questions using evidence from the text</li><li>Making inferences/relevant connections</li><li>Retelling using key details and information from the text</li><li>Determining theme or main idea</li><li>Analyzing text structure</li><li>Summarizing</li><li>Characterizing</li><li>Comparing and contrasting information</li><li>Determining meaning from unknown vocabulary</li><li>Understanding texts with increased complexity</li></ul>	<ul><li>Asking and answering questions using evidence from the text</li><li>Making inferences/relevant connections</li><li>Retelling using key details and information from the text</li><li>Determining main idea</li><li>Analyzing how an author presents information (including bias and point of view)</li><li>Analyzing text features (captions, images, illustrations, etc.)</li><li>Analyzing text structure</li><li>Determining meaning from unknown vocabulary</li><li>Comparing and contrasting information</li><li>Understanding texts with increased complexity</li></ul>

Management Tip: If you are new to teaching, or new to teaching a particular grade level, check out *The Fountas and Pinnell Literacy Continuum: A Tool for Assessment, Planning, and Teaching, PreK–8* (Fountas & Pinnell, 2016). This valuable resource provides an in-depth look at all of the skills that go into developing proficient readers across the grades. Regardless of what standards your state has adopted, this updated tool provides helpful information about what to expect from readers at your specific grade level.

Before You Can Teach a Mini-Lesson

Once a teacher decides on the purpose of planning a comprehension lesson, he or she is ready to lay the groundwork for a successful mini-lesson. The major components of a reading workshop lesson include the connection, teaching point and demonstration (mini-lesson), active engagement, and links to ongoing work (Collins, 2004). Based on our ongoing professional development in schools, we revised the lesson plan template in Figure 8.1 (see pp. 146–147) to assist teachers with the planning process. After linking the lesson to the appropriate grade-level standards, it is important to reflect on what the students have recently learned in your classroom, or what they should have learned in the previous grade. In the Common Core State Standards, information regarding comprehension instruction can be found under Reading Literature and Reading Information. Two options described in Table 8.2 are popular for getting students ready for more explicit comprehension instruction (Gunning, 2013).

Planning and Teaching the Mini-Lesson

Once students are familiar with a text, opportunities are endless for teaching comprehension-focused mini-lessons. At the beginning of the lesson, consider providing an opportunity for students to turn and talk about questions that tap into

TABLE 8.2. Getting Students Ready for Explicit Instruction

Read-aloud day

Select a book to read for enjoyment that is slightly above grade level. During the read-aloud, model the "think-aloud" process for your students, making your thinking visible to them. Prepare your reading in advance and determine how long it will take. Reading aloud can often take up 10–30 minutes of time.

Shared reading

Using a Big Book or large text displayed on a document camera, encourage students to join in by reading repeated lines, phrases, sentences, etc. At first, the teacher may choose to have students echo-read the text. Students can practice choral reading at the same time once the text is more familiar.

students' background and prior knowledge related to the text/topic of study. The lesson should include a connection that explains to students how the lesson fits into the larger curriculum. During this part of the lesson, it is important for the teacher to state, in student-friendly language, what strategy is being taught to help with achieving a comprehension skill. For example, if students will be working on the skill of using illustrations to gain more information about characters, setting, plot, and the like, the teacher might state, "Today I'm going to teach you how good readers take their time to zoom in on illustrations to better understand the text." Keep in mind that most standards were written for educators. Taking the time to explain the importance of what the students are learning will create more owner-ship as students begin to invest in the lesson. Then, the gradual release of respon-sibility can take place, with a carefully scaffolded lesson designed so that students succeed. Because students need their teacher, time is set aside for the teacher to model the strategy being taught. Students are invited to help as the modeled les-son continues. Of course, research also shows that students learn through social interaction with their peers, in addition to working with the teacher. This is why time is included for students to work with partners or in small groups. The tips outlined below will assist you with forming partnerships and small groups.

- Use your assessment data and classroom observations to determine who will work best together.
- Mix it up—allow students of different ability levels to work together, but in a "just right" partnership students will support one another. Prior to let-ting students work together, take the time to model a successful partnership with the rest of the class looking on as they work together. Debrief what the expectations of partner work and accountability are in your classroom.
- Monitor partnerships and small groups to ensure that all students are work-ing and respectfully intervening with one another.
- Finally, provide opportunities for students to practice the strategies being learned on their own. Students can be held accountable to do this during independent reading, which is discussed later in this chapter. Throughout the lesson, ask yourself, "What am I noticing about the readers and how they are grasping today's workshop lesson?" If a trend is noticed, this may be the perfect opportunity for a midworkshop check-in.

Management Tip: When interrupting in the middle of the workshop, make sure that you always gain students' attention. The teacher states, "1–2–3, look at me." Stu-dents respond, "1–2, look at you." Once all eyes are on the teacher, selectively acknowl-edge and praise their efforts and their commitment to the learning process. *—Angie Rosen, Director of Curriculum, Little Silver, NJ*

Guiding language is included in the lesson template (Figure 8.1) for sharing observations, flexibly offering alternative ways of understanding, or to praise excellent examples of mastering a skill using a specific strategy. If time permits, allow students to go back to their texts with increased attention for working on a strategy. Finally, provide opportunities for students to openly share their successes and challenges. The lesson should always conclude with the teacher asking the students how the lesson helps them as readers. Keep in mind that if this is a new strategy, the students may not be able to articulate how the instruction has helped them as readers. Comprehension develops over time, and students may need multiple exposures before they truly understand how a strategy works.

Where Will You Conduct the Lesson in Your Classroom?

Now that the format of the reading comprehension workshop has been fleshed out, it is crucial to determine how your classroom space can best support this type of instruction. Far too often, schools seek out professional development for high-quality workshop lessons, requesting that instruction be modeled in rooms that are not physically (and sometimes emotionally) supportive of this type of approach to teaching and learning. In *Around the Reading Workshop in 180 Days*, Serafini (2006) suggests that teachers start the school year by getting students used to gathering in a whole-class area to listen to read-alouds and interact through collaborative conversations about text. He explains the four decisions teachers can make so that implementing the whole-class lesson is flawless:

1. Where will students sit?
2. How will they get there?
3. When will the read-aloud occur?
4. What materials should students bring?

Because reading comprehension lessons often involve creating anchor charts and modeling instruction explicitly, it is important to choose a whole-class area that is visible to all learners. If technology is an important consideration for your lesson, you might be limited in choosing your whole-class area, as interactive whiteboards are often mounted in a permanent location in the classroom. If this is the case, a large rug area in front of the interactive whiteboard should provide enough space for the whole class to gather. However, a popular gathering place involves creating an "open concept" in the library area with an easel and chart paper for creating anchor charts.

Unit of study: _____	Date: _____

Mini-lesson topic: _____

Standard(s) addressed: _____

Connection	*Recently, you've learned about . . .*
Optional: Build in opportunities for students to turn and talk.	
Name the strategy being taught.	
	Today I'm going to teach you about/how to . . .
Mini-Lesson	*Now, I'm going to show you how to do this . . . watch me . . .*
Gradual release of responsibility	
(I do—you watch; I do—you help)	
Use a mentor text or authentic writing sample to model instruction.	*Can you help me . . . ?*

(continued)

FIGURE 8.1. Reading workshop lesson template.

Active Engagement Gradual release of responsibility, continued . . . (You do—with a partner or small group; You do—alone) The teacher has an opportunity to confer with readers individually, or meet with small groups for differentiated instruction.	*Now it's your turn to try (with a partner or in a small group) . . .* *When you are independently reading today, see if you can . . .*
Midworkshop Check-In The teacher uses class observations, anecdotal notes, etc., to check in with the whole class.	*So far, I've been noticing that . . .* *I notice that some of us are struggling with . . . let me show you another strategy I have to help . . .* *When you go back to reading, see if you can . . .*
Link Include opportunities for students to share their learning. Celebrate successes.	*Today I taught you how to . . .* *When you go off to read today, and every time you read, you're going to . . .* Concluding the lesson: *How does this strategy help you as a reader?*

FIGURE 8.1. (*continued*)

Transitioning to the whole-class area:

> Everybody have a seat, have a seat, have a seat,
> Everybody have a seat on the floor.
> Not on the ceiling, not on the door . . .
> Everybody have a seat on the floor.

Transitioning to students' desks:

> Everybody have a seat, have a seat, have a seat,
> Everybody have a seat on your chair.
> Not on the ceiling, not on the stair . . .
> Everybody have a seat on your chair.

(from *www.songsforteaching.com*)

Once you have determined where to gather for whole-class instruction, it is important to decide how students will get there. This is often the part of the lesson that causes the most stress for teachers, as many behavior problems occur among students during transitions within the classroom. Many teacher evaluation systems also include a component for classroom procedures, setting high expectations for teachers to seamlessly transition the students from one task to the next. In early childhood classrooms, teachers might consider introducing a song to assist with transitions to the whole-class area for instruction. These two examples below engage students of all ages, allowing them to fluently sing lyrics that foster a community of learners.

Recommended Materials

- Comfortable seating: whole-class rug, beanbag chairs, etc.
- Self-adhesive anchor charts
- Easel
- Permanent markers
- Sticky pads
- Clipboards (for students to use with graphic organizers, mentor texts, etc.)
- Graphic organizers (according to strategies being taught)

SAMPLE LESSON

Based on a sample lesson available through the Teaching Channel (*www.teachingchannel.org/videos/student-run-lesson*), we drafted a reading comprehension workshop lesson in Figure 8.2 that teaches students to make and confirm/adjust predictions when reading.

Unit of study: *Varies*		Date: _____

Mini-lesson topic: *Making and confirming/adjusting predictions*

Standard(s) addressed: *Varies*

Connection	*Recently, you've learned about . . .*
Optional: Build in opportunities for students to turn and talk. Name the strategy being taught.	*How third graders make thoughtful predictions prior to reading. These predictions can be based on illustrations, book titles, prior knowledge, etc.* *Today I'm going to teach you about/how to . . .* *Monitor your comprehension when reading. Good readers monitor their predictions when they read. We check to see if our initial thoughts are indeed what we uncover when we read.*
Mini-Lesson Gradual release of responsibility (I do—you watch; I do—you help) Use a mentor text or authentic writing sample to model instruction.	*Now, I'm going to show you how to do this . . . watch me . . .* *Keep It or Junk It! This strategy can be used for monitoring predictions. I'm going to use the sticky note to make a thoughtful/purposeful prediction based on the title and illustration on the cover of Crenshaw, a novel by Katherine Applegate.* *Can you help me . . . ?*
Active Engagement Gradual release of responsibility, continued . . . (You do—with a partner or small group; You do—alone) The teacher has an opportunity to confer with readers individually, or meet with small groups for differentiated instruction.	*Now it's your turn to try (with a partner or in a small group) . . .* *Turn and talk to your neighbor about what you predict the text will be about. Based on your discussions, jot down your prediction on this sticky note. I'm going to read the first chapter to get us started. Then you can partner-read chapter 2 since the chapters are short. During your partner reading, you should be deciding whether to keep or junk your sticky note. If you junk your prediction, it's important to think about why. What happened to change your thinking?* *When you are independently reading today, see if you can . . .*
Midworkshop Check-In The teacher uses class observations, anecdotal notes, etc., to check in with the whole class.	*So far, I've been noticing that . . .* *I notice that some of us are struggling with . . . let me show you another strategy I have to help . . .* *When you go back to reading, see if you can . . .*
Link Include opportunities for students to share their learning. Celebrate successes.	*Today I taught you how to . . . Keep It or Junk It.* *When you go off to read today, and every time you read, you're going to . . . apply this strategy to confirm or adjust your predictions.* *Concluding the lesson: How does this strategy help you as a reader?*

FIGURE 8.2. Sample reading workshop lesson: "Keep It or Junk It."

READING CONFERENCES

Purpose for Conferences

The reading conference is a time set aside for teachers to meet with individual students one-on-one. The purpose of the conference is to:

- Use formative assessments to drive instruction
- Notice students' reading strengths
- Notice students' reading behaviors
- Set goals for reading
- Determine next steps for reading instruction

Where Does Conferring Take Place?

Choose a location in your classroom where you are able to keep track of and observe the rest of the class working. You should have access to your anecdotal records and other notes/data collected about the readers in your class. Create a comfortable space where you can sit next to, and not across from, students. Ensure that the atmosphere is relaxed so that the teacher and student can positively interact with one another to discuss reading.

Recommended Materials

- Reading conference forms (see example in Figure 8.3)
- Sticky notes
- Browsing boxes—for students to store choice reading materials
- *Conferring with Readers: Supporting Each Student's Growth & Independence* (Serravallo & Goldberg, 2007)

How to Organize a Reading Conference

The form in Figure 8.3 will assist teachers when organizing and planning high-quality reading conferences with students. In addition to making students feel comfortable and encouraged to read, an overarching goal of the reading conference is to hold students accountable and to help them track their growth as readers. Therefore, a valuable conference cannot occur "on the fly." The teacher should use a plethora of data to determine each reader's focus. This information can come from guided reading anecdotal notes, formative and summative assessments, and the like. Conferences should begin with a compliment, noting the reader's strengths. In many instances, young readers will need to be encouraged to

Student's Name	Needs Instruction Focusing on . . .				
	Based on Guided Reading Anecdotal Notes/Data	Compliment STRENGTHS	Tracking the Text CHOICE/STAMINA/ RECALL	Skills/Strategies CHALLENGES/ APPLIED SKILLS AND STRATEGIES LEARNED	Next Steps WHOLE-CLASS/ SMALL-GROUP/ CONFERENCE

FIGURE 8.3. Reading conference form.

stay focused on finishing a text. The information collected under "Tracking the Text" allows the teacher to answer the following questions:

- What types of choices is the reader making when it comes to independent reading?
  - Do these choices include a healthy variety of genres and a balance of fiction and informational texts?
- Does the reader have *stamina,* or the energy to stay focused during independent reading? When the reader is focused, is her or she committing energy to sticking with a text? If not, what is causing the reader to abandon texts?
- Can the reader retell and recall information from his or her choice text?

These questions will assist the teacher in determining an appropriate focus for reinforcing strategies and skills taught in class. While the teacher might make note of the student applying skills and strategies learned, opportunities can also be seized for addressing gaps in knowledge. Finally, next steps can be determined. Rich data gleamed from high-quality reading conferences will reap many benefits for teachers:

- More intentional whole-class lessons
- Purposeful planning for guided reading and small-group activities
- Holding students accountable when the next conference takes place
- Communicating information to parents about their readers
- Tracking growth for grading purposes (especially with standards-based report cards)

INDEPENDENT PRACTICE

What Is the Purpose for Independent Reading?

Like athletes training for the Olympics, readers need plenty of opportunities to practice and to build stamina. Opportunities built into the daily agenda should include independent reading, with additional independent reading assigned for homework. For many teachers, the term "independent reading" brings back a certain nostalgia for what is often referred to as DEAR time, or a designated time to "Drop Everything and Read." This sustained silent reading (SSR) activity has often been linked to reading celebrations occurring during Read Across America Week and author Beverly Cleary's birthday. Despite efforts to make this sacred time a celebration for reading enjoyment, our coaching and professional development in schools has led us to witness many independent reading not-so-best practices that are cited in many observational research studies. In some instances, students are asked to read without accountability, often resulting in "fake reading" across classrooms, where teachers often perform various nonrelated reading tasks while children read. With this in mind, the following criteria highlight our beliefs about independent reading:

1. Independent reading time should be protected. Ensure that students are engaging in "eyes on the page" reading with a purpose.
2. Confer with students during this time to set goals, to monitor progress, and to demonstrate that you value independent reading and learning more about your readers.
3. When students choose books to read, do not solely rely on students' reading levels. Students are individual readers, not levels. If a student is interested in a topic, he or she will be motivated to read, even if the text provides a challenge. "Just right" books are not just about level: they also take interest into consideration.
4. Students deserve 30–40 minutes a day for independent reading in school. Building stamina is important to help students achieve this goal.

At the beginning of the year, achieving 30 minutes of focused independent reading time will be quite a challenge, so creating a staircase of complexity shows that 15 minutes is a starting-point goal to aim for.

> *Management Tip:* Using sticky notes, write each student's name and post all of them on their desks. Remind students that readers are not in "race," but to use independent reading time to practice their skills and strategies. Use a stopwatch while observing their behaviors. When students appear disengaged, place their sticky note on the anchor chart next to the appropriate "step." Debrief how the students did as a whole class. Ask students, "What interrupts your focus?" Collect the sticky notes and revisit the activity as necessary to build stamina with the class. As the year progresses, you can increase the goal incrementally until you reach 30–40 minutes.

Where Does Independent Reading Take Place?

Because independent reading time is so important and needs to be protected, it is critical to ensure that students are focused and on task, despite where they are reading. While many teachers insist that students read independently at their desks, answer for yourself the following question: When you decide to read for pleasure at home, do you formally sit in a chair at a desk? The answer is likely that you do not. Many readers choose comfortable locations (both inside and outside of the home) for getting lost in a good read. While you likely cannot allow students to read anywhere, comfortable spaces should be provided for independent reading. If needed, creating assigned reading spots will result in smoother transitions.

Recommended Materials and Book Selections

- *Reading journals* allow students to keep their own reading notebooks. They become a space for practicing skills and new strategies learned. Allow students to doodle and "stop and jot" important thoughts, reactions, etc., when reading. Provide opportunities for classmates to "tour" one another's notebooks to compare learning and applied use of comprehension strategies.

- *Browsing bags or boxes,* using strong plastic bags or old cereal boxes, is a great way for students to keep track of their choice reading materials. Review the appropriate steps for shopping for books. When teaching students about "just right" books, go beyond focusing on a student's level. Be sure that students are interested in the various genres and topics that they are choosing.

> *Management Tip:* Choosing an on-level book is just one option. Students should also choose quick reads, books that challenge, and books that pique their interest. Each student's browsing box, or personal collection of materials for independent reading, has a variety of texts that engage the reader.

SHARING

What Is the Purpose of Sharing?

The cornerstone of a high-quality lesson is the closure, a chance for the teacher to assess student learning, celebrate successes, and troubleshoot challenges. Sharing creates an environment of respect and rapport, reinforces a culture of learning, and holds students accountable for staying on task during independent reading.

Where Should Sharing Take Place?

Many teachers bring the class back to the whole-class area for share time. It is important to have a space large enough to gather the entire class back for a recap

Choosing "Just Right" Books	
• Choose an author you like. • Choose a book that the teacher has read aloud. • Choose a book in a series that you are reading. • Look at the cover page and title. • Look at the first page. • Look at another page.	• Use the "five-finger rule": If only two or three words on a page are unknown, students will know they have chosen a "just right" text. If four or five words on the page are unknown, the text may prove to be a difficult challenge to read without support. • Be sure to choose some books within your level for fast, fun, and easy reading
(Diller, 2003).	

of today's strategy focus. If you have a document camera, this is a great tool for digitally displaying student work that the whole class can see. Keep in mind that the share time should take approximately 20% of the entire scheduled workshop time.

Overall workshop time	Approximate share time
60 minutes	12 minutes
45 minutes	9 minutes
30 minutes	6 minutes

Organizing Share Time

Because of time constraints, it is helpful to intentionally choose which students will share their learning during this time. Share time is an opportunity to allow students to share their successes, which can include applying a reading strategy, further developing a reading skill, meeting a goal, or overcoming a challenge.

> **Management Tip:** Keep a clipboard near your whole-class area and keep track of which students in your class have shared their learning. Tally marks can be used to ensure that high-achieving students/proficient readers are not the only learners being featured during this time. If you notice that a student has not shared, find a reason for highlighting his or her accomplishments.

The "Ted Talk"

Inspired by the popular series of talks on spreading ideas (*www.ted.com/talks*), many teachers have turned to Ted Talks, allowing students to create short "hooks" and engaging talks about books that they are passionate about. During this share-time format, students excite their classmates about the books that they are reading and "bless the books" in a way that encourages other readers to consider new choices for independent reading (Gambrell, 1996).

MORE SAMPLE STANDARDS-ALIGNED LESSONS

Comprehension-Sort Activity

If students can learn to organize their thinking through word sorts, why not include lessons where students organize their comprehension of text? The sample activity below includes a comprehension sort for main idea, setting, and summarization using the children's book *The Story of Ruby Bridges* (Coles, 2010). Each sort includes directions about how to further develop students' thinking about text. While these examples are focused on three specific areas of comprehension, check out the skills/strategies at the beginning of this chapter to create your very own comprehension sort activities.

Comprehension Sort 1: The Main Idea

Cut out and read the six possible main ideas. Choose two that best match the text. Then cut out and read the supporting details. Choose one detail to match each of the main ideas you have chosen.

Possible Main Ideas

There are some who judge people based on the color of their skin.	It just isn't fair when people are treated differently.
It is against the law to receive a separate education from others.	One determined person can change history.
Being the first to accomplish something isn't always easy.	Being polite can make all the difference.

Supporting Details from the Text

The people carried signs that said they didn't want black children in a white school.	Ruby Bridges was the only black student to attend the William Frantz Elementary School.
The judge ordered four black girls to go to two elementary schools.	Ruby would hurry through the crowd and not say a word.
"We were very poor, very, very poor."	"She was polite and she worked well at her desk."

Comprehension Sort 2: Setting

Cut out and read the six details from the story. Choose two that best describe the setting.

Using Details to Build the Setting

In 1957, the family moved to New Orleans.	Ruby's parents were proud that their daughter had been chosen to take part in an important event in American history.
Ruby kept saying she was doing fine.	As Ruby approached the school, she saw a crowd of people marching up and down the street.
The marshals carried guns.	We prayed long and we prayed hard.

Comprehension Sort 3: Summarizing the Text

Cut out and read the eight sentences from the text. Choose three that help to summarize the story. Put them in the order in which they occurred.

Creating a Summary

Every day, Ruby went into the classroom with a big smile on her face.	Every morning, Ruby prayed for those who hated her, asking for God's forgiveness.
Angry mobs gathered and shouted in protest.	Ruby began learning how to read and write in an empty classroom.
They went to church.	Ruby Bridges was born in a small cabin near Tylertown, Mississippi.
Weeks turned into months.	Six-year-old Ruby Bridges was sent to first grade in the William Frantz Elementary School.

Comprehension Spinner Activity

To avoid students choosing the same activities for independently reading at home and in school, we designed a spinner activity that can be used with a copy of the spinner, paperclip, and pencil to hold the clip in place. The example activities in Figure 8.4 are aligned to the standards and skills for readers. Teach each of the activities as a mini-lesson during whole-class instruction. Once students become comfortable with the tasks, they can work on them during literacy stations or independent reading.

 Management Tip: Take a look at your state/district/school standards and create your own tasks based on the spinner in Figure 8.4.

ADAPTING THE UPPER-LEVEL WORKSHOP: SOCRATIC SEMINAR

Why Use Socratic Seminars?

There is a famous quote about teaching by Benjamin Franklin: "Tell me and I forget. Teach me and I remember. Involve me and I learn."

It is this philosophy of teaching that inspires many teachers in the upper grades to weave Socratic seminars into time set aside for reading workshop. Through this approach, students are moved to the forefront of the classroom, while the teacher moves into the background as a facilitator. When implemented in the classroom (especially on a regular basis) the students reap a number of benefits. For example, Socratic seminars . . .

- Give students a voice in the classroom.
- Increase student engagement by actively involving students in the classroom.
- Enable students to take control of their learning by practicing strategies/ skills.
- Encourage students to develop higher-level questioning and thinking skills.
- Help students develop speaking and listening skills.

How Do Socratic Seminars Work?

Socratic seminars require some prep work, both for the teacher and for the students. First, the classroom desks are organized into an outer circle and a "fishbowl." The fishbowl is a series of desks (typically four to six) placed in the center of the outer circle. Depending on the class, teachers may also want to consider a "hot seat," or designated desk that allows the student to immediately initiate a debate or an insightful topic.

For Socratic seminars that are more formal or designed to take place during longer class periods, it is often helpful to give students the opportunity to prepare discussion topics and responses in advance. For example, students can take notes while reading or prepare for the seminar the day before it takes place. These topics may come, in part, from the teacher, but students should also be encouraged to develop their own topics. The more ownership that students have over the

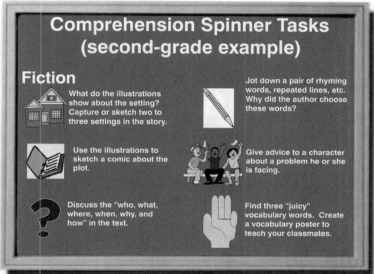

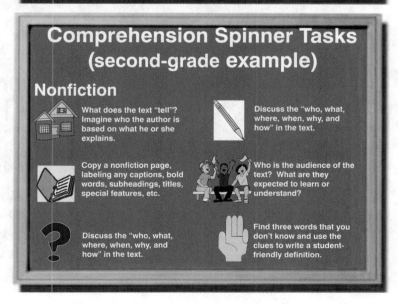

FIGURE 8.4. Sample spinner with fiction and nonfiction tasks.

discussion, the more invested they are in the seminar and the more they learn about the texts or topics being studied.

During Socratic seminars, students in the fishbowl lead the discussion; students in the outer circle engage in active listening and raise their hands to make brief comments or to ask questions. To enter the fishbowl, participants tap on a student's shoulder in order to switch places with him or her. If incorporating a "hot seat," students may use that seat to immediately start a relevant debate or share an

Students comprehend and collaborate in a classroom
designed to support the Socratic seminar approach.

important insight. Students should be encouraged to contribute to the seminar as many times as they want. However, you may want to encourage students to contribute at least twice.

> **Management Tip:** *Todaysmeet.com* is a powerful tool for creating a digital platform for students to engage in the Socratic seminar. After creating this free space, students can log in for free to add their ideas and thoughts related to the text in a chatroom-like function.

For Socratic seminars to run effectively, teachers should encourage students to maintain a "flow" in and out of the fishbowl, rather than halting the Socratic seminar to replace the entire fishbowl at once. In addition, students may need guidance on how to speak *to* peers rather than *at* them. In successful seminars, the students in the fishbowl are able to collaborate with their peers by connecting to and building on each other's ideas, rather than focusing only on their own agenda.

CLOSE READING: WHAT AND WHY?

Literacy comprehension strategies can and should be employed across content areas, and content-area reading and writing not only reinforce knowledge and understanding of the subject matter, but increase our students' ability to read, write, and think. As content grows, many elementary literacy teachers are now teaching only reading, writing, and social studies, while others teach math and science. The overlay of specific comprehension strategies, usually introduced in the literacy portion of the day, on content-area reading and writing makes the most of the limited time teachers have. Since literacy strategies can be used on any text, the use of content-area texts makes a great deal of sense.

Any project-based or interdisciplinary project requires instruction and practice in *close reading*. This is not a new method; it has existed for many decades as the practice of reading a text for a level of detail not used in everyday reading (Richards, 1929). Frey and Fisher (2013) agree with Newkirk (2011) that "not all texts demand this level of attention" (p. 57). In fact, the texts that require close reading must be "complex enough to warrant repeated reading and detailed investigation" (Frey & Fisher, 2013, p. 57). Close reading is necessary in complex text because student interaction with detailed material is called for. It necessitates analysis of aspects and perspectives that are not evident without careful focus. It is necessary for teachers to train students how to analyze this type of text for deeper meaning.

CLOSE READING: HOW?

Frey and Fisher (2013, p. 58) posit that all close reads should have these things in common: the passages should be *short* (three to nine paragraphs) and *worthy* (complex, and requiring sophisticated analytic skills). They state that the passages must be read and *reread*. Sometimes the teacher reads the text aloud the first time, and students reread or partner-read after that. Students should *annotate*, or "read with a pencil," during the second reading so that they can mark passages that are important, confusing, or surprising. Passages should be followed by *text-dependent questions*, which require students to provide evidence from the text in their answers. *After-reading tasks* should exist to deepen student comprehension.

Annotation is a powerful tool for close reading, and requires explicit instruction as a new strategy. The annotation marks themselves can be determined with each teacher's class, but often take the form shown in Figure 8.5. In elementary school, close reading might look more like Figure 8.6.

CONCLUSION

Although many school districts will adopt a basal reading series or anthology-based program, research has shown that many of these programs are a one-size-fits-all approach to teaching reading comprehension. Designed to build confidence and stamina in readers, the reading workshop model empowers teachers to determine what skills and strategies need to be taught and when. More important, instruction is delivered through engaging and high-impact mini-lessons with time set aside for partner/independent practice and small group and one-on-one support from teachers. Anthologies and collections of children's literature should be seen as resources for designing and delivering quality comprehension instruction.

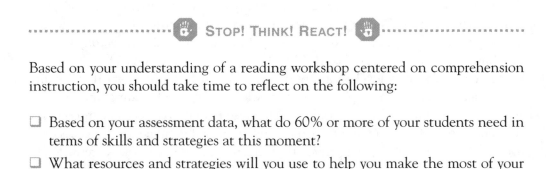

Based on your understanding of a reading workshop centered on comprehension instruction, you should take time to reflect on the following:

- ❏ Based on your assessment data, what do 60% or more of your students need in terms of skills and strategies at this moment?
- ❏ What resources and strategies will you use to help you make the most of your mini-lessons?

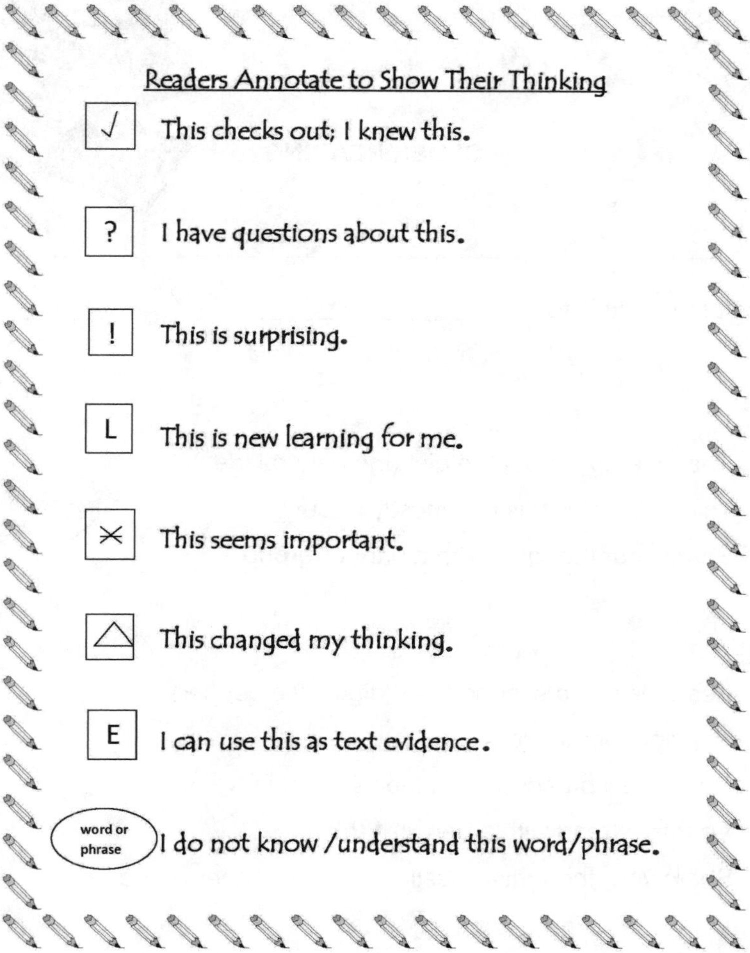

FIGURE 8.5. Annotation marks.

❑ What parts of the workshop model do you feel most comfortable with? What areas are in need of focus?

❑ In what ways can you use a close-reading approach responsibly, without overrelying on this one practice?

❑ Choose an activity from the chapter that you would like to adapt for use with your own students.

CLOSE READING

Title: _____

The purpose of this text is to: _____

FIRST READ

- Read the text to get the gist (the general idea).
- Think: "What is this text mostly about?"
- Share your thoughts with a partner/group.

SECOND READ

- Read the text a second time (dig a little deeper).
- Highlight headings.
- Number all paragraphs in the left margin.
- Annotate (read with a pencil) * ? !
- Share your thoughts/questions with a partner/group.

THIRD READ

- Read the text a third time (put it all together).
- Look for evidence that helped you understand.
- Make inferences about the text.
- Ask: "Why did the author write this piece?"
- Share thoughts with partner/group/class.

FIGURE 8.6. Close reading form for elementary students.

CHAPTER 9

Writing Workshop

CLASSROOM VIGNETTE

Similar to making decisions for reading comprehension workshop lessons, Ms. Tapia analyzes data to determine the next steps for meaningful writing instruction. She uses professional planning time to collect students' writing portfolios and takes notes about progress made and areas that are in need of improvement. Immediately, she sees that her students have written excellent leads, but, like many learners, need more instruction focused on elaborating their ideas. Despite having plenty of time for other areas of literacy instruction, she finds that there is not enough time each day for students to write. So she decides to make all writing lessons as student-centered and as authentic as possible.

WHAT IS WRITING WORKSHOP?

According to Cassidy and Cassidy (2010), the International Reading Association "What's Hot for 2010" survey found that at least 75% of educators felt that writing was not a "hot topic," yet all survey respondents agreed that it should be. When the National Reading Panel (2000) released its research-based findings, focused on five areas of literacy instruction, writing was one of the important components of a comprehensive literacy program omitted from the list. Shortly thereafter, literacy educators and advocates argued their beliefs about how important it is for students to be able to communicate through writing. These principles are outlined in *The Art of Teaching Writing* (Calkins, 1994), a writing workshop legacy tool that echoes our sentiments about the importance of high-quality writing instruction within an exemplary literacy program:

- Every writer has essential needs.
- One essential need is a productive, student-centered approach to instruction.
- The curriculum within a high-quality writing program is important.
- The teaching of writing occurs within a larger context, extending beyond the responsibility of the language arts teacher.

These ideals are best embedded within a writing workshop format, designed to stand the test of time when it comes to writing research and theory. A unique feature of the writing workshop model is that students are engaged through immersion and demonstration as they are surrounded by examples and models within an environment where expectations are modeled and writing is carried out in realistic and authentic ways (Bromley, 2015).

The components and timing of the writing workshop are similar to that of the reading workshop (see Figure 9.1):

1. A high-quality mini-lesson with strategies modeled (30% of the allotted time).
2. Independent/partner practice with a taught writing strategy or skill (50% of the allotted time).
3. Conferring with the teacher.
4. Sharing learning (20% of the allotted time).

HOW TO PLAN FOR THE WORKSHOP

What Is the Purpose of the Lesson?

Similar to our thoughts about reading comprehension instruction, we strongly believe that if 60% or more of the students are in need of working on a writing

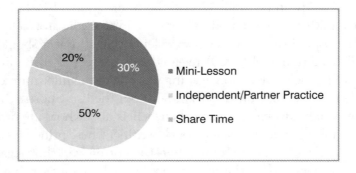

FIGURE 9.1. Components of the writing workshop.

strategy or skill, then the time is right for planning a workshop lesson. The writing workshop should include the major components of the writing *process*:

- *Brainstorming*—Opportunities should be provided daily for students to pre-write and organize their thoughts.
- *Drafting*—Similar to how a runner builds stamina to run a marathon, a writer must also start off by just writing, and then incrementally increasing his or her amount of time spent on task.
- *Revising*—Using the six traits of writing, students can assess their work for quality of ideas, organization, voice, word choice, sentence fluency, and conventions.
- *Editing*—Time to check for grammar, spelling, and punctuation (a sample lesson is included in Figure 9.4 later in the chapter).
- *Collaborating*—Students share their ideas with other classmates and confer with the teacher to seek feedback about their writing.
- *Publishing*—Now it is time to share student writing with an authentic audience of readers.

Within these steps, we emphasize the word *process* because all too often students are provided writing prompts and asked to create finished products. To develop confident writers, researchers have long argued for collaborative discussions around writing, using children's literature as a mentor text, modeling how to write, focusing on ideas and not mechanical errors, and collecting/recording daily observations (Graves, 1983). These values, combined with a student-centered

---

Research-Based Strategies for Writing

1. *Partner writing.* Students in the same grade/classroom are partnered to co-create writing drafts and build on one another's thinking.
2. *Buddy writing.* Students in the upper grades team up with "buddies" in the younger grades to read their writing samples and to help younger writers gain confidence with their own writing.
3. *Using graphic organizers.* The teacher models how to use various graphic organizers for gathering ideas and prewriting.
4. *Using visuals and artifacts to inspire ideas.* Pictures and student belongings are used to inspire new ideas for writing stories, essays, etc.
5. *Digital writing communities.* In a digital environment, students share their writing drafts and work within a web-based program to elaborate on ideas and revise/edit writing samples
6. *The writer's notebook.* Students use writing notebooks to reflect on their lives as writers, to gather new ideas and inspirations for writing, and to draft samples. Selected pieces are brought to the publishing stage.

A student works with a graphic organizer and a laptop computer to write a discovery draft.

approach and various forms of conferring with readers, contribute to the benefits of a writing workshop format within an exemplary literacy day (Atwell, 1998; Calkins & Harwayne, 1991).

Unlike when teaching reading comprehension, teachers are likely to find that searching for writing strategies will lead to an overwhelming list of resources and ideas for helping students to become better writers. Based on our professional development in schools, we highlight six key strategies below that have proven to be successful with blossoming writers.

Choosing a strategy, or "how-to" plan of action, requires the teacher to reflect on what the writers in the classroom need at this time in their writing careers. The teacher should ask him- or herself:

- "What skills and strategies have the students previously learned?"
- "What is the purpose for the lesson?"
- "What is the writing unit of study that is being explored?"
- "Have I exposed my students to a plethora of forms of writing?"
- "Are students writing for authentic purposes and audiences?"
- "What additional strategies will assist students with the skills being addressed?"

Although there are many resources, a few preferred ones for writing instruction top our list of recommendations for planning great writing lessons:

- *The Writing Strategies Book: Your Everything Guide to Developing Skilled Writers* (Serravallo, 2017).

- *A Writer's Notebook: Unlocking the Writer within You* (Fletcher, 2003)
- *Units of Study in Opinion, Information, and Narrative Writing* (Calkins, 2013)
- *Writing Workshop: The Essential Guide* (Fletcher & Portalupi, 2001)
- *Using Literature to Enhance Writing Instruction: A Guide for K–5 Teachers* (Olness, 2005)
- *Writing Pathways: Performance Assessments and Learning Progressions, Grades K–8* (Calkins, 2014)

 Breaking Through the Block: As students learn new information in the content areas, encourage them to keep a small "wonder notebook." Using this notebook, students can jot down ideas that they would like to learn more about. Schedule a "genius hour" for your class and allow students to read about the topics they have drafted. The more students read, the more they will become experts. Then students can have an opportunity to write about what they have learned and to choose a format to present their information to the class.

Introducing a class to selected strategies matched to the specific needs of young writers will allow them to stretch their muscles and build confidence and endurance for increasingly difficult writing tasks. Although standards vary across local school districts and states, common skills expected from writers are listed in the box below. These skills are developed across a continuum of learning and become increasingly complex as students proceed throughout the grades. A writer who is unable to master these skills will likely struggle in the middle grades; therefore, teachers must work within their communities of practice to ensure that strategy development is consistent and that the expectations of what it means to achieve each of the writing standards is agreed upon.

Ten Skills for Developing Writers

1. Draw, dictate, organize, and write opinion pieces.
2. Compose and organize informative/explanatory texts.
3. Narrate events that take place.
4. Use feedback to strengthen writing.
5. Explore digital tools to publish writing within a classroom community.
6. Conduct research.
7. Gather information to problem-solve or answer questions/wonderings.
8. Understand various writing tasks and purposes.
9. Use evidence from text to support writing.
10. Write over extended periods of time to build stamina.

Before You Can Teach a Mini-Lesson

One essential need that every writer is entitled to is a teacher who perceives him- or herself as a writer (Murray, 2004). As teachers, we need to draw from everything that we know, feel, and believe in order to make instruction meaningful for our students, even before attempting to teach mini-lessons in the writing classroom. Many teachers identify with the perils of writing papers for graduate school and the purposes of receiving a grade, so we must readjust with our surroundings and hone in on the purpose of K–6 writing instruction so that we think of ourselves as writers, reconnecting with a former joy for writing in its purity. Teachers, like authors, need to notice the smallest details that an ordinary person would pass by. These ideas become sparks that light the way for future stories and essays. Students are often encouraged to decorate their writing notebooks with significant people, places, and life events.

Once a teacher decides on the purpose of planning a writing lesson, he or she is ready to lay the groundwork for a successful mini-lesson. Like reading comprehension, the major components of the writing workshop lesson include the connection, teaching point and demonstration (mini-lesson), active engagement, and links to ongoing work. During the planning phase, a perfect place to get started is to find the perfect mentor text. Three options for working with mentor texts are described in Table 9.1.

> *Management Tip:* Be sure to save your students' published writing. These can be laminated and bound into books for future classes to reference as mentor texts. Create a "published authors" bin in your classroom library so that students can read one another's writing. Many professional companies like Studentreasures Publishing will allow you to create a hardbound book for your classroom, with ordering options available for parents and families.

TABLE 9.1. Three Ways to Find the Perfect Mentor Texts

Before I Can Teach a Mini-Lesson:

1. *Children's books.* A quick online search for writing mentor texts will yield a variety of high-quality children's books that help writers grow. Using children's books, the teacher can expose writers to the strategies published authors use to keep their audiences engaged. Encourage students to emulate these techniques in their own writing. Check out a favorite resource: *http://writingfix.com/picture_book_prompts.htm.*

2. *Student work samples.* Of course, some of the best mentor texts come from the published writing that students in your classroom produce. These authentic samples will expose students to grade-level expectations and allow them to set goals to achieve mastery of skills.

3. *Standardized test exemplars.* While teaching to the test is not condoned, teachers are often pressured to prepare students for the demands of these high-stakes assessments. Many states release writing samples that can be used as models of strong writing with students in the classroom (*https://prc.parcconline.org/assessments/parcc-released-items*)

Planning and Teaching the Mini-Lesson

The same key ingredients discussed in the reading comprehension workshop chapter apply to teaching high-quality writing mini-lessons:

- *Connection*—Connect your writers about what they have been previously learning and working on in the classroom. Name the writing strategy that you will be focusing on with this lesson.
- *Mini-lesson*—Now is your chance to use a mentor text to model what you would like your writers to try. To gradually release responsibility, show them how you do it first. Many teachers draft their own writing samples in a "teacher's writing notebook" to model lessons. Encourage students to help you make your writing better or to apply a new strategy learned.
- *Active engagement*—Once you teach a strategy, your students will be motivated to practice writing with each other within a community of writers. Initially, students will benefit from working with their peers to write, but the teacher should keep track of prime opportunities for students to write independently.
- *Optional midworkshop check-in*—At this point in the lesson, refocus the students and gather them to discuss noted strengths and areas of needed improvement.
- *Focus on grammar*—To help students strengthen their skills with grammar, try *sentence combining* with them. Using a student's writing sample, show how a sentence can be manipulated or rewritten into more varied and syntactically mature forms (Bromley, 2015). Encourage students to identify and

*Partner reading and collaborative research
to produce informational writing in fourth grade.*

correct one another's uses of grammar by sharing and discussing writing drafts.

- *Link*—Include opportunities for students to share their writing samples. Celebrate successes and restate what students have learned. Students should be asked how the strategy lesson helps them to become better writers.

The writing workshop planning template in Figure 9.2 helps teachers to organize their implementation of a lesson. Sample sentence stems are included for thinking about the language that will be used to guide students through writing instruction.

> *Management Tip:* Helpful tips for determining where to conduct whole-class lessons are discussed in the Reading Comprehension Workshop chapter. Be sure that your meeting place is a comfortable space suitable for the entire class to meet. Think carefully about your space and make sure that you have all of the necessary tools for writing at your fingertips (Fletcher & Portalupi, 2001).

Recommended Materials

- Paper, pencils, colored pencils, notebooks, and computers (tablets, laptops, etc.)
- Self-adhesive anchor charts
- Scissors, tape, staplers
- Mentor texts: children's literature, student work samples, standardized test exemplars
- Easel
- Permanent markers
- Sticky pads
- Clipboards (for students to use with graphic organizers, mentor texts, etc.)
- Graphic organizers (according to strategies being taught)
- Dictionaries, thesaurus, word-study notebooks, "Word Nerd" journals, etc.

WRITING CONFERENCES

What Is the Purpose for Conferences?

The writing conference is a time set aside for teachers to meet with individual students one-on-one. The purpose of the conference is to:

- Use formative assessments to drive instruction.
- Notice students' writing strengths and writing behaviors.
- Listen and be present when students are discussing their writing.

Unit of study: _____	Date: _____
Mini-lesson topic: _____	
Standard(s) addressed: _____	

Connection	*Recently, you've learned about . . .*
Optional: Build in opportunities for students to turn and talk. Name the strategy being taught. *Recently, you've learned about . . .*	
	Today I'm going to teach you about/how to . . .
Mini-Lesson Gradual release of responsibility (I do—you watch; I do—you help) Use a mentor text or authentic writing sample to model instruction.	*Now, I'm going to show you how to do this . . . watch me . . .* *Can you help me . . . ?*

(continued)

FIGURE 9.2. Writing workshop lesson template.

Active Engagement Gradual release of responsibility, continued . . . (You do—with a partner or small group; You do—alone) The teacher has an opportunity to confer with readers individually, or to meet with small groups for differentiated instruction.	*Now it's your turn to try (with a partner or in a small group) . . .* *When you are independently reading today, see if you can . . .*
Midworkshop Check-In The teacher uses class observations, anecdotal notes, etc., to check in with the whole class.	*So far, I've been noticing that . . .* *I notice that some of us are struggling with . . . let me show you another strategy I have to help . . .* *When you go back to reading, see if you can . . .*
Link Include opportunities for students to share their learning. Celebrate successes.	*Today I taught you how to . . .* *When you go off to read today, and every time you read, you're going to . . .* Concluding the lesson: *How does this strategy help you as a reader?*

FIGURE 9.2. *(continued)*

- Set goals for writing, taking the writer's inspirations into consideration.
- Determine next steps for writing instruction.

Recommended Materials

- Writing conference form (see Figure 9.3)
- Sticky notes
- *One to One: The Art of Conferring with Young Writers* (Calkins, Harkman, & White, 2005)
- *How's It Going?: A Practical Guide to Conferring with Student Writers* (Anderson, 2000)

HOW TO ORGANIZE A WRITING CONFERENCE

Similar to reading workshop, the conference form ensures that the writing conference is brief and focused. Few teachers have the luxury to spend more than a few minutes checking in with writers, so this valuable interaction must include planning that occurs ahead of time. After reviewing previous notes about a student:

- Begin with a compliment and ask the writer to explain what he or she has been working on.
- To build stamina, get the student talking so that he or she can share ideas about his or her goals for individual writing pieces.
- Track the writer to determine:
  - What types of choices is the writer making when it comes to independent writing?
  - Do these choices include a healthy variety of genres and purposes for writing?
  - Does the writer have stamina, or the energy to stay focused during independent writing? If not, what is the most important thing that the writer could be working on?
- Determine next steps for instruction. Ask, "When I meet with this writer next time, what is the one thing that I can teach?"

INDEPENDENT PRACTICE

What Is the Purpose of Independent Writing?

A daily and predictable amount of time for writing is important for the K–6 student. Calkins (1994)) asserts, "If students are going to become deeply invested in

Student's Name	Needs Instruction Focusing on . . .				
	Based on Anecdotal Notes/Data/Small-Group Instruction	Compliment STRENGTHS	Stamina	Skills/Strategies CHALLENGES/APPLIED SKILLS AND STRATEGIES LEARNED	Next Steps WHOLE CLASS/SMALL-GROUP/CONFERENCES

FIGURE 9.3. Writing conference form.

their writing, and if they are going to live toward a piece of writing and let their ideas grow and gather momentum, if they are going to draft and revise, sharing their texts with one another as they write, they need the luxury of time" (p. 186). A unique aspect of the workshop model is that 50% of the time is dedicated to allowing students to actually write. Therefore, if a teacher sets aside 30 minutes a day for writing instruction, students should be observed writing for at least 15 minutes. This independent writing time should respect students' individual choices, as not everyone will be writing about the same topic or responding to a prompt. Instead, students will be revisiting past drafts in their notebooks, trying out new strategies based on their previous work, and working toward individualized goals. For many teachers, this approach requires a shift in thinking, because students are valuing their independent writing time to discover many new avenues for growing as writers. Not all drafts are published and ownership and responsibility are placed in the writer's hands.

 Management Tip: Refer to the stamina anchor chart in the Reading Comprehension Workshop. Stamina is also needed for writing!

Where Does Independent Writing Take Place?

Unlike independent reading, which can occur throughout the classroom in relaxing locations, writers will need tools and space for writing at their desks. If the purpose of the lesson is to have student independently apply a strategy to work on a skill, students should work at their individual desks. However, if the students are still grasping a new strategy or learning a new concept, independent writing should take place in more collaborative ways:

- Putting two desks together will allow students to work with writing partners.
- Forming a cluster of three or four desks will encourage more collaborative discussions about writing samples.

The organization of the furniture in the classroom should reflect the purpose of the day's writing lesson.

SHARING

What Is the Purpose of Sharing?

Like readers, writers also need a chance to reflect on their learning, celebrate successes and milestones, and troubleshoot challenges. However, the writing workshop brings its own unique challenges to share time. Because developing writers are delicate, students will need to be guided in how to give and receive responses about each other's original writing (Fletcher & Portalupi, 2001). See Figure 9.4 for a sample lesson for editing writing.

> *Management Tip:* During share time, have your students practice PQP: Praise, Question, Polish. Students can share what they like about one another's writing, ask questions that encourage writers to elaborate on their ideas, and determine areas of writing that need to be revisiting for fine-tuning.

Where Should Sharing Take Place?

Again, ensure that your space is large enough to gather the entire class back for a recap of today's strategy focus. If you have a document camera, this is a great tool for digitally displaying student writing samples that the whole class can see. Because writers are motivated by authenticity, mix up your share time to include opportunities where writers can share their learning with audiences that extend beyond the classroom:

- *Twitter*—Using a class Twitter account, tweet a picture of a student's writing sample or tweet a children's book author to show how students in your class emulated their writing style
- *Inviting guests*—Invite members of your school community to attend a share-time session with students. To show the importance of community involvement, encourage all members of the school to visit your classroom (teachers, principals, custodians, administrative assistants, cafeteria employees, etc.).
- *Writing celebrations*—Celebrate the end of a unit of study or special writing focus with a high tea or publishing party to feature your writers. Send an invitation to parents and community members to hear students feature their selected pieces brought to publication.

FROM THE NATIONAL WRITING PROJECT: SAMPLE LESSONS

Quick Writes

Although the writing workshop model promotes student choice, there are many instances where students are asked to produce writing on demand. The "quick-write" strategy allows writers to write in response to specific writing topics within a given time frame. These are also lessons that are great for building writing stamina. Writers can reflect on their writing and share their writing with partners and make revisions.

Unit of study: _N/A_ Date: _____	
Mini-lesson topic: _Editing writing_	
Standard(s) addressed: _Varies_	

Connection *Optional:* Build in opportunities for students to turn and talk. Name the strategy being taught.	[*Students should gather around a whiteboard and follow classroom procedures in order to participate in the lesson.*] Recently, you've learned about . . . *recognizing when to put a capital letter that allows the writer to "go" and when to add proper punctuation that tells the writer to "stop."* Today I'm going to teach you about/how to . . . *take this learning one step further to make our writing even better! We're going to be working with a checklist that will train us to act like real writers.* *Let's turn and talk. Have you ever had to fix anything before? Talk to your neighbor about something you had to fix.* [*The teacher informs the students that writers also often have to "fix" things in their writing.*] *We refer to this part of the writing process as editing.*
Mini-Lesson Gradual release of responsibility (I do—you watch; I do—you help) Use a mentor text or authentic writing sample to model instruction.	*Now, I'm going to show you how to do this . . . watch me . . .* [*The teacher writes a message on the board (filled with mistakes) and introduces a strategy known as "COPS"*] *Using a checklist, you will be able to check for capitalization, order, punctuation, and spelling mistakes.* I think I have found a few capitalization, order, punctuation, and spelling errors. Can you help me . . . ? [*The teacher encourages the students to help find additional errors for fixing.*]

(continued)

FIGURE 9.4. Sample writing workshop: "Editing Fix-It Tickets."

Active Engagement	*Now it's your turn to try (with a partner or in a small group) . . .*
Gradual release of responsibility, continued . . . (You do—with a partner or small group; You do—alone) The teacher has an opportunity to confer with readers individually, or to meet with small groups for differentiated instruction.	*[The students will meet with their writing partners to review a writing sample. They will follow the directions on the COPS fix-it ticket to search for capitalization, order, punctuation, and spelling errors.]* *When you are independently writing today, see if you can . . . read with a writer's eye to find what needs to be fixed.]*
Midworkshop Check-In	*So far, I've been noticing that . . .*
The teacher uses class observations, anecdotal notes, etc., to check in with the whole class.	*I notice that some of us are struggling with . . . let me show you another strategy I have to help . . .* *When you go back to reading, see if you can . . .*
Link	*Today I taught you how to . . . use the COPS checklist to improve our skills with editing writing.*
Include opportunities for students to share their learning. Celebrate successes.	*When you go off to write today, and every time you write, you're going to . . . take note of what could be fixed in your writing.* Concluding the lesson: *How does this strategy help you as a reader?*

FIGURE 9.4. *(continued)*

- Provide the students with a prompt, writing materials, and a time frame for completing the writing task (e.g., 5 minutes).
- Invite your students to write independently.

After writing, students are encouraged to review their work and share their writing with a partner. The writing partner's role is to hear the writer read their work and thank them for sharing their writing. Writers can optionally choose to revise their work or write in response to their original quick write.

Wordless Picture Books

Endless possibilities exist for students when teachers use the genre of wordless picture books. For this sixth-grade lesson, students will need:

- Writing notebooks
- Copies of *Window* by Jeannie Baker (1991)
- A framed picture or image
- A large poster board or other large sheets of paper
- Large brown envelopes for group materials
- Sticky notes, pencils/pens/markers
- Direction sheets (see Figure 9.5)

The teacher begins the lesson by discussing how authors make choices and explaining that they need to use words to convey details to their readers. Students

---

Activity Directions

1. Choose a reader to carefully read the directions to the group. The reader will be responsible for making sure the directions are read aloud and followed. You should each have your own color of sticky notes. Choose another person who should be responsible for handing out the materials found in the envelope. (Looks good!)

2. Please follow the directions in order. Most of all, everyone must participate!

3. Please list the names of the members in your group:

   _____

   _____

   _____

   _____

4. Look through the book *Window* by Jeannie Baker. Look carefully at each picture. What do you notice about this book? What is actually happening as you move to the ending of the book? Discuss your ideas within your group.

5. Use your sticky notes. Go through the book again page by page. Look at each page carefully. Be sure to notice details and changes that occur as you move from one page to the next. Write as many of your observations about each page as you can on your sticky notes. On the sticky notes, write all the details of anything else you can find that seems important to the story. Stick the notes on the pages that you are discussing so that they can be referenced later.

6. Great job taking so many notes! Now, you will each be transferring your notes to a large piece of white paper. Try to keep the notes in an order which shows how the story moves from the beginning to the resolution. Please also place all of the other materials back into the envelope.

FIGURE 9.5. Sample direction sheet for *Windows* by Jeannie Baker.

are encouraged to discuss topics that they have explored through narrative writing. Then students use their writer's notebooks to write a description of a framed picture. Students later share these descriptions with partners. A brief discussion follows about sequence and how it relates to literature. Students will focus on elements of a story through their exploration of a wordless picture book.

For group work:

- Students use sticky notes to write their ideas about the details they find in "something to explore" in the envelopes their group receives.
- Students are reminded to read the directions sheet in their envelopes.

At the conclusion of the lesson, all of the students' sticky notes are placed on large poster boards following the sequence of *Window*.

Some other great wordless picture books to use for writing instruction include:

- *A Boy, a Dog, and a Frog* (Mayer, 1967)
- *Alphabet City* (Jenkins, 1995)
- *The Arrival* (Tan, 2006)
- *Chalk* (Thomson, 2010)
- *Flotsam* (Wiesner, 2006)
- *Fossil* (Thomson, 2013)
- *Free Fall* (Wiesner & Lothrop, 1988)
- *Home* (Baker, 2004)
- *Journey* (Becker, 2013)
- *Looking Down* (Jenkins, 1995)
- *Mirror* (Baker, 2010)
- *Quest* (Becker, 2014)
- *The Red Book* (Lehman, 2004)
- *Sector 7* (Wiesner, 1999)
- *Sidewalk Circus* (Fleischman & Hawkes, 2004)
- *Time Flies* (Rohmann, 1994)
- *Tuesday* (Wiesner, 1991)
- *Unspoken: A Story from the Underground Railroad* (Cole & Kostiw, 2012)
- *Window* (Baker, 1991)
- *Yellow Umbrella* (Liu & Sheen, 2002)

CONCLUSION

Similar to reading workshop, the writing workshop is a model that empowers teachers to determine what skills and strategies need to be taught and when. Rather than simply "assigning" writing tasks to be completed and turned in, teachers take the time to model authentic writing through high-quality mini-lessons. The classroom becomes a bustling learning environment where writers are valued, given time to engage in the writing process collaboratively, and provided support through meaningful conferences. Both the teacher and students identify as writers and seek opportunities to improve communication through the written word using appropriate strategies and techniques.

······················ ✋ STOP! THINK! REACT! ✋ ··························

Based on your understanding of the writing workshop, you should take time to reflect on the following:

❏ Based on your assessment data, what do 60% or more of your students need in terms of skills and strategies at this moment?

❏ What resources and strategies will you use to help you make the most of your mini-lessons?

❏ What parts of the workshop model do you feel most comfortable with? What areas are in need of focus?

❏ Choose an activity from the chapter that you would like to adapt for use with your own students.

CHAPTER 10

Interdisciplinary Literacy Instruction

CLASSROOM VIGNETTE

Ms. Tapia is a teacher who keeps up with research. She belongs to the International Literacy Association and her state-affiliate group, so she often reads articles about newly researched information. She has worked with her students for a few months, and believes that this year's class would benefit from more independent small-group work. She recalls a workshop she attended dedicated to project-based instruction (PBI), and locates her notes from that workshop to guide her as she begins work to set up a project based on locally available fish. She is friendly with a family that owns a big seafood restaurant on the waterfront, and she has asked them whether they would like to have student products about fish and the waterfront available for families to read as they wait for their meals. They were enthusiastic about the projects. She presents this idea at a professional learning community (PLC) meeting and finds a great deal of interest from her grade-level colleagues. They decide how to begin PBI, assigning themselves tasks that each will research before the next meeting. They realize that this might be exactly what their students need to reengage with learning, and just what the teachers need to reenergize their teaching!

USING INFORMATIONAL TEXT IN LITERACY: WHAT AND WHY?

Over the course of the past few years, teachers have been reminded of the importance of using informational text for instructional purposes in literacy. It is recommended that elementary teachers utilize a 50–50 mix of fiction and informational text in the classroom. This advice has been justified by Duke (2014), whose research demonstrates that, although we certainly live in the age of information, Americans, both students and adults, experience difficulties gleaning information from text. Duke also found that low-income and minority students are particularly likely to struggle. Since much of the reading and writing done by adults in this country is informational, the stress on the use of such text in the classroom is logical. Duke suggests that there are several paths teachers need to follow to correct this problem (see Table 10.1).

We already know what good readers do when they read. Good readers are active readers, and they interact with text. They have goals in mind before they read, and they integrate prior knowledge with the material. Good readers monitor their own understanding, they evaluate the text's quality and value, and they read different kinds of text differently. Explicit instruction in comprehension strategies during mini-lessons and in guided reading lessons increases the likelihood that students will achieve adequate comprehension of informational texts.

Students are required to work with informational text for half of the reading and writing that they do in the classroom. It makes sense for teachers to use written content from the work they are also teaching in social studies, science, math, and technology as the passages on which they base their explicit instruction in comprehension strategies. In this way, the purposes of literacy and coverage of content-area material are both attained.

TABLE 10.1. Problem Solving in the Use of Informational Texts

Problem	What teachers can do
• Lack of availability of informational text	• Gather more informational books for your library.
• Limited exposure to informational text	• Use informational texts for half of your read-alouds.
• Inconsistent instructional time spent with informational text	• Have students work with informational text at stations and during independent reading.
• Uneven explicit teaching of comprehension strategies	• Use informational books during guided reading, pointing out important strategies for this type of reading.
• Lack of attention paid to the unique features of informational text	• Teach mini-lessons about the usefulness of captions, glossaries, headings, graphs and charts, etc.
• Informational texts are often not used for authentic purposes	• Ask children to read and write to solve problems, to give opinions, and to persuade people other than their teacher.

USING INFORMATIONAL TEXT: HOW?

As always, we begin our work with informational text by identifying pertinent teaching goals. These goals may come from weaknesses demonstrated by our students, from specific standards that guide our practice, and from our knowledge of student interests. Many of our objectives in literacy are based on a set of comprehension strategies. While these strategies occur automatically in the minds of accomplished readers, they must be the subject of explicit instruction in the elementary years. The following strategies are identified as necessary for comprehension:

- Monitoring comprehension
- Activating and connecting to background knowledge
- Setting a purpose for reading a text
- Predicting
- Inferring
- Relying on visualization
- Identifying text structure
- Evaluating content
- Summarizing and synthesizing information

The important knowledge for us as teachers is that most children do not do these things with automaticity. They need to be taught. In her book *Inside Information*, Duke (2014) warns that the teaching of strategies is not an end in itself, but a means to an end. "The value of comprehension strategies lies in using them to better comprehend what one is reading and . . . to put comprehension to use to serve a compelling purpose" (p. 79). She details how to instruct children in strategies to benefit their comprehension while conducting an inquiry project at the same time. She stresses the use of the gradual-release-of-responsibility model, and advises teachers about scaffolding and offering support.

Beers and Probst (2016) list several "signposts" for readers to look for as they work through informational text. When they notice these indicators, students are taught to STOP and ask themselves a specific question. The signposts Beers and Probst describe are:

- *Contrasts and contradictions* (Ask: "What does this make me wonder about?")
- *Absolute or extreme language* (Ask: "Why did the author use this language?")
- *Numbers and statistics* (Ask: "Why did the author choose to include these numbers?")
- *Quoted words* (Ask: "Why was this person quoted, and what did the quote add?")
- *Word gaps* (Ask: "Are there clues that can help me figure this word out?")

The authors also remind students to ask themselves as they read:

- "What surprised me?"
- "What does the author think I already know?"
- "What changed, challenged, or confirmed what I already know?"

Being on the lookout for these signposts and answering the questions above cause student readers to slow down and interact with text. Only then will they truly comprehend the text, which is every teacher's goal.

The use of an R.A.N. chart (reading and analyzing nonfiction) can also help make informational text come alive for children. The R.A.N. is an expanded version of the KWL chart (what we *know*, what we *want* to know, and what we *learned*) teachers have used for decades. Here's how it works:

- Step 1. Activate prior knowledge by introducing the topic and calling on students who believe they know something about it.
- Step 2. Have each student write his or her fact on a sticky note and stick it on the chart in the first column. Do this without commenting on the quality of student "facts."
- Step 3. Read the text orally yourself or have small groups read it aloud. Ask students to raise a hand when they notice confirmation of a fact, a new piece of learning, or a misconception from the first column.
- Step 4. Physically move the sticky notes that contain confirmations and

Sixth-grade scientists explore new learning using the R.A.N. strategy.

misconceptions to the appropriate columns. Ask a capable student to write "new learning" on another set of sticky notes and place them accordingly.

- Step 5. When the reading has been completed, note and move unanswered "facts" to the "I Still Wonder" column.
- Step 6. To complete the last column, ask the question, "How could we find out more about . . . ?" The answers are always the same: look in a book, ask an expert, or check the Internet. These unanswered questions can become topics for further student research.

 Breaking Through the Block: What students "still wonder" about can be turned into research they do independently when they complete other classwork early.

THEMATIC UNITS

Children will become engaged in reading and writing with content-area themes in social studies, sciences, art, music, math, etc. Themes are about topics such as bugs, dinosaurs, animals, and the like. Themes include topics of interest to children. Teachers plan projects that involve experiments and exploration. John Dewey (1966) was largely responsible for bringing the concept of an interdisciplinary approach to teaching to educators' attention. This approach, which is referred to as the "integrated school day," teaches skills from all content areas within the theme being studied.

The themes that are studied at school derive from children's real-life experiences and topics that they demonstrate an interest in. Learning experiences are socially interactive and process-oriented, giving children time to explore and experiment with varied materials. If, for example, a class is studying dinosaurs, the students talk, read, and write about them; do art projects related to dinosaurs; and sing songs related to the theme. According to Dewey (1966), when children are taught this way they learn about dinosaurs and develop skills in literacy and content areas.

WHAT IS THE DIFFERENCE BETWEEN PBI AND THEMATIC INSTRUCTION?

Children are engaged when they read and write about themes since they are interesting topics and often children get to select what theme they will study. Themes and PBI are similar, but there are differences. Themes last a month or shorter, whereas PBI can be conducted over an entire year. Themes are topics such as animals, volcanoes, seasons, and so on. PBI are student-driven research into topics where the children can accomplish something to help the school, neighborhood, and beyond. A PBI topic might be to improve the school's playground. This requires getting approval to do so, raising money, investigating playgrounds in other schools, and arranging for putting the playground together.

PREPARING A THEMATIC UNIT

Unit themes can be selected by the teacher and the children. Giving students choices concerning what they will learn is important. When a topic is selected, allow the children time to brainstorm what they would like to know about. You might begin by suggesting categories to focus on and letting them fill in subheadings (Katz & Chard, 2000; Tompkins, 2003). In preparation for a unit on nutrition, we asked a class of kindergarten children to help decide what they might like to learn. We used a web to chart their ideas and started it for them with nutrition as the theme and four categories to focus on: Why is food important? What foods are good for you? Where do we get food from? How are different foods prepared to eat?

In planning a unit, the teacher needs to include activities in all content areas. Create a plan and select activities related to the unit from different content areas to schedule throughout the school day. Following is a mini-unit written by Ms. Ngai, a first-grade teacher. As you will see, she integrates content-area activities throughout the day that and utilizes literacy skills as well.

Thematic Instruction: Good Food

"An interesting theme can make learning come alive for children. With food as our theme and popcorn as our weeklong focus, things were really 'popping' in our first-grade classroom! Here are some exciting ways to make learning about popcorn fun, while tying in content-area instruction and literacy.

"[The Friday before] We read about how to make popcorn and made a sequence chart of what to do first, second, etc. Then we followed the chart and planted popcorn kernels in cupcake pans lined with paper towels. Next we spread popcorn in the pans, then watered the seeds, and finally covered the pans with plastic wrap. In a few days, the roots began to sprout (science).

"[Monday] Using a log, we recorded the growth of the seedlings over the weekend. We read *The Popcorn Book* by Tomie dePaola [1978]. We discussed how the Native Americans introduced popcorn to the colonists. We used the compound word *popcorn* to trigger a list of other food compound words, such as *cupcake* and *milkshake*, which we wrote on a chart. Anytime a student thought of or came across a new compound word, he or she would write it down on the chart. By the end of the week, the chart paper was full (science, language arts, social studies).

"[Tuesday] We set up an experiment chart for making popcorn. We asked ourselves, 'What do I want to find out?' (How does a corn kernel change to popcorn?); 'What do I think will happen?'; 'How will I find out?'; 'What actually happened?'; and 'What did I learn?' We answered the first two questions. We used an air popper to pop the corn and then completed the experiment chart, answering the remaining questions. We also enjoyed the popcorn for our snack. We planted our seedlings in paper cups filled with soil (science).

"[Wednesday] We made more popcorn to create an estimation lesson for math. Each child grabbed a handful of popcorn from a large bowl and guessed how many kernels were in his or her hand. Next we used a simple record sheet to log estimations. We then counted to find the actual number. We tried it a second time to see if we arrived at a more accurate estimation (mathematics).

"[Thursday] One way Native Americans popped corn was to put an ear of dried corn on a stick and hold it over a fire until the kernels popped. Another way was to throw kernels into the fire until they popped out all over the place. Still another way was to use clay pots filled with hot sand, in which the kernels were mixed until they eventually popped to the top of the pot. We illustrated the method we thought was the best and wrote a few sentences as to why we felt that way. We discussed how the Native Americans made necklaces out of popcorn. Using the popcorn from Wednesday, we gave it a try. We used large, blunt needles and heavy thread and created necklaces (writing, art, social studies).

"[Friday] As a culminating lesson, we had parent volunteers come into our classroom to make popcorn balls. We checked for any growth of our corn plants and recorded the information in our science logs (science, cooking).

"In these activities, the children are learning content and engaging in literacy activities as well."

INTERDISCIPLINARY PBI: WHAT AND WHY?

PBI is a classroom approach in which students explore relevant real-world problems over an extended period of time and present their work to an audience. Today's classrooms are extremely busy places. In fact, as content and curriculum expand and the time to teach the material does not, "covering" the curriculum can become an added stress for teachers. Interdisciplinary teaching means using the language and methodology from several academic disciplines to study a single theme or topic. When teachers design interdisciplinary project-based work we create logical connections among disciplines that are usually taught separately. We allow our students to discover the relationships across subject areas and topics.

Interdisciplinary teaching is valuable for several reasons. *It is engaging.* The world is an interdisciplinary place, which makes this type of teaching relevant and authentic for students. Farmery (2015) has determined that interdisciplinary work makes meaningful links between subject areas in order to make learning coherent and to be motivational, relevant, and real for students. *Work that is authentic leads to greater transfer of knowledge.* Interdisciplinary units teach and *require critical thinking and reasoning on the part of students.* By allowing pupils to delve into multiple perspectives of a topic, *we teach them to live with the ambiguity of complex issues.* They begin to learn that people hold differing ideas, and that all of these ideas contribute to their own understanding of the world. *They synthesize information,* creating larger and more comprehensive thoughts than they previously held. *Their self-efficacy develops and grows.*

Interdisciplinary instruction also supports cognitive growth in the following areas:

- Recognizing bias
- Thinking critically
- Tolerating ambiguity
- Acknowledging and appreciating ethical concerns (Repko, 2009)

Project-based learning is a part of the inquiry-oriented curriculum model. It mimics today's real-world work in that small groups of interested students are formed to work on a problem or project. The projects may be suggested or required by the teacher, or developed by the students themselves. In the classroom, inquiry groups are often based on true student interest and choice. Groups are heterogeneous and diverse and require student responsibility and peer leadership (Harvey & Daniels, 2009).

Management Tip: Before beginning any group work, each group should create its own set of ground rules outlining how they will work together, what they will expect from each other, and how they will solve problems when they arise.

Nell Duke (2014) defines the PBI method: "In a project-based approach, students work over an extended time period for a purpose beyond satisfying a school requirement—to build something, to create something, to respond to a question they have, to solve a real problem, or to address a real need" (p. 11). In order for inquiry groups to work in the classroom, children must know how to think and how to work together (see Chapter 1). They must utilize the above-mentioned *comprehension strategies* we teach in literacy each day to allow readers to make sense of text.

These strategies can be taught at the same time as teachers inculcate lessons in *collaboration,* the other key ingredient in inquiry- or project-based learning. Collaboration instruction can be broken down into a list of "social strategies of small-group learning" (Duke, 2014, p. 43):

Class Rules for Active Discussion

- Be responsible to the group.
- Listen actively.
- Speak up.
- "Share the air" and encourage others to speak out.
- Show tolerance and respect.
- Reflect and correct.

The inquiry approach stresses the fact that what children study in school should be based on questions in which they have a sincere interest or on authentic problems. It also requires that the students will be doing much of the work. We often hear critics of education state that school needs to be more 'rigorous.' Here is one response to the critics: teachers utilizing project-based instruction are not delivering knowledge to their pupils. Students take the responsibility to research, create and present the knowledge they have synthesized. Most importantly, the focus in the project-based classroom is always on "the development of kids' thinking" (Duke, 2014, p. 57).

According to Brigid Barron and Linda Darling-Hammond (2008), children will be made college- and career-ready by their immersion in "complex, meaningful projects that require sustained engagement, collaboration, research, management of resources, and the development of an ambitious performance or product," (p. 12). McTighe, Seif, and Wiggins (2004), and Wilhelm (2007) agree, and have found that children taught using an inquiry- or project-based structure do better on standardized tests than those who were taught using the old transmission model of curriculum.

Duke (2015b) stresses the point that project-based instruction is of particular importance now for several vital reasons:

- *Research supports it.* "Students who experienced the project-based approach . . . developed greater content knowledge and reported much higher engagement . . . than students receiving more traditional instruction" (p. 1). Her research also shows that the authenticity of project-based learning is motivating for many diverse groups: young students, children with learning disabilities, and pupils living in poverty, and that these children develop comprehension more quickly than with traditional methods of instruction.

- *Higher standards and skills demand it.* Standards require that students write for "different tasks, purposes, and audiences" (p. 2). PBI provides "opportunities for students to problem solve, collaborate, and think creatively" (p. 2).

- *Today's students need it.* Children are highly motivated and remain engaged when they are involved in problem-based instruction. "In fact, people seem to be built for learning through projects" (p. 2).

- *Students are motivated and teachers energized.* Engaged students produce more and deeper work. Teachers who instruct using project-based instruction report that the enthusiasm of students for the practice has reenergized their teaching.

INTERDISCIPLINARY PROJECT-BASED LITERACY INSTRUCTION: HOW?

PBI begins with the teacher and/or her class coming up with areas they'd like to study further. These areas could stem from student interest or from local or world issues that present a problem that can be researched and worked on by the children and one that is highly relevant to them. This alone takes time to plan thoughtfully and thoroughly. Larmer, Mergendoller, and Boss (2015) remind us to plan work that embraces these elements:

- Sustained inquiry (requiring a longer period of time to accomplish)
- Authenticity (being real and relevant to children)
- Student voice and choice (allowing students to help decide the topics or how to demonstrate the knowledge they glean)
- Reflection (for teachers: allowing them to be flexible and to make adjustments along the way; and for students: learning self-regulation)
- Critique and revision (building in the time for self- and peer revision)

As we set about beginning work in PBI, we need to be mindful of the steps involved. Harvey and Daniels (2009, pp. 61–62) recommend that teachers follow a small-group inquiry model, which includes four stages:

1. Immerse.
2. Investigate
3. Coalesce.
4. Go public.

The first step, *immersion*, finds us as teachers expressing and inviting students to express their own curiosity. As the children wonder, ask questions, read, listen, and view teacher-gathered material, we demonstrate how to ask questions and find topics, we organize resources, and we confer with small groups.

Students are beginning research by reading about their topics.

During the *investigation* period, we, as teachers, surround our students with relevant information (books, photographs, films, newspapers, magazines, journals, maps, websites, etc.) and model note taking, determining importance, and the synthesis of information. Children are reading, listening, talking, and using materials to develop questions and answer them. Questions center on what the students already know and what they need to research to learn. We need to locate and gather for our students the best websites, film clips, and so on, in order to set them up for success.

The *coalesce* phase engages students in delving into more intense research, checking sources, synthesizing information, conducting interviews, and meeting with their team while their teacher conducts mini-lessons in how to evaluate sources, models how to draw conclusions, teaches interviewing, and confers with groups. During this phase we are overseeing each group, helping to delve deeper into resources. We are also setting check-in times for each group, so that they can stay on track and not become overwhelmed by the amount of information they have at a click of the mouse.

In the *go public* stage, students share their learning, demonstrate their understanding, and take action. Their teacher makes clear her expectations for final projects (creating and sharing rubrics), helps groups and individuals reflect on both content and process, and assists as her students locate a wide range of performance possibilities and determine their preferred method of demonstration of what they have learned. She will later assess all of the work done over the life of the project.

Duke (2014) suggests that problem-based instruction can be made more accessible for teachers if a consistent structure for both all projects and all sessions within the project work is used. The structure she proposes for each session is quite similar to the organization of the writing workshop, and therefore should be familiar to many teachers. Each session begins with a short *whole-class lesson* around a particular teaching point (10–15 minutes); continues with *small-group, partner,* or *individual work,* during which the teacher circulates and confers with groups or individuals (25–30 minutes); and closes with a *whole-class wrap-up,* which might include sharing or review of the original lesson (5 minutes), (Duke, 2014, p. 23). A typical lesson about this topic in a project-based setting might look like this:

- Teacher delivers a mini-lesson in how to write questions for an interview.
- Teacher circulates to do small-group work with each group to scaffold the practice of writing questions for their particular needs.
- Teacher and students participate in a wrap-up, during which several interview questions are shared with the whole class.

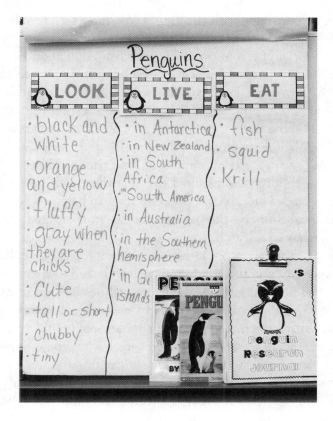

A kindergarten class conducts research on penguins.

In their book *Comprehension and Collaboration,* Harvey and Daniels (2009) detail 40 lessons in the two areas mentioned in the book title, both of which are needed to support learners during project-based work. They also include much work with the concept of inquiry. The lessons run the gamut from "Activating and Building Background Knowledge" to "I Beg to Differ: *Disagreeing Agreeably*" (pp. 151–191).

> *Management Tip:* It is imperative that teachers (or the teacher in conjunction with students) set up check-in dates: preset dates when groups will confirm their status with the teacher. Without these weekly check-ins, students can easily get off track or fall behind. A student calendar can be very helpful here, so that children are able to visualize schedules.

Let's set the stage for this section: Ms. Tapia has already visited the library, begged, borrowed and, well, let's say borrowed again, all of the resources she could locate on the local waterfront and the fish that are caught there. She has displayed several books, cover outwards, on the chalk tray or in a specific spot for children to view. The room is also filled with artifacts specifically relating to the local waterfront. Continuing with the idea of Ms. Tapia's study of fish in this area, she has displayed newspaper articles, maps of fishing grounds and fishing patterns throughout the year, and recent problems with fish population since a hurricane 2 years earlier. She has taught some basics; she has asked children to collect news articles about the hurricane, local businesses, and, most importantly, the fish that are local to the area. The children have viewed several short films about the local fishing industry, and the teacher has planned for a visit and interview with a local fisherman. She calls her students "ichthyologists" and has piqued their interest by talking about how many communities around the world depend on the fishing industry. The children are psyched to study their own locale and to create work that will be placed on tables in the restaurant to help people understand the waterfront, the local fish, and the fishing industry in their area. They move into the next phase, ready to research.

One of her PLC members has chosen a different topic. A local dentist visited the classroom recently, and the children have been asked to create pamphlets that families could read about caring for their teeth while they are waiting to see the dentist. This teacher also borrowed books from her local library, set up various websites for student research, and combed the newspaper and various magazines about new research about teeth. The children break into groups to research several different topics: one group studies what causes cavities and makes recommendations; another writes about the importance of seeing a dentist early and often in life; a third investigates what it takes to become a dentist and will create a pamphlet about that.

The interest of older students can be piqued by a bigger set of ideas. Much in the way that Google allows their employees 20% of their time to "dabble" in ideas that interest them, students can now take part in "Genius Hour." We have seen this idea beautifully carried out in a local middle school. The assistant principal and the town's literacy coach had talked about this concept extensively, and had set up the parameters of the project work and decided, with a team of teachers, who would do what. Because this was in a middle school, students moved from teacher to teacher for different subjects, so buy-in from all of the teachers was important. Once the structure had been roughed out, the administrator created a video presentation of inspirational clips from many movies (*Rocky, Rudy,* etc.). He gathered one grade level of students together in the auditorium to view this 20-minute presentation, and then talked to them about how important inspiration was for inventors, scientists, and others who have helped to cure illnesses or save the world in some other way. He pumped the students up to believe that even they could contribute to saving the world if they put their whole mind and effort toward one topic. Students returned to homeroom to begin to flesh out ideas that they would like to investigate as part of their plan to save the world. Topics ranged from music therapy for troubled children, to saving animals from being used for research, to raising money to buy mosquito nets for children in countries where much disease is carried by insects.

The teachers presented the proposed schedule to the students for their input and began to teach lessons that the groups or individuals would need to research, to work together, and to create their projects. Social studies teachers covered social interactions, teaching how to get along in a group, how to speak up in a group, etc. Math teachers took the role of teaching students how to read statistical material, so that they would know when an idea was backed by good research. Science teachers took over the area of locating resources and presenting the bibliographical data. Language arts teachers worked with comprehension skills, demonstrating how to ask questions of the author, how to take notes by determining importance, and how to best present the material discovered. Related arts teachers contributed when students needed to learn how to present their findings.

Teachers using the project-based method will have already determined when to use various formative assessments. This discussion continues later in this chapter.

Literacy comprehension strategies can and should be employed across content areas. Content-area reading and writing not only reinforce knowledge and understanding of the subject matter, but increase our students' ability to read, write, and think. The overlay of specific comprehension strategies, usually introduced in the literacy portion of the day, on content-area reading and writing makes the most of the limited time teachers have. Since literacy strategies can be used on any text, the use of content-area texts makes a great deal of sense.

There are many wonderful authors of nonfiction for children. Among our favorites are Seymour Simon, Aliki, Melissa Sweet, Steve Jenkins, Patricia MacLachlan, and David Macaulay. These authors provide an abundance of knowledge in readable and enjoyable formats for our students.

USING TECHNOLOGY WITH PBI: WHAT AND WHY?

The technology available to teachers and students in the classroom has forever changed the manner in which we teach. Facts, opinions, photographs, videos, and even primary source documents are readily accessible. The most up-to-date research is as close as a keyboard click. If we hope to teach our students to be prepared to learn new information, we must teach them to be wary of using certain sources, how to know which websites are valuable and which are biased, and how to search and sift through the phenomenal amount of information available. Therefore, we need to lead them through the steps of locating, evaluating, paraphrasing, and quoting valid source material using the computer.

USING TECHNOLOGY: HOW?

Many wonderful Web resources are set up for children to use. Some of these include:

- *http://wonderopolis*
- *https://newsela.com*
- *www.ducksters.com*
- *www.sweetsearch.com*
- *http://scholar.google.com*
- *www.sciencenewsforstudents.com*
- *www.icivics.org*
- *www.timeforkids.com*
- *www.cnn.com/studentnews*
- *www.dogonews.com*
- *http://gws.ala.org/tags/nonfiction*
- *news.nick.com*
- *https://whyfiles.org*
- *www.choosito.com*

We can and should teach lessons in how to evaluate websites. Useful for this are two fake sites we can use to show students that they need to be diligent in checking their Internet sources:

http://zapatopi.net/treeoctopus/help.html
www.youtube.com/watch?v=yflTu150QZw

Many teachers use Google Classroom to inform and keep children aware of their requirements. Teachers conduct mini-lessons in how to set up an account, how to share a document with websites, and how to save websites as favorites.

Management Tip: Once we have determined that PBI is right for our classroom, we can create bins for each group of investigators. These might include:

- Pens, markers, pencils
- Scissors
- Books
- Badges or lanyards that indicate who is in charge of what

- Flash drives
- Index cards
- Magazines
- A calendar with important project dates already designated

PBI ASSESSMENT: WHAT AND WHY?

PBI is a highly relevant and authentic practice; it requires assessment that is designed and executed carefully. Formative and summative assessments are essential if students are to gain what we hope for them as they work through this process. Student work-product should be considered and discussed during the project launch. Rubrics should be shared before work begins.

Before students even begin work on their projects, their input should be sought as the teacher designs the rubric he or she will use to assess their work. As work proceeds, student understanding and growth must be measured frequently to check for understanding and for both teacher and student reflection. Checklists and calendars are helpful when conducting formative assessment in this structure.

PBI ASSESSMENT: HOW?

As we launch our PBI, we need to show students exemplars. Projects that were created by last year's students and judged to be of excellent caliber should be shared with our pupils. Children should be encouraged to dream up new ways to demonstrate their understanding. Sometimes a presentation to local authorities is appropriate, while other times the creation of a short film would be considered best. The website *www.teachthought.com/learning/60-things-students-can-create-to-demonstrate-what-they-know* gives teachers and children 60 different ways to show what they know. Whichever format they choose, the product should be authentic and relevant, and delivered to the correct audience.

The creation of a rubric is an excellent way to assess students' final projects, although we must take care to include measurement of all of the standards and all of the lessons we taught along the way. A typical rubric might only consider organization, content, and presentation, but we should not forget to include to plan to assess the following pieces as well:

- Time management
- Teamwork

- Problem solving
- Use of technology
- Critical thinking.

Teachers may assign a grade in literacy and in the subject areas touched on by the project, as well. Giving a group grade and an individual grade in each area is also a fair way to assess. In order to best judge student growth over time, we should periodically include some forms of formative assessment. They might include checklists, graphic organizers, exit cards, and the like. These may not be scored, but will allow the teacher to see where and when he or she needs to scaffold or teach a mini-lesson, and give him or her insight into each student's understanding of the research he or she is conducting. Of course, the final project is scored and graded.

CONCLUSION

In this chapter, we detailed the difference between thematic units and PBI by presenting examples of each. We discussed the importance of using informational text in the classroom and stressed the importance of explicit instruction in comprehension strategies. We detailed the phases of PBI. We also introduced the use of technology with PBI and how to assess student work.

·· 👋 STOP! THINK! REACT! 👋 ··

❑ Determine a period of time within your school year during which PBI might fit. Plan out the project time, which usually means 3–6 weeks of class time.

❑ Gather a list of subjects of importance to your students. Many classes respond well to "How I Can Make the World a Better Place," which could include a vast number of ideas and topics of relevance to your children.

❑ Remember to ask yourself just how willing you are to give up the reins as project-based work proceeds.

❑ Try to enlist the help of a colleague; working together is very helpful.

❑ Keep things relevant to your students; relevance leads to transfer of learning.

Concluding Thoughts

In this book we have presented an approach to organization and management for building best practice in literacy development. We emphasize the importance of literacy-rich environments; social interaction; peer collaboration; whole-class, small-group, and individual learning with explicit instruction; and problem-solving experiences. The activities we suggest underscore the concurrent, integrated nature of learning how to *use* reading, writing, listening, and speaking. We discuss making literacy experiences functional and connected to real-life experiences, and thereby meaningful and interesting to the child. Our book fosters the integration of literacy activities into content areas through themes and project-based learning that add enthusiasm, motivation, and meaning. We have suggested careful monitoring of individual growth through direct instruction and frequent assessment, using multiple measures and allowing ample space for children to learn through exploration.

New information about learning is constantly being generated, subsequently changing the strategies we use to help children learn. Teachers must stay abreast of the constant stream of literature that is available after they complete their formal education. They need to engage in multiple forms of professional development to be up-to-date with the latest research, theory, policy, and practice. Teachers can also continue their education to receive a master's or doctorate degree or another teaching certification—or simply take a course to strengthen their knowledge in a particular area of concern. Teachers need to join professional organizations that have local, state, and national conferences. These organizations publish practical and research journals with the current information, and some also publish books.

Through these organizations, teachers connect with each other and have opportunities to talk and reflect. In addition to these individual initiatives, we encourage you to work on a professional development plan with your school, whether by grade level or for the entire school. This can be a 1-year plan that continues as long as it works. The plan is based on what teachers and administrators believe they need to work on in literacy.

Try to use a collaborative model with your peers, as this has proven to work well. Both teacher and administrative support are needed to succeed. The goals of a professional development program in a school are to:

- Change classroom practice.
- Change teacher attitudes toward professional development.
- Create a school that is composed of a community of learners.

How can this be done?

- Focus on changing classroom practices.
- When teachers can observe changes in student learning as a result of changing classroom practice, changes in teacher beliefs and attitudes will follow.
- Bring in experts to model the teaching practice you wish to implement.

COMPONENTS OF A GOOD PROFESSIONAL DEVELOPMENT PROGRAM

Good professional development programs include:

1. Administrative support for the project prior to beginning.
2. Professional development workshops to provide information about new strategies from motivating and knowledgeable consultants.
3. Goals to accomplish set by teachers.
4. A coach in the school to model new strategies in the classroom and to support teachers.
5. Accessible materials.
6. Classroom observations by other teachers, the coach, etc., to determine progress.
7. Teacher discussion groups to foster collaboration and reflection with reading materials to provide new ideas.
8. Time to change.

Another aspect of professional development is when a teacher acts as a researcher to reflect upon his or her own teaching. In doing this, you can discover your own strengths and weaknesses while exploring important questions about teaching your students. To be a teacher-researcher means to formulate questions about teaching strategies, child development, classroom environment, curriculum development, and other relevant topics that help to clarify issues or generate new information. Questions should originate from your daily experiences in the classroom and interest you personally. When teachers are researchers, they increase their knowledge and skill.

After deciding on an area of inquiry, the teacher should focus on collecting data that will help answer the questions posed. Data can be collected in many ways: by observing and recording anecdotes of classroom experiences that are relevant to the question being asked; by videotaping classroom segments; by collecting samples of children's daily work over a period of time; by interviewing children, teachers, and parents; by administering formal and informal tests; and by trying new techniques.

As a teacher-researcher, you will always be on the cutting edge of what is current and effective. You will always find teaching interesting because you will learn about new things on a daily basis. You will enjoy your work more because you have extended your role to include additional professional activities. As a teacher-researcher, you are practicing both the art and the science of teaching. The science involves inquiry, reading, observing, and collecting data. The art involves reflecting on your findings and making appropriate changes. Teacher-researchers empower themselves to be decision makers and catalysts for change in their schools. As they study questions for which they have tangible data, they are more likely to be heard when they propose new ideas and changes. Each year that you teach, select another area of inquiry to study. When appropriate, collaborate with your colleagues on research projects. Collaboration with adults, as with children, results in projects that you might not have been able to do alone. Much of what we have learned over the years about learning theory and early literacy development is due to collaborative research by college professors and classroom teachers.

This book is meant to be motivating for teachers and children. Motivation allows teachers to work with vigor and enthusiasm, and it allows children to associate literacy with a school environment that is pleasurable, positive, and designed to help them succeed. One of the most important elements in literacy development is a teacher who encourages children to want to read and write. This desire motivates them to learn the skills necessary to become proficient in literacy. As proficiency develops, so does a lifelong interest in refining and using these literacy skills.

Exemplary Literacy
Day Planning Example

Olga Pryymak
Shira Wasserman

The following unit plan demonstrates a 2-day sample rollout of exemplary literacy instruction that is comprehensive, interconnected, and taking place beyond the traditional "reading block." Although this plan serves as an example of what instruction might look like, the best planning takes place when teachers collaborate and use curricula and standards to design lessons that best match the needs of current students. This plan matches the exemplary day outline introduced in Chapter 1.

Note: The plan included below is a draft of the beginning of instruction that can take place across 2 days in a second-grade classroom. For each component of the exemplary day, consult earlier chapters in the book to orchestrate comprehensive instruction.

GETTING STARTED

Prior to drafting the exemplary day, it is important to find materials that best match the standards being addressed. The following mentor texts were chosen for 2 days of instruction in this second-grade classroom:

Choosing Mentor Texts for Reading Comprehension Workshop

- *Why Do Bears Hibernate?*—a nonfiction book that takes the reader through the process of why animals hibernate, focusing on the bear. All the subtitles on the pages are questions. It is full of facts about winter and how different plants and animals react to the changing seasons. This book poses questions not only through the title, but also through the subtitles.

- *The Mitten*—a translated Ukrainian folktale that relates the story of Nikki, a boy who loses his mitten. The book tells about what the animals do when they find it. This fiction story is great for both sequencing and retelling, allowing the student to think creatively. Having the students reenact the story as the different characters provides ample fluency practice. This book opens the mind to different possibilities to compare and contrast animals in winter with the nonfiction book introduced above.

- *The Thing about Yetis*—a sweet book about Yetis who love winter . . . but even they get tired of winter sometimes. So, they do activities that remind them of summer. Yetis are full of surprises. This book is a great vehicle for text-to-self and text-to-text connections. It allows for creative thinking about implicit comprehension. Students can write a story about a day they spent with their Yeti friend or draft letters to the Yetis about different activities they enjoy doing in both the summer and the winter.

DIFFERENTIATING FOR ALL STUDENTS:
PREPARING FOR HIGH-QUALITY GUIDED READING

Although classrooms will have students with a plethora of needs, this sample schedule was designed with four possible reading groups in mind:

Group A

Students need to work on sequencing and retelling.

- Leveled text: *Baltic Rescue* is about a dog that travels on ice and his 75-mile adventure through the Baltic Sea. His adventure ends when a ship's crew rescues him and adopts him, giving him the name "Baltic."
- Possible lesson extensions: Write a letter to Baltic about your favorite part of his adventure and how you felt reading about it.
- Leveled readers for extending learning: *Hibernation* is a nonfiction book that connects well to the informational text *Why Do Bears Hibernate?* It expands on the book we read as a class and allows the students to think deeply and add to their KWL chart. This book will be a good challenge for advanced readers.

Group B

Students need to work on comparing and contrasting, making predictions, and retelling.

- Leveled text: *Wonderful Winter* is about a boy who is sad that winter has come because he likes to play outside. After a friend invites him to play in the snow, the young boy quickly realizes that winter activities are also enjoyable. Students in this reading group can compare and contrast the summer and winter activities that the boy talks about.

- Possible lesson extensions: Students can write about text-to-self connections about activities they enjoy doing outside or write a letter to the boy, giving him more ideas about new activities to do outside in the winter.

- Leveled readers for extending learning: *The Igloo* is a story about a rabbit family with different personalities and how they solve problems that arise. This book is good for making predictions and retelling. Our on-grade-level readers will enjoy this book because the characters have fun and engaging personalities. They can choose a character that is their favorite and retell using textual evidence to explain why they chose that specific character.

Group C

Students need to work on using adjectives for more descriptive writing.

- Leveled text: *Monster Snow Day* is about a group of monsters that are eagerly awaiting the arrival of snow. They play winter activities inside, and a fight is averted when the monsters notice it's finally snowing.

- Leveled readers for extending learning: *Monster on Wheels* is about a group of monsters that like to ride bicycles and rollerblade. They are upset when it snows because they can't use their wheels, so they buy a shovel to make a path to be able to use their wheels again. This book includes opportunities for struggling readers to be able to identify a problem and a solution as well as to retell using descriptive adjectives. With prompting, students should be able to retell the story by using a five-finger retell strategy and answer the five "W" questions: who, what, where, when, and why.

Group D

Students need to work on using context clues.

- Leveled text: *I Need a Snow Day* is about a girl who has a math test, but she wants it to snow so she doesn't have to take it. It doesn't snow, so she has to take the test, but she does well on it. Then it snows that night. Readers in this group will use context clues along with pictures to help figure out what is happening in the story. With prompting, the students will be able to answer the five "W" questions and make text-to-self connections.

- Leveled readers for extending learning: *Runaway Snowball* is about a boy whose snowball gets away from him and causes problems for all the people at the bottom of the hill. This book can be used to model cause-and-effect relationships and serve as a text for reviewing adjectives. With prompting, the students should be able to make connections about a problem they have caused and how these problems affect others.

DAY 1

Do-Now
Students are invited to take one another on a short tour of each other's reader's notebooks. A sticky note is placed on each student's desk so that he or she can collaborate on a focus question of the day: *What do you know about hibernation?*

Vocabulary Meeting
1. New vocabulary terms are embedded in a "morning meeting" letter to students from the teacher. Explain hibernation and ask the students to think about why animals hibernate, what types of animals hibernate, and whether or not they have heard of any animals who hibernate.   2. Weekly vocabulary words written on index cards are posted on the board and discussed verbally.   3. Vocabulary list: *hemisphere, rodents, burrow, migrate, hibernate, den, mammals,* and *equator*

Reading Comprehension Workshop	
Materials	*Why Do Bears Hibernate?* by Darice Bailer Anchor chart paper
Reading Objective(s)	• **Objective #1:** Determine or clarify the meaning of unknown and multiple-meaning words and phrases by using context clues, analyzing meaningful word parts, and consulting general and specialized reference materials, as appropriate. • **Objective #2:** Read and comprehend complex literary and informational texts independently and proficiently with scaffolding as needed.
Sequence of Instruction	1. Introduce the book. Start a KWL chart on chart paper with the class. Assess what the class *Knows* and *What* they want to *Learn* about hibernation on the chart paper. Be able to refer back to the chart paper when necessary. Students can refer to the sticky notes that they worked on during the morning Do-Now. 2. **Mini-Lesson:** Explain to the students that this is a nonfiction book and that the author's purpose is to give information about hibernation. The teacher will demonstrate how to navigate the book and its text features. The mini-lesson topic will focus on how noticing and appreciating new vocabulary words will extend students' knowledge about a topic. 3. Read the book aloud, stopping at each vocabulary word to elaborate and question students about the words. (*Why do animals burrow?*) A think-aloud can be modeled to support students.

	4. After reading the book, students will help the teacher to fill out what they *Learned* on the KWL chart. 5. **Reflection:** How does noticing and appreciating new vocabulary words help you understand more about a topic?
	<div align="center">**Guided Reading**</div>
Group D	**Materials:** *I Need a Snow Day* from Reading A–Z **Literacy Goals:** Describe information provided by illustrations. **Sequence of Instruction:** 1. Give each student a copy of *I Need a Snow Day* and introduce the book. Show the students the title page and the back cover. Show the students where the title of the book is, who the author is, and who the illustrator is. 2. Ask the students to look at the front cover and use the title of the book to predict what they think the book is about. 3. Students will whisper-read and stop at words they don't know so that the teacher can help them. The teacher will focus primarily on the student that is closest to him or her that day to monitor that student's reading. 4. When all the students are done reading, explain that good readers use the illustrations in the book they are reading to give them additional information about the story. 5. Model a think-aloud about how to get additional information from an illustration using page 7. 6. Ask the students to turn to the page with their favorite picture on it and turn and talk with their partner about any additional information they might get from the illustration they are looking at. 7. Spotlight one of the groups and ask them to share what they learned from the illustration they picked with the rest of the group.
Group C	**Materials:** *Monster Snow Day* from Reading A–Z **Literacy Goals:** Identify and understand the use of adjectives. **Sequence of Instruction:** 1. Give each student a copy of *Monster Snow Day* and introduce the book. Show the students the title page and the back cover. Show the students where the title of the book is, who the author is, and who the illustrator is. 2. Ask the students to look at the front cover and use the title of the book to predict what they think the book is about.

3. Students will whisper-read and stop at words they don't know so that the teacher can help them. The teacher will focus primarily on the student that is closest to him or her that day to monitor that student's reading.
4. Write the following sentence so the group can see it: "Bonk makes paper snowflakes." Ask the students to read the sentence aloud with the teacher.
5. Review nouns by explaining that they name a person, place, or thing. Have the students identify the nouns in the sentences.
6. Explain adjectives as describing words that describe a noun.
7. Ask the students to look at the word *snowflake* and come up with describing words for it.
8. Discuss with the students how using adjectives/describing words makes us visualize the story better.
9. To check for understanding, have the students read page 5 and identify the nouns and the adjectives describing the nouns.
10. Each student can share an adjective he or she found that describes the noun he or she chose.

Literacy Work Stations

- Word work: Nouns versus adjectives review (sorting activity)—Students will sort nouns into one bucket and adjectives into another one. Then they pick a noun and an adjective and write a sentence with them. Students can refer to an "I Can" list for additional activities to complete.
- Listening comprehension—*The Mitten* (Students will use a computer-assisted program and laptops to participate.)
- Compare and contrast nonfiction and fiction animals.
- Library station—Independent reading (The class library also includes a display of winter books and books related to the science unit of study.)
- Writing station—Students can choose to write a letter to the Yetis about what they can do to not miss summer or consult the "I Can" list for other choices.

Writing Workshop

Writing Objective(s)	Objective #1: Write narratives to develop real or imagined experiences or events using effective technique, well-chosen details, and well-structured event sequences.
Sequence of Instruction	1. Brainstorming: Students will brainstorm a list of animals that hibernate based on the book *Why Do Bears Hibernate?* 2. **Mini-Lesson:** The teacher will model how writers can develop narratives based on information gained when reading. The teacher will share a sample story draft and engage students in a mini-lesson on whether the unfolding events are real or imagined.

3. Students will then partner-write, using their brainstormed list of animals to decide on a purpose: creating a real or an imagined piece.
4, The teacher will spotlight select students and have them share their stories. As students listen, they will determine if the narratives are real or imagined.
5. **Reflection:** Based on our writing today, how does a variety of real and imagined stories make narratives interesting?

Interdisciplinary Project-Based Instruction

Second-grade students have been studying the environment and what parts of the environment are included in their local community. Based on this unit of study, students will:

- Create a "Passion List" of things they are interested in learning more about involving their local neighborhood environment.
- Read and conduct research about the local community (including information about parks, animals, nature, etc.).

On Day 1, the teacher will use the interactive whiteboard to review what students have been learning in science. Based on a recent study of living and nonliving things, the teacher will engage the students in a short presentation about living and nonliving things found around the school outdoors. Students will collect information in their science notebooks and reflect on their learning.

Math Instruction

In math class, students are working on number stories throughout the week. Students will collaborate using a digital app to write and illustrate number stories, explaining what they know.

Specials

In today's schedule, students are scheduled to attend art. The art teacher will read aloud a short biography of a famous artist that they are studying. Time will be set aside for students to independently read to learn more about the artist.

Wrap-Up

What stuck with you today?:

The students will think back to what they worked on during guided reading, reading comprehension workshop, or writing workshop. On a sticky note, they will reflect on what they did well today.

Read-aloud:
The teacher will read aloud a short poem from Brod Bagert entitled "The Homework Guarantee." Students will be reminded to complete their independent reading at home.

DAY 2

Do-Now	
Students begin the day by independently reading and shopping for new books in the classroom library. Students are asked to share what they read at home with a partner. After taking attendance and organizing for the day, the teacher conducts a short book talk based on a new book that has been added to the library.	

Vocabulary Meeting	
In today's lesson, students are asked to complete a graphic organizer by choosing one of the featured vocabulary words from the weekly list: *hemisphere, rodents, burrow, migrate, hibernate, den, mammals,* and *equator.* *Note:* Students can complete part of the graphic organizer based on time (approximately 15 minutes).	

Reading Comprehension Workshop	
Reading Objective(s)	**Objective #1:** Read with sufficient accuracy and fluency to support comprehension. Read grade-level text with purpose and understanding.
Sequence of Instruction	1. The teacher will introduce the book and explain that the class will be working on sequencing events in the story and practicing fluent reading. 2. The teacher will assign roles to each of the students using the animals in the book to build their fluency. 3. As a short warm-up, the students will be given time to read their lines and become more familiar with the text. 4. **Mini-Lesson:** The teacher will model how fluent reading can help a reader better understand the key events taking place in the story. 5. Students will partner-read and complete a sequencing worksheet by cutting out the different animals and putting the animals in the order in which they appear in the book. 6. Once students complete the worksheet they will gather back in the whole-class area to reflect on their learning. 7. **Reflection:** How did reading like the character (with fluency and expression) help you as a reader?

Guided Reading	
Group D	**Leveled Text:** *Runaway Snowball* from Reading A–Z **Literacy Goals:** Determine cause and effect.

Sequence of Instruction:

1. Give each student a copy of *Runaway Snowball* and introduce the book. Show the students the title page and the back cover. Show the students where the title of the book is, who the author is, and who the illustrator is.

2. Ask the students to look at the front cover and use the title of the book to predict what they think the book is about.

3. Focus: Read today to find out what happens with the snowball.

4. Students will whisper-read and stop at words they don't know so that the teacher can help them. The teacher will focus primarily on the student who is closest to him or her that day to monitor that student's reading.

5. Students will turn and talk to each other to discuss their response to the focus question. The teacher will explain to the students that cause is "the action" and effect is "the result of the action."

6. Using the text: The teacher will have students go to the last page of the book and turn and talk with their partner about the effect of the snowball getting to the bottom of the hill.

Group B	**Leveled Text:** *The Igloo* **Literacy Goals:** Identify story elements—focus on problem and solution. **Instructional Sequence:** 1. Give each student a copy of *The Igloo* and introduce the book. Show the students the title page and the back cover. Show the students where the title of the book is, who the author is, and who the illustrator is. 2. Ask the students to look at the front cover and use the title of the book to predict what they think the book is about. 3. Focus: As you read, come up with the elements that are important to a story. Write these on your sticky note. 4. Students will turn to each other and talk about what they have collected once they are finished reading. The teacher will explain that *characters* are people or animals in a story. The *setting* is when and where the story takes place. The *problem* is something difficult to deal with that must be worked out, and the *solution* is the answer to the problem. *Events* are the things that happen to characters as they find the solution. The teacher will list these terms on a whiteboard. 5. The teacher will ask students to name the character and the setting. The problem and the solution are not usually stated: you have to use clues from the story to find them.

6. Explain that identifying story elements such as the problem and the solution helps the reader to organize the information he or she reads.
7. Go through the book with students and discuss with them how to find clues for what a problem might be.
8. Go through the book and show students how the events in the story can be the solution to the problem you identified.
9. Direct the students to work in pairs to identify another problem in the story and the solution for it. Have students share with the rest of the class.
10. Explain to students that the more they read, the more story elements they will find and the better they will get at spotting them.
11. **Reflection:** How does spotting story elements help you as a reader?

Literacy Work Stations

- Word work: Nouns versus adjectives review (sorting activity)—Students will sort nouns into one bucket and adjectives into another one. Then they pick a noun and an adjective and write a sentence with them. Students can refer to an "I Can" list for additional activities to complete.
- Listening comprehension—*The Mitten* (Students will use a computer-assisted program and laptops to participate.)
- Compare and contrast nonfiction and fiction animals.
- Library station—Independent reading (The class library also includes a display of winter books and books related to the science unit of study.)
- Writing station: Students can choose to write a letter to the Yetis about what they can do to not miss summer or consult the "I Can" list for other choices.

Writing Workshop

Writing Objective(s)	Objective #1—Write narratives to develop real or imagined experiences or events using effective technique, well-chosen details, and well-structured event sequences
Sequence of Instruction	1. **Mini-Lesson:** Yesterday, students used their brainstormed lists to create real or imagined stories using the mentor text *Why Do Bears Hibernate?* Today, the teacher will use *The Mitten* to help students determine how this text fits in with the narrative unit of study. Students will create a t-chart to collect narrative elements and determine how they impact the story. 2. Students will work with partners to revisit their drafts from yesterday. Students will be encouraged to embed a new narrative element in their stories.

3. The teacher will spotlight a few students to share their narratives with the class.
4. **Reflection:** Today you took some creative liberties in trying out what you noticed in the Ukrainian folktale. In what ways did you enhance your story?

Interdisciplinary Project-Based Instruction

Using Google Earth, the students will zoom in on a local park in the neighborhood. Students will complete a graphic organize to list all of the living and nonliving things that they can see in the park. The teacher will assist students to think about how these things interact within the local ecosystem.

Partners will have an opportunity to use Google Earth to explore other local areas within the community. Students will explore the following question: Are there any living and nonliving interactions within our environment that pose a problem? *Note:* This will set the stage for future reading and using the Next Generation Science Standards to engineer solutions to potential problems within the local environment.

Math Instruction

In math class, students are working on number stories throughout the week. Students will collaborate using a digital app to write and illustrate number stories, explaining what they know.

Specials

Today, students are scheduled to attend music class. The teacher will introduce a new song and teach five featured vocabulary words to students. The music teacher has a Word Wall entitled, "Mozart's Words."

Wrap-Up

The teacher will read aloud a short article based on a local problem within the environment. Students will be encouraged to read and research for homework and to bring in their findings to use during tomorrow's lesson.

Fry (1980) Sight Words Grouped by Relative Difficulty

FIRST 100 WORDS

the	this	which	into
of	have	she	time
and	from	do	has
a	or	how	look
to	one	their	two
in	had	if	more
is	by	will	write
you	word	up	go
that	but	other	see
it	not	about	number
he	what	out	no
was	all	many	way
for	were	then	could
on	we	them	people
are	when	these	my
as	your	so	than
with	can	some	first
his	said	her	water
they	there	would	been
I	use	make	call
at	an	like	who
be	each	him	oil

now	down	get	may
find	day	come	part
long	did	made	over

SECOND 100 WORDS

new	great	put	kind
sound	where	end	hand
take	help	does	picture
only	through	another	again
little	much	well	change
work	before	large	off
know	line	must	play
place	right	big	spell
year	too	even	air
live	mean	such	away
me	old	because	animal
back	any	turn	house
give	same	here	point
most	tell	why	page
very	boy	ask	letter
after	follow	went	mother
thing	came	men	answer
our	went	read	found
just	show	need	study
name	also	land	still
good	around	different	learn
sentence	form	home	should
man	three	us	America
think	small	move	world
say	set	try	high

THIRD 100 WORDS

every	plant	city	saw
near	last	earth	left
add	school	eye	don't
food	father	light	few
between	keep	thought	while
own	tree	head	along
below	must	under	might
country	state	story	close

something	important	state	almost
seem	until	once	let
next	children	book	above
hard	side	hear	girl
open	feet	stop	sometimes
example	car	without	mountain
begin	mile	second	cut
life	night	late	young
always	walk	miss	talk
those	while	idea	soon
both	sea	enough	list
paper	began	eat	song
together	grow	face	leave
got	took	watch	family
group	river	far	body
often	four	Indian	music
run	carry	real	color

References

Adams, M. J. (1990). *Beginning to read: Thinking and learning about print*. Urbana: University of Illinois Center for the Study of Reading.

Adams, M. J. (2001). Alphabetic anxiety and explicit, systematic phonics instruction: A cognitive science perspective. In S. B. Neuman & D. K. Dickinson (Eds.), *Handbook of early literacy research* (Vol 1, pp. 66–80). New York: Guilford Press.

Allington, R. L., & Cunningham, P. M. (2007). *Schools that work: Where all children read and write*. New York: HarperCollins.

Almasi, J. F., & Hart, S. J. (2015). Best practices in narrative text comprehension instruction. In L. B. Gambrell & L. M Morrow (Eds.), *Best practices in literacy instruction* (5th ed., pp. 223–248). New York: Guilford Press.

Alvermann, D. E., Phelps, S. F., & Gillis, V. R. (2010). *Content area reading and literacy: Succeeding in today's diverse classroom*. Boston: Allyn & Bacon.

Anderson, C. (2000). *How's it going?: A practical guide to conferring with student writers*. Portsmouth, NH: Heinemann.

Antonacci, P., & O'Callaghan, C. (2003). *Portraits of literacy development: Instruction and assessment in a well-balanced literacy program, K–3*. Upper Saddle River, NJ: Merrill/ Prentice/Hall.

Ashton-Warren, S. (1986). *Teacher*. New York: Simon & Schuster.

Atwell, N. (1998). *In the middle: New understandings about writing, reading, and learning*. Portsmouth, NH: Heinemann.

Bahlmann Bollinger, C., Kleppe Graham, K., Kelly, C., Kunz, K., McManus, M., Miller, S., et al. (2016, Nov. 30–Dec. 2). *Understanding and breaking through the noise: Literacy leaders in the face of accountability, evaluation, and reform*. Paper presented at the 66th annual Literacy Research Association conference, Nashville, TN.

Baker, J. (1991). *Window*. New York: Greenwillow Books.

Baker, J. (2004). *Home*. New York: Greenwillow Books.

Baker, J. (2010). *Mirror*. Somerville, MA: Candlewick Press.

Barron, B., & Darling-Hammond, L. (2008). *Teaching for meaning*. San Francisco: Wiley.

Base, G. (1987). *Animalia*. New York: Abrams.

Bear, D., Invernizzi, M., Templeton, S., & Johnston, F. (2008). *Words their way* (6th ed.). Upper Saddle River, NJ: Pearson Education.

Beaver, J., & Carter, M. (2013). *Developmental Reading Assessment* (2nd ed.). Upper Saddle River, NJ: Pearson Education.

Beck, I. L., McKeown, M. G., & Kucan, L. (2003). *Bringing words to life: Robust vocabulary instruction*. New York: Guilford Press.

Beck, I. L., McKeown, M. G., & Kucan, L. (2013). *Bringing words to life: Robust vocabulary instruction* (2nd ed.). New York: Guilford Press.

Becker, A. (2013). *Journey*. Somerville, MA: Candlewick Press.

Becker, A. (2014). *Quest*. Somerville, MA: Candlewick Press.

Beers, K., & Probst, R. E. (2013). *Notice and note: Strategies for close reading*. Portsmouth, NH: Heinemann.

Berenstain, S., & Berenstain, J. (1987). *The Berenstain bears and too much birthday*. New York: Random House

Blachowicz, C., & Fisher, P. J. (2015). *Teaching vocabulary in all classrooms* (5th ed.). Upper Saddle River, NJ: Pearson Education.

Brenner, B. (1972). *Three little pigs*. Boston: Grolier Books.

Bromley, K. (2015). Best practices in teaching writing. In L. B. Gambrell & L. M. Morrow (Eds.), *Best practices in literacy instruction* (5th ed., pp. 288–314). New York: Guilford Press.

Brown, M. (1947). *Goodnight moon*. New York: HarperCollins.

Brownwell, R. (2011). *Receptive One-Word Picture Vocabulary Test (ROWPVT)*. Austin, TX: PRO-ED.

Calkins, L. M. (1994). *The art of teaching writing*. Portsmouth, NH: Heinemann.

Calkins, L. M. (2013). *Units of study in opinion, information, and narrative writing*. Portsmouth, NH: Heinemann.

Calkins, L. M. (2014). *Writing pathways: Performance assessments and learning progressions, grades K–8*. Portsmouth, NH: Heinemann.

Calkins, L. M. (2016). *Units of study for teaching reading, K–5*. Portsmouth, NH: Heinemann.

Calkins, L. M., Hartman, A., & White, Z. (2005). *One to one: The art of conferring with young writers*. Portsmouth, NH: Heinemann.

Calkins, L. M., & Harwayne, S. (1991). *Living between the lines*. Portsmouth, NH: Heinemann.

Cassidy, J., & Cassidy, D. (2010). What's hot for 2010. *Reading Today, 28*(3), 1, 6–8.

Center for Responsive Schools. (2015). *The first six weeks of school* (2nd ed.). Turners Falls, MA: Author.

Clay, M. M. (1993a). *An observation survey of early literacy achievement*. Portsmouth, NH: Heinemann.

Clay, M. M. (1993b). *Reading Recovery: A guidebook for teachers in training.* Portsmouth, NH: Heinemann.

Clay, M. M. (2000). *Running records: For classroom teachers.* Portsmouth, NH: Heinemann.

Cole, H., & Kostiw, M. (2012). *Unspoken: A story from the Underground Railroad.* New York: Scholastic.

Coles, R. (2010). *The story of Ruby Bridges.* New York: Scholastic.

Collins, K. (2004). *Growing readers: Units of study in the primary classroom.* Portland, ME: Stenhouse.

Combs, M. (2009). *Readers and writers in primary grades: A balanced literacy approach K–3* (3rd ed.). Upper Saddle River, NJ: Pearson Education.

Cook-Cottone, C. (2004). Constructivism in family literacy practices: Parents as mentors. *Reading Improvement, 41*(4), 208–216.

Cronin, D. (2000). *Click, clack, moo: Cows that type.* New York: Simon & Schuster.

Cunningham, H. (2017). *Children and childhood in western society since 1500.* New York: Routledge.

Cunningham, P. (2009). *Phonics they use* (5th ed.). Boston: Pearson.

de Paola, T. (1978). *The popcorn book.* New York: Holiday House.

Deci, E. L., & Flaste, R. (1995). *Why we do what we do: Understanding self-motivation.* New York: Penguin.

Deno, S. (1985). *Dynamic Indicators of Basic Early Literacy Skills (DIBELS).* Eugene, OR: Dynamic Measurement Group.

Deno, S., & Fuchs, L. S. (1987). *Dynamic Indicators of Basic Early Literacy Skills (DIBELS).* Eugene, OR: Dynamic Measurement Group.

Deno, S., & Mirkin, P. K. (1977). *Dynamic Indicators of Basic Early Literacy Skills (DIBELS).* Eugene, OR: Dynamic Measurement Group.

Denton, P. (2015). *The power of our words: Teacher language that helps children learn* (2nd ed.). Turners Falls, MA: Center for Responsive Schools.

Dewey, J. (1966). *Democracy and education.* London: Collier-Macmillan.

Dickinson, D. K., & Tabors, P. O. (2002). Fostering language and literacy in classrooms and homes. *Young Children, 57*(2), 10–18.

Diller, D. (2000). *Practice with purpose: Literacy work stations for grades 3–6.* Portland, ME: Stenhouse.

Diller, D. (2003). *Literacy work stations: Making centers work.* Portland, ME: Stenhouse.

Diller, D. (2008). *Spaces and places.* Portland, ME: Stenhouse.

Dolch, W. (1948). *Problems in reading.* Champaign, IL: Garrand Press.

Duke, N. K. (2014). *Inside information: Developing powerful readers and writers of informational text through project-based instruction, K–5.* New York: Scholastic.

Duke, N. K. (2015a, March 3). Now is the time for project-based learning. *Phi Delta Kappa International, The Blog: Learning on the Edge.*

Duke, N. K. (2015b). Project-based learning in Michigan. *Michigan Reading Journal, 48*(1), 13–17.

Duke, N. K., & Martin, N. M. (2015). Best practices for comprehension instruction in the elementary classroom. In S. R. Parris & K. Headley (Eds.), *Comprehension instruction: Research-based best practices* (3rd ed., pp. 211–223). New York: Guilford Press.

Dunn, L. M., & Dunn, D. M. (2007). *Peabody Picture Vocabulary Test, Fourth Edition (PPVT-4)*. Upper Saddle River, NJ: Pearson.

Duvoisin, R. (2002). *Petunia*. New York: Dragonfly.

Dweck, C. (2006). *Mindset: The new psychology of success*. New York: Ballantine Books.

Farmery, C. (2015). The cross-curricular approach in Key Stage 2. In T. Kerry (Ed.), *Cross-curricular teaching in the primary school: Planning and facilitating imaginative lessons* (2nd ed., pp. 73–82). New York: Routledge.

Fleischman, P., & Hawkes, K. (2004). *Sidewalk circus*. Cambridge, MA: Candlewick Press.

Fletcher, R. (2003). *A writer's notebook: Unlocking the writer within you*. New York: HarperCollins.

Fletcher, R., & Portalupi, J. (2001). *Writing workshop: The essential guide*. Portsmouth, NH: Heinemann.

Flippo, R. R., Holland, D. D., McCarthy, M. T., & Swinning, E. A. (2009). Asking the right questions: How to select an informal reading inventory. *The Reading Teacher, 63*(1), 79–83.

Fountas, I. C., & Pinnell, G. S. (1996). *Guided reading: Good first teaching for all children*. Portsmouth, NH: Heinemann.

Fountas, I. C., & Pinnell, G. S. (2012). *Guided reading: The romance and the reality*. Portsmouth, NH: Heinemann.

Fountas, I. C., & Pinnell, G. S. (2016). *The Fountas and Pinnell literary continuum: A tool for assessment, planning, and teaching, PreK–8*. Portsmouth, NH: Heinemann.

Frey, N., & Fisher, D. (2013). Close reading. *Principal Leadership, 13*(8), 57–59.

Fry, E. B. (1980). The new Instant Word List. *The Reading Teacher, 34*, 284–289.

Fukijawa, A. (1980). *Jenny learns a lesson*. New York: Grosset & Dunlap.

Gambrell, L. (1996). Creating classrooms cultures that foster reading motivation. *The Reading Teacher, 50*, 4–25.

Gambrell, L., Morrow, L. M., & Pressley, M. (Eds.). (2007). *Best practices in literacy instruction*. New York: Guilford Press.

Gay, G. (2010). *Culturally responsive teaching: Theory, research, and practice*. New York: Teachers College Press.

Graves, D. H. (1983). *Writing: Teachers and children at work*. Portsmouth, NH: Heinemann.

Gunning, T. G. (2003). *Creating literacy instruction for all children* (4th ed.). Boston: Allyn & Bacon.

Gunning, T. G. (2014). *Creating literacy instruction for all children* (8th ed.). Boston: Allyn & Bacon.

Hallinan, M. T., & Sorenson, A. B. (1983). The formation and stability of instructional groups. *American Sociological Review, 48*, 838–851.

Hanlon, A. (2012). *Ralph tells a story*. Las Vegas, NV: Amazon Children's Books.

Hart, B., & Risley, T. B. (1995). *Meaningful differences in the everyday experiences of young American children*. Baltimore: Brookes.

Harvey, S., & Daniels, H. (2009). *Comprehension and collaboration: Inquiry circles in action.* Portsmouth, NH: Heinemann.

Harvey, S., & Goudvis, A. (2008). *The primary comprehension toolkit: Language and lessons for active literacy.* Portsmouth, NH: Heinemann.

Harvey, S., & Goudvis, A. (2013). Comprehension at the core. *The Reading Teacher, 66*(6), 432–439.

Hasbrouck, J., & Tindal, G. (2006). Oral reading fluency norms: A valuable assessment tool for reading teachers. *The Reading Teacher, 59,* 636–644.

Hills, T. (2012). *Rocket writes a story.* New York: Schwartz & Wade.

Hoban, R. (1964). *Bread and jam for Frances.* New York: Harper & Row.

Hoberman, M. A. (2001). *You read to me, I'll read to you.* New York: Little, Brown.

Hurd, E. (1980). *Under the lemon tree.* Boston: Little, Brown.

International Literacy Association and National Association for the Education of Young Children. (1998, July). *Young Children, 53*(4), 30–46.

Jalongo, M. R. (2007). *Early childhood language arts* (4th ed.). Boston: Allyn & Bacon.

Jenkins, J., Stein, M., & Wysocki, K. (1984). Learning vocabulary through reading. *American Educational Research Journal, 21,* 767–787.

Jenkins, S. (1995). *Looking down.* Boston: Houghton Mifflin.

Johns, J. (2012). *Basic Reading Inventory: Pre-primer through grade twelve and early literary assessment.* Dubuque, IA: Kendal Hunt.

Johns, J., & Berglund, R. L. (2002). *Fluency: Evidence-based strategies.* Dubuque, IA: Kendall/Hunt.

Johnson, S. T. (1995). *Alphabet city.* New York: Viking.

Johnston, P. (2004). *Choice words: How our language affects children's learning.* Portland, ME: Stenhouse.

Johnston, P., & Costello, P. (2005). Principles of literacy assessment. *Reading Research Quarterly, 40*(2), 256–267.

Katz, L., & Chard, S. (2000). *Engaging children's minds: The project approach.* Stamford, CT: Ablex..

Keats, E. J. (1974). *Pet show.* New York: Aladdin Books.

Keats, E. J. (1996). *The snowy day.* New York: Viking.

Kuhn, M. R., Schwanenflugel, P. J., & Meisinger, E. B. (2010). Aligning theory and assessment of reading fluency: Automaticity, prosody, and definitions of fluency. *Reading Research Quarterly, 45,* 230–251.

Kuhn, M. R., & Stahl, S. A. (2003). Fluency: A review of developmental and remedial strategies. *Journal of Educational Psychology, 95,* 3–21.

Larmer, J., Mergendoller, J., & Boss, S. (2015). *Setting the standard for project-based learning: A proven approach to rigorous classroom instruction.* Alexandria, VA: ASCD.

Lehman, B. (2004). *The red book.* Boston: Houghton Mifflin.

Leslie, L., & Caldwell, J. (2010). *Qualitative Reading Inventory–5.* Upper Saddle River, NJ: Pearson.

Leu, D. J., Jr., Kinzer, C. K., Coiro, J., & Cammack, D. (2004). Toward a theory of new literacies emerging from the Internet and other information and communication technologies. In R. Ruddell & N. Unrau (Eds.), *Theoretical models and processes of reading* (5th ed., pp. 1568–1611). Newark, DE: International Reading Association.

Levin, I., Snatil-Carmon, S., & Asif-Rave, O. (2006). Learning of letter names and sounds and their contribution to word recognition. *Journal of Experimental Child Psychology, 93*(2), 139–165.

Linder, R. (2014). *K–2 chart sense: Common sense charts to teach K–2 informational text and literature.* Atlanta, GA: Literacy Initiative.

Lionni, L. (1987). *Swimmy.* New York: Dragonfly Books.

Liu, J. S., & Sheen, D. I. (2002). *Yellow umbrella.* La Jolla, CA: Kane/Miller Books.

Mariotti, A., & Homan, S. (2009). *Linking reading assessment to instruction: An application worktext for elementary classroom teachers* (5th ed.). New York: Routledge.

Martinelli, M., & Mraz, K. (2012). *Smarter charts: Optimizing an instructional staple to create independent readers and writers.* Portsmouth, NH: Heinemann.

Marzano, R. J. (2004). *Building background knowledge for academic achievement: Research on what works in schools.* Alexandria, VA: Association for Supervision and Curriculum Development (ASCD).

Mayer, M. (1967). *A boy, a dog, and a frog.* New York: Dial.

McAfee, O., & Leong, D. (1997). *Assessing and guiding young children's development and learning.* Boston: Allyn & Bacon.

McClosky, R. (1948). *Blueberries for Sal.* New York: Viking.

McCormick, C., & Mason, J. (1981). What happens to kindergarten children's knowledge about reading after summer vacation? *The Reading Teacher, 35,* 164–172.

McGee, L. M., & Morrow, L. M. (2005). *Teaching literacy in kindergarten.* New York: Guilford Press.

McKenna, M. C., & Stahl, K. A. D. (2009). *Assessment for reading instruction.* New York: Guilford Press.

McKenna, M. C., & Stahl, K. A. D. (2015). *Assessment for reading instruction* (3rd ed.). New York: Guilford Press.

McKeown, M. G., Beck, I. L., Omanson, R. C., & Perfetti, C. A. (1985). The effects of long-term vocabulary instruction on reading comprehension: A replication. *Journal of Reading Behavior, 15*(1), 3–18.

McTighe, J., Seif, E., & Wiggins, G. (2004). *You can teach for meaning.* Available from *www.ascd.org/publications/educational-leadership/sept04/vol62/num01/You-Can-Teach-for-Meaning.aspx*

Miller, D. (2002). *Reading with meaning: Teaching comprehension in the primary grades.* Portland, ME: Stenhouse.

Morrison, T. G., & Wilcox, B. (2013). *Developing literacy: Reading and writing to, with, and by children.* Upper Saddle River, NJ: Pearson Education.

Morrow, L. M. (1996). Story retelling: A discussion strategy to develop and assess comprehension. In L. B. Gambrell & J. F. Almasi (Eds.), *Lively discussions: Fostering engaged reading* (pp. 265–285). Newark, DE: International Reading Association.

Morrow, L. M. (2003a). *Organizing and managing the language arts block: A professional development guide.* New York: Guilford Press.

Morrow, L. M. (2003b). *The Literacy Center.* Portland, ME: Stenhouse.

Morrow, L. M. (2015). *Literacy development in the early years* (8th ed.). Upper Saddle River, NJ: Pearson Education.

Morrow, L. M., Kuhn, M., & Schwanenflugel, P. J. (2006). The family fluency program. *The Reading Teacher, 60*(4), 322–333.

Morrow, L. M., Tracey, D. H., Woo, D. G., & Pressley, M. (1999). Characteristics of exemplary first-grade literacy instruction. *The Reading Teacher, 52,* 462–476.

Moustafa, M. (1997). *Beyond traditional phonics: Research discoveries and reading instruction.* Portsmouth, NH: Heinemann.

Murray, D. M. (2004). *A writer teaches writing.* Boston: Cengage Learning.

National Reading Panel Report. (2000). *Report of the National Reading Panel: Teaching children to read.* Washington, DC: National Institution of Child Health and Human Development.

Neuman, S., & Roskos, K. (Eds.). (1998). *Children achieving: Best practices in early literacy.* Newark, DE: International Reading Association.

Newkirk, T. (2011). *The art of slow reading: Six time-honored practices for engagement.* Portsmouth, NH: Heinemann.

Olness, R. (2005). *Using literature to enhance writing instruction: A guide for K–5 teachers.* Newark, DE: International Reading Association.

Overturf, B., Montgomery, L., & Smith, M. H. (2013). *Word nerds: Teaching all students to learn and love vocabulary.* Portland, ME: Stenhouse.

Paris, A. H., & Paris, S. G. (2007). Teaching narrative comprehensive strategies to first graders. *Cognition and Instruction, 25*(1), 1–44.

Potter, B. (1902). *The tale of Peter Rabbit.* New York: Scholastic.

Pressley, M., Rankin, J., & Yokoi, L. (1996). A survey of instructional practices of primary teachers nominated as effective in promoting literacy. *Elementary School Journal, 96*(4), 363–383.

Pressley, M., Wharton-McDonald, R., Hampston, J. M., & Echevarria, M. (1998). The nature of literacy instruction in ten grade-4 and -5 classrooms in upstate New York. *Scientific Studies of Reading, 2,* 150–191.

Purcell-Gates, V., Duke, N. K., & Martineau, J. A. (2007). Learning to read and write genre-specific text: Roles of authentic experience and explicit teaching. *Reading Research Quarterly, 42*(1), 8–45.

Repko, A. (2009). *Interdisciplinary research process and theory.* Los Angeles: Sage.

Reutzel, D. R., & Clark, S. (2011). Organizing literacy classrooms for effective instruction. *The Reading Teacher, 65*(2), 96–109.

Reutzel, D. R., & Cooter, R. B. (2009). *Teaching children to read: Putting the pieces together* (4th ed.). Upper Saddle River, NJ: Pearson/Merrill/Prentice Hall.

Ricci, M. C. (2013). *Mindsets in the classroom: Building a culture of success and student achievement in schools.* Waco, TX: Prufrock Press.

Richards, I. A. (1929). *Practical criticism.* London: Cambridge University Press.

Risko, V. J., & Walker-Dalhouse, D. (2010). Making the most of assessments to inform instruction. *The Reading Teacher, 63*(5), 420–422.

Roberts, K., & Roberts, M. B. (2016). *DIY literacy: Teaching tools for differentiation, rigor, and independence.* Portsmouth, NH: Heinemann.

Robertson, C., & Salter, W. (2018). *Phonological Awareness Test (PAT)*. Austin, TX: PRO-ED.

Rohmann, E. (1994). *Time flies*. New York: Random House.

Roswell, F. G., Chall, J. S., Curtis, M. E., & Kearns, G. (2017). *Diagnostic Assessments of Reading with Trial Teach Strategies (DAR-TTS)*. Boston: Houghton Mifflin.

Schotter, R. (1997). *Nothing ever happens on 90th Street*. New York: Orchard Books.

Serafini, F. (2006). *Around the reading workshop in 180 days: A month-by-month guide to effective instruction*. Portsmouth, NH: Heinemann.

Serravallo, J. (2015). *The reading strategies book: Your everything guide to developing skilled readers*. Portsmouth, NH: Heinemann.

Serravallo, J. (2017). *The writing strategies book: Your everything guide to developing skilled writers*. Portsmouth, NH: Heinemann.

Serravallo, J., & Goldberg, G. (2007). *Conferring with readers: Supporting each student's growth and independence*. Portsmouth, NH: Heinemann.

Seuss, Dr. (1960). *Green eggs and ham*. New York: Random House.

Shinn, M. (1989). *Dynamic Indicators of Basic Early Literacy Skills (DIBELS)*. Eugene, OR: Dynamic Measurement Group.

Slavin, R. E. (1987). Ability grouping and student achievement in elementary schools: A best-evidence synthesis. *Review of Educational Research, 57*, 292–336.

Snow, C. E., Burns, M. S., & Griffin, P. (Eds.). (2009). *Preventing reading difficulties in young children*. Washington, DC: Department of Education, National Academy of Sciences National Research Council, Commission on Behavioral and Social Sciences and Education.

Soderman, A. K., & Farrell, P. (2008). *Creating literacy-rich preschools and kindergartens*. Boston, MA: Allyn & Bacon.

Sorenson, A. B., & Hallinan, M. T. (1986). Effects of ability grouping on growth in academic achievement. *American Educational Research Journal, 23*, 519–542.

Spiegel, D. L. (1992). Blending whole language and systematic direct instruction. *The Reading Teacher, 46*, 38–44.

Stahl, S. A. (2003). Vocabulary and readability: How knowing word meanings affects comprehension. *Topics in Language Disorders, 23*(3), 241–247.

Stanovich, K. E. (1986). Matthew effects in reading: Some consequences of individual differences in the acquisition of literacy. *Reading Research Quarterly, 21*, 360–407.

Strickland, D. S., & Schickedanz, J. A. (2009). *Learning about print in preschool: Working with letters, words, and beginning links with phonemic awareness*. Newark, DE: International Reading Association.

Strickland, D., & Snow, C. (2002). *Preparing our teachers: Opportunities for better reading instruction*. Washington, DC: Joseph Henry Press.

Tan, S. (2006). *The arrival*. New York: Levine.

Taylor, B. M. (2008). Tier 1: Effective classroom reading instruction in the elementary grades. In D. Fuchs, S. Fuchs, & S. Vaughn (Eds.), *Response to intervention: A framework for reading education* (pp. 5–25). Newark, DE: International Reading Association.

Taylor, B. M., Pearson, P. D., Clark, K. F., & Walpole, S. (1999). Effective schools/accomplished teachers. *The Reading Teacher, 53*(2), 156–159.

Thomson, B. (2010). *Chalk.* New York: Marshall Cavendish Children.

Thomson, B. (2013). *Fossil.* Las Vegas, NV: Amazon.

Tompkins, G. E. (2003). *Literacy for the 21st century: Teaching reading and writing in prekindergarten through grade 4.* Upper Saddle River, NJ: Pearson Education.

Wagner, R. K., Torgesen, J. K., Rashotte, K. A., & Pearson, N. A. (2013). *Comprehensive Test of Phonological Processing, Second Edition (CTOPP-2).* Austin, TX: PRO-ED.

Walpole, S., & McKenna, M. C. (2007). *Differentiated reading instruction: Strategies for the primary grades.* New York: Guilford Press.

Walpole, S., & McKenna, M. C. (2016). *Organizing the early literacy classroom: How to plan for success and reach your goals.* New York: Guilford Press.

Wasik, B. A., & Bond, M. A. (2001). Beyond the pages of a book: Interactive book reading and language development in preschool classrooms. *Journal of Educational Psychology, 93*(2), 243–250.

Weinstein, C. S., & Romano, M. E. (2015). *Elementary classroom management: Lessons from research and practice.* New York: McGraw-Hill Education.

Wharton-McDonald, R., Pressley, M., & Hampston, J. M. (1998). Literacy instruction in nine first-grade classrooms: Teacher characteristics and student achievement. *The Elementary School Journal, 99*, 101–128.

Wheelock, W., Silvaroli, J., & Campbell, C. (2012). *Classroom Reading Inventory* (12th ed.). New York: McGraw-Hill.

White, T. G., Graves, M. F., & Slater, W. H. (1990). Growth of reading vocabulary in diverse elementary schools: Decoding and word meaning. *Journal of Educational Psychology, 82*(2), 281–290.

Whitehurst, G. J., & Lonigan, C. J. (2001). Emergent literacy: Development from prereaders to readers. In S. B. Neuman & D. K. Dickinson (Eds.), *Handbook of early literacy research* (pp. 11–29). New York: Guilford Press.

Wiesner, D. (1991). *Tuesday.* New York: Clarion.

Wiesner, D. (1999). *Sector 7.* New York: Clarion.

Wiesner, D. (2006). *Flotsom.* New York: Clarion.

Wiesner, D., & Lothrop, L. (1988). *Free fall.* New York: Lothrop, Lee, & Shepard.

Wilhelm, J. (2007). *Engaging readers and writers with inquiry.* New York: Scholastic.

Woodcock, R. W. (2011). *Woodcock Reading Mastery Tests—Revised (WRMT-R).* Upper Saddle River, NJ: Pearson Education.

Woods. M. J., & Moe, A. (2011). *Analytical Reading Inventory: Comprehensive standards-based assessment for all students* (9th ed.). Boston: Allyn & Bacon.

Xu, Y., & Drame, E. (2007). Culturally appropriate context: Unlocking the potential of response to intervention for English language learners. *Early Childhood Education Journal, 35*(4), 305–311.

Young, C., & Rasinski, T. (2009). Implementing readers' theatre as an approach to classroom fluency instruction. *The Reading Teacher, 63*(1), 4–13.

Index

Note. *f* or *t* following a page number indicates a figure or a table.